W9-CJN-508

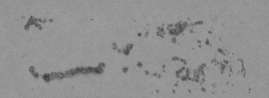

The Role of Woman in the Middle Ages

Contributors

David Herlihy

Harvard University

Franz H. Bäuml

University of California, Los Angeles

Gerard J. Brault

Pennsylvania State University

Aldo S. Bernardo

State University of New York, Binghamton

Charity Cannon Willard

Ladycliff College

Philippe Verdier

Université de Montréal

The Role of Woman
in the Middle Ages

Papers of the sixth annual conference
of the Center for Medieval and
Early Renaissance Studies
State University of New York at Binghamton
6–7 May 1972

Edited by Rosmarie Thee Morewedge

State University of New York Press
Albany 1975

The Role of Woman in the Middle Ages
First Edition

Published by State University of New York Press
99 Washington Avenue, Albany, New York 12210
© 1975 State University of New York
Printed in the United States of America

Library of Congress Cataloging in Publication Data
Main entry under title:

The role of woman in the Middle Ages.

Includes bibliographical references.
1. Women—History—Middle Ages, 500–1500—Congresses.
2. Women—Social conditions—Congresses.   3. Women
in literature—Congresses.   I. Morewedge, Rosmarie
Thee, 1943–   ed.   II. New York (State).   State Uni-
versity at Binghamton.   Center for Medieval and Early
Renaissance Studies.   III. Title.
HQ1143.R73   301.41'2'0902   74-23227
ISBN 0-87395-274-X
ISBN 0-87395-275-8 microfiche

Contents

Introduction

In spite of the tremendous influence woman is known to have exerted upon numerous facets of medieval civilization, until now her role has not been the subject of a special concerted effort using critical perspectives gained from multidisciplinary approaches. The papers in this volume represent an attempt to develop and to demonstrate the use of such critical perspectives. Before turning to these methodological considerations, let us briefly outline aspects of her role stressed in this work.

Taken as a whole, the six essays collected in this volume paint a diversified portrait of the medieval woman. They cover these topics: (1) the factors influencing the span of her life and the value placed upon her existence by society; (2) the interaction of those sociological, historical, anthropological, and literary factors which determined her possible functions in illiterate as well as in literate medieval narrative communities and the literary representations corresponding to these functions; (3) the complex relational possibilities emerging out of various ambivalent thematic, motivic, and structural relationships of her role in the courtly romance; (4) the idealized personal as well as suprapersonal feminine image capable of resolving the apparent and potentially conflicting impulses pulling the artist in bifarious directions of antiquity and Christianity; (5) a study of France's first professional woman of letters who was aware that written history has been masculine history, convinced that women are able to play an important role in the body politic of France, and adamant in her demand that women learn to adapt to ever-changing circumstances; (6) the typological portrayal of woman in idealized as well as in caricatured depictions with correspondence to the vertical structure of the hierarchical ladder, studded with rungs positioned at unequal intervals so as to discourage upward mobility, and to the horizontal structure of the manuscript page which discriminated unmistakably between that which was depicted in the center and in the marginalia. The essays corroborate Karl D. Uitti's perceptive portrayal of the women in Chrétien's romances: "What a picture of the Lady one might derive from juxtaposing and comparing Énide, Guenevere, Soredamor, Fénice, Laudine, Lunete, Blanche-fleur, and others! The creation is overwhelming in its nuance, its sophistication, and in its sympathy; and, of course, it is profoundly literary." *

With regard to methodology, historical, economic, socio-logical, anthropological, and literary data as well as material taken from the visual arts have been consulted for clues as to how woman's role was conceived and depicted by medi-eval society. Conversely, the typologies emerging out of such traditional depictions—seen through their evolution into conceptual and normative constructs—are examined in turn for evidence as to how they function within works of art and, upon acquiring an independent role, shape succes-sive works. The existence of such constructs, e.g., the Lady or the ideal Lover, which depend upon and correspond to the level of expectation of medieval intellectual communi-ties (i.e., the medieval perceivers responding to works of art) made for possible irony and satire within these works of art. Moreover, the emergence of such constructs, either ac-knowledged implicitly within works of art or formulated explicitly in treatises like Andreas Capellanus's *De amore libri tres*,** prepared the way for the evolution and the creation of new genres, genres which naturally followed the realiza-

---

* *Story, Myth, and Celebration in Old French Narrative Poetry 1050–1200* (Princeton, N.J.: Princeton University Press, 1973), p. 219.
** Cf. also *The Meaning of Courtly Love*, ed. F. X. Newman (Albany: State University of New York Press, 1967).

tion that particular overly systematized conceptual constructs like "courtly love" had outrun their course and deserved to be earmarked for the shelves of history.

Amour courtois and *chevalerie* as understood in the High Middle Ages were recognized by some thinkers in the late Middle Ages as inapplicable to that society in view of a new consciousness and new constructs corresponding to it. Christine de Pizan, for instance, regards these older constructs as cumbersome strictures actually inimical to the healthy functioning of the body politic. Irony and an ironic perception of woman's role can enter the realm of literature, Franz H. Bäuml informs us, upon the transition from oral to written literature. Because literature is endowed with a different function in illiterate and in literate medieval societies, the particular function of woman is to a large extent a function of the level of literacy of a narrative community and that community's place in the given social stratification. The development of the courtly romance—whose celebration of *chevalerie,* the *clergie,* and the Lady reaches a high point with Chrétien according to Karl Uitti—hinges on irony and on the ambiguous narrator.*

In the visual arts a similar process unfolds before our eyes. Illuminations occupying the center of manuscript pages accord generally in tone and attitude with the text they illustrate; such ocular guidelines or strictures appear to have lost their binding force as they shifted off-center, that is, were located in the marginalia and the *bas-de-page* which began to be filled out after 1250. Here, in a new physical position, the conventional idealized depictions are questioned, declared invalid, and turned around; impulses for the creation of new genres in art given by the bizarre inhabitants of the marginalia reveal an irreverence and intellectual detachment from the text on the part of the artists. The literary outgrowth of such forms is discussed, for instance, in Klaus Lazarowicz's *Verkehrte Welt;* ** the progeny

* See also Dennis H. Green, "Irony and Medieval Romance," *Forum for Modern Language Studies* 6 (1970): 49–64.
** *Vorstudien zu einer Geschichte der deutschen Satire,* Hermaea, Germanistische Forschungen, no. 15 (Tübingen: Niemeyer, 1963).

of the grotesques and drôleries is found in Hieronymus Bosch and grotesque *emblemata* of the Renaissance. The methodological considerations of such cross-fertilization and its implications are evident in the majority of the volume's essays, but are developed for literature particularly by Franz Bäuml and for the visual arts by Philippe Verdier.

Taken individually, the papers disclose the multifarious facets of the role of woman, many of which have as yet been examined only tangentially.

David Herlihy presents evidence related to the life span of woman in classical antiquity, in the early Middle Ages, as well as in the High and late Middle Ages. He establishes an inverse relationship between her longevity and her favorable numerical ratio over men on the one hand, and the value society placed on her on the other. He correlates, moreover, the reversal in life expectancies of women during the High and late Middle Ages with other changes taking place in the fabric of medieval society: the rise of the cities, wars which decimated the numbers of men, the deterioration of the social position of woman, various religious movements (*Frauenbewegungen*), and other transformations. In following woman from the cradle to the tomb from classical antiquity (and its dearth of women) to the late Middle Ages (with a higher number of women than men), David Herlihy has advanced our knowledge in a field where objective evidence is sparse and difficult to come by.

By linking textual analysis with historical, cultural, sociological, and anthropological determinants of the medieval work of art, Franz H. Bäuml demonstrates that the role accorded to woman in a particular medieval literary text is contingent upon these very factors. Kriemhild, the "heroine" of the *Nibelungenlied,* is the vehicle by which he demonstrates the concurrent and interdependent transformations taking place in the narrative community, a community which progresses from "functional illiteracy" to the level of a disadvantaged illiterate subgroup in a literate medieval society, and finally to the literate community. In the context of the heroic oral epic Kriemhild's actions illustrate the mores and cultural values of her community, but in the written *Nibelungenlied* she is transformed into a villainess whose actions are inimical and disruptive to society. The recognition that changes in the representation of women (and of men) as well as changes in the attitude of the narrator, are direct functions of historical, sociological, anthropological, and cultural factors, is gaining more and more ground—in no small part because of Bäuml's efforts.

Although he draws on extra-textual data, Gerard J. Brault favors the analysis of the thematic and motivic texture of the works he considers, so as to allow the multifaceted and multiassociational contours of Isolt's and Guenevere's complex roles to emerge more fully. His choice of the ring motif in Thomas's *Tristan* allows an analysis of convergent motif, theme, and structure. The motif is shown to assume an organic function in relationship to the theme of sadness and the circular narrative structure; more importantly for this investigation, the ring motif establishes Isolt's primary function as magical healer and idealized lover. A similar motivic analysis of the comb, the well, and the carol in Chrétien's *Chevalier de la Charrette* reveals the highly religious nature of Guenevere's role in this romance. The exploration of symbolic ambivalences associated with these motifs discloses the artistry of narration, realistic detail in depiction, and great complexity in the portrayal of the fictional role of the heroine. Last but not least, it opens an avenue of access to the perception of woman by men, by revealing to us clerical fantasies about women at that time. Such fantasies about woman and attitudes toward her are ultimately reflected in the bifarious conception of woman as Eve/Ave, chattel/Lady. In time these conceptions, fantasies, and attitudes crystallized into various poetic myths and constructs. As such, they played a demonstrable function in the literary genres which emerged around them, the courtly lyric and the pastourelle for instance, which ceased to function organically in the society only when the older poetic constructs dissolved or gave way to others more in accord with new aesthetic sensibilities, historical necessities, sociological factors, and other forces.

Aldo S. Bernardo begins his presentation with the divergent medieval conception of woman as the "creature of extremes," a source of sin on the one hand, but a source of perfection on the other. The resolution of this dualism translated by Petrarch into a dualism between the classical impulse and Christianity—Mt. Parnassus and Mt. Calvary— constitutes the difficulty but also the great poetic resource of the *Canzoniere*. Bernardo addresses himself to this transformation of a personal encounter into a supra-personal poetic construct by tracing the evolution of Laura's image through five forms of the *Canzoniere*. Having become integrated into the poet's very being, Laura functions as rejuvinating, spiritualizing poetic mainspring; the potential contradictions utilized in the casting of each form of the poems intersect in her image and in doing so, bestow depth and conviction on it. Laura evolves into a poetic construct capable of generating a *rapprochement* between Mt. Parnassus and Mt. Calvary, capable of bridging—though not fully reconciling—the two extremes, which, in the final form of the *Canzoniere*, are no longer found to be mutually exclusive.

Christine de Pizan has been hailed as an early herald of the feminist movement; for this claim Charity Cannon Willard finds little substantiation in Christine's *opera*. Nevertheless, while choosing the traditional medieval form of the *enseignement* or the *chastisement*, she does so with a new purpose in mind: to correct the distorted satires which men have directed against woman, satires such as are found in the *Roman de la Rose*. The reasons for which Christine deserves to be known are many; for our purposes a brief listing will have to do. Her awareness that literature has in the main been written from the masculine perspective is as astute as it is surprising. What does her reliance on prose rather than verse betoken, if not a conscious departure from the well-established didactic mold of the past and a readiness to participate in the forging of a new tool? Not only was she gifted with a fine scent for the winds of change blowing within the hierarchical social structures, but she was also able to draw the far-reaching conclusion that such currents were an enjoinder to women to adapt intelligently to the inevitable changes of the times by seeking to educate themselves as best they could. In contrast to the traditional political, social, and cultural interests a woman of her station can be expected to have had, stands her abiding concern for the internal difficulties of the body politic of France and the place of women within this organism. Last but not least among her achievements is her analysis of the position women actually held in society and the possible positions they could secure. Christine's work carries the imprint of the Middle Ages but reveals also the emergence of new forms characteristic of later times. While she employs the traditional didactic instrument designed to keep woman in her place, Christine de-emphasizes the traditional restraints placed on woman and emphasizes instead the need for woman to educate herself. She makes use of the medieval allegorical vehicle but instead of using religious personifications, she presents a new cast with the secular personifications of Reason, Honesty, and Justice. Willard's study of the author of *Le Livre des Trois Vertus,* of the content of this work, of the educational precepts formulated within its structural subdivisions (which correspond to the divisions of the social hierarchy), and of its public—particularly the Burgundian court—allows us to gain insight into a late medieval woman who perceives many of the complexities of her time and responds to them in her writings. Her work, her ideas, and her influence challenge Gustave Lanson's description of the fourteenth and fifteenth centuries as periods of sterility and disintegration, as well as Johan Huizinga's portrayal of these times as periods of decadence.

The longing of medieval man to embody every conception in a concrete shape is established beyond the need of comment. Whereas most studies focus on the medieval concern with order, harmony, and balance, which led, for instance, by a process of analogy to the creation of nine worthy women to balance the original nine worthies (*les neuf preux,* to which a tenth was subsequently added),* Philippe Verdier focuses on another aspect and another product of medieval mentality. Its offsprings are the reverse of the conventional idealized depictions: they are the vignettes or *drôleries* [drolleries referring to all types of animated

---

* Cf. Horst Schroeder, *Der Topos der Nine Worthies in Literatur und bildender Kunst* (Göttingen: Vandenhoek and Ruprecht, 1971).

marginal configurations] and grotesques [referring to the more beastly and monstrous apparitions in the latter category] covering the marginalia and the *bas-de-page* [used for more elaborate compositions] of medieval manuscripts. Revealing often a topsy-turvy world, these drawings focus particularly on the role of woman as it is socially perceived; however, they may also reveal a perception of woman by women who filled the margins with fantastic, hybrid shapes as well as with caricatures and realistic detail. These renderings do not show signs of misogyny; instead, they constitute more often than not a tongue-in-cheek symbolical commentary on the text in question and an indulgence in satirical comment absent from the text they "adorn." The typological exploitation of poliguities traditionally associated with aspects of the text provides often the *point d'appui* for the irreverent drawings in which woman may hold equal footing with man only on the highest rungs of the social hierarchy but considerably less than that on lower rungs. The pictorial punning undercutting the main text—though at times apparently unrelated to it—and the patent marginal irony which lampoons all authority, are described by Verdier as the "naive exponents of a women's freedom movement against the definition of her condition by the church or against rules edicted by man." The *drôleries* and grotesques, which attract as much as they repel, reveal a medieval mentality able to see woman in contradistinction to conventional stereotypes. The vast array of these bizarre, hybrid depictions (with which Lilian Randall regales the reader in her definitive work on the subject,*) offer alternative ways of depicting the role of woman. As these alternatives gained greater foothold and became increasingly typological, they condensed into genres of their own. As typological constructs propelled by a force of their own which enabled them to leave the marginalia for the center, they emerge on the European horizon of art with the onset of the grotesque *emblemata* in the Renaissance.

The six essays presented in this collection constitute the

---

* *Images in the Margins of Gothic Manuscripts* (Berkeley and Los Angeles: University of California Press, 1966).

papers delivered at the Sixth Annual Conference of the Center for Medieval and Early Renaissance Studies of the State University of New York at Binghamton held on The Role of the Woman in the Middle Ages on 6–7 May 1972. Apart from the addition of notes and some other minor changes, the original versions have not been altered. Not included are the numerous questions put to speakers by the audience, the responses to such questions, or the records of the informal discussions—to which the format of the conference proved so conducive. An author and subject index will facilitate the use of this text.

The editor wishes to acknowledge a debt of gratitude to the co-directors of the Center, Aldo S. Bernardo and Bernard F. Huppé, for their active help and advice in the planning of the conference and in activities related to it; to the speakers for their gracious cooperation in matters related to the delivery of the papers and the submission of the MSS; to Dorothy Huber, secretary of the Center, for attentive help willingly rendered; to William Snyder, chairman of the Department of Germanic Languages and Literatures for his encouragement, to Norman Mangouni, director of the State University of New York Press, for his advice, to W. Bruce Johnson of the State University of New York Press for editorial assistance, and to Mary Savo of the Department of Germanic Languages and Literatures for typing the final MS.

It is hoped that the results of this conference—the first of its kind to focus on the role of woman in the Middle Ages from a multi-disciplinary perspective—may stimulate further critical investigation of aspects touched on but not fully explored in these essays.

Rosmarie Thee Morewedge

Life Expectancies for Women in Medieval Society

DAVID HERLIHY

Harvard University

In every epoch and in every society, the duration of her life deeply influences the social position and social experiences of woman. This factor determines at all ages the proportions of women and men in a population. This in turn affects the chances that a girl has for marrying, and, indirectly, how she is trained and how she is treated by her parents, her suitors and her husband. Within marriage, her longevity fixes the length of her contact with her household and with her children, and magnifies or diminishes the influence she is likely to exert upon them. The number of widows in the community and the role they play in its life will again be set by how long women live. In this paper we shall seek to examine the relative life expectancies which women seem to have enjoyed—or endured—in medieval society. Our data are understandably sparse, and almost always difficult to interpret. But enough information is available to offer a crude but accurate appraisal of the survival of women during the Middle Ages. We shall also hazard some comment concerning how this factor seems to

1

have affected the treatment which women received and the attitudes concerning them in the medieval world.

The period has left us two quite different kinds of documents, which throw some illumination on the mortalities of women. The scholars of the age, especially those with an interest in medicine and biology, produced a fairly abundant comment on the aging process and on dying, and occasionally they related aging and death to the factor of sex. Their scientific theories are questionable, but their observations and impressions retain considerable historical interest. Moreover, the Middle Ages, from as early as the eighth century, have left us several revealing censuses of serfs or taxpayers, which describe households and which give us a hard look into the inner structure of medieval communities; in particular, they show the relative distributions of men and women across various status and age categories. However, before consulting this properly medieval material, it is first essential to cast a brief glance at the ancient Mediterranean world, at that classical society which intellectually and socially helped prepare the Middle Ages. From antiquity too, learned opinions and some data have survived which cast light on the longevity of women.

Among the scholars of antiquity, the most prominent figure was without doubt Aristotle, and in one of his short biological tracts, entitled "On Length and Shortness of Life," he described how animals age and why they die, and how sex influences senescence.[1] "By nature and as a general rule," Aristotle concluded, "the male lives longer than the female, the reason being that the male is a warmer creature than the female." [2] In Aristotle's theory of the stages of life, old age, and death itself, were "cold and dry." [3] Females, colder and dryer than the males, at all stages of life were thus closer to senescence and death. Aristotle did note certain exceptions to this general rule. Those males given to frequent sexual intercourse, as among the sparrows, age sooner, because they dry up quicker, and so also do males who labor excessively. There is, however, no suggestion that these exceptions applied generally to human beings, among whom, Aristotle implicitly affirmed, the warmer and moister males normally outlive the females.

In spite of some disagreement whether females were moister or dryer than the males, the opinion that they died sooner seems to have enjoyed wide currency among the biologists and doctors of antiquity. The Roman naturalist Pliny the Elder, for example, affirmed that females were born more quickly, and passed through life more rapidly, than the males.[4] The physician Galen similarly stated that women are conceived more quickly and more quickly pass through childhood, youth, and old age than do men.[5] Males, as warmer animals, also more nearly approached the perfection of their species than did the females.

This prevalent antique opinion concerning the inferior nature, more rapid aging and earlier death of women raises the intriguing question: in ancient society, did men in fact live longer than women? Tens of thousands of surviving gravestone inscriptions, dating in the main from the opening centuries of the Christian era, have held out hope of answering this question, for many of them record both the sex and the age of the decedent. Grossly surveyed, for all provinces of the empire from which such inscriptions have been collected, the average age of recorded death is lower for women than for men.[6] In 1953 A. R. Burn summarized the then available data, and concluded that in the period of late antiquity men could expect to outlive women by some four to seven years. Of groups of 100 boys and girls alive at age ten, 36 males, but only 28 females, could hope to reach their sixties.

More recently, another student of ancient populations, Keith Hopkins, has called into question the use made of these inscriptions by Burn and others.[7] He isolates for special examination the gravestones raised by a husband or a wife in memory of a deceased spouse, on the assumption that only inscriptions of the same character and provenience can yield consistent and comparable information. The age of recorded deaths from this subset of inscriptions is 34 years for the deceased wives and 46.5 years for the husbands. But the inscriptions, Hopkins contends, mislead us. To restate his argument, we may consider that at marriage both husband and wife enter a competition to determine who will get the single tombstone that the marriage is likely to produce. Success in the competition goes to the partner who dies before the other. But the wife is at a disadvantage, as she is on the average nine years younger than her husband, and therefore likely to outlive him. Only those wives who die at abnormally young ages, when their husbands are still living, have a good chance of being recorded. Most wives who live out a normal span of years will also outlive their husbands and pass into the grave unremembered in stone. The inscriptions recording the age of death for wives are thus biased in favor of those fortunate or unfortunate enough to pass away at an untimely age. Hopkins adds the telling comment that gravestone evidence from other periods has proved similarly unreliable. He concludes that it is entirely possible that women died sooner than men in ancient society, but that the inscriptions give no sure proof of this. His criticisms are well taken, but we may still hope that classical scholars, through heightened ingenuity and more refined methods, may yet be able to gain from this enormous fund of inscriptions reliable data concerning life and death under the Roman empire.

Those scholars have already ventured some conclusions concerning the life experience of women in Roman society. There seems to have been fewer women than men.[8] According to the historian Cassius Dio, there were fewer females than males among the free-born population in 18 B.C., and a considerable volume of scattered allusions indicates that girl babies were more likely to be exposed at birth than boys. According to a purported "law of Romulus," the Roman father was required to raise all his male children, but only the firstborn girl. Moreover, on the basis of the inscriptions, the average difference in age between wives and husbands was nine years.[9] This great difference would assure, under normal conditions, that the population would contain a large number of spinsters—unmarried and unmarriageable women, as grooms were selected from higher and narrower levels of the age pyramid. This is clearly the situation in medieval Italian towns, where a comparable age difference separated the spouses and deprived many young girls of all statistical chance of gaining a husband. But classical Latin has not even a word for spinster, and classical society seems to have had no institutions, comparable to the medieval convents, able to provide a haven for unmarriageable girls. This indicates that comparatively fewer girls were reaching adulthood than boys, although we cannot yet determine whether female infanticide or a harder and shorter life for little girls primarily explains the shortage. Whatever the explanation, ancient society seems marked by a dearth of women.

How, if at all, did the treatment and survival of women change in the new world of the Middle Ages? Unfortunately, before the thirteenth century, we have almost no learned comment on aging, death, and the role of sex in advancing or retarding senescence. On the other hand, the surveys of peasant communities, which have survived from the late eighth century, present a comprehensive view of those communities. Here we shall single out for special attention two of these surveys from the Carolingian epoch, which describe the dependent peasants of the church of St. Victor of Marseilles in southern France and of the monastery of Farfa in central Italy.[10] The survey of the serfs of St. Victor includes 128 households, in which the members are identified, and was redacted probably between 813 and 814. The households of Farfa number 299, and this inventory was taken sometime between 789 and 822. The lists of St. Victor give the ages for male children between two and fifteen and for females between one and fifteen—between the time the children were weaned and the time they reached age of marriage. The document also identifies the marriageable members of the population with the terms *baccularius* or *baccularia*. It is possible, therefore, to calculate sex ratios for different status levels of the population —children, those of marriageable age, and those married or widowed—which approximately reflect age levels.

Among the peasants of St. Victor, men slightly outnumber women by a ratio of 102 to 100.[11] But the females are not evenly distributed among the various status and age levels of the population. They dominate the ranks of children. There are 106 female children but only 99 males, a ratio of 93.40. For those children with a stated age, the proportion is even more tipped in favor of girls, as their ages are recorded seventy-four times and only fifty-three times for boys. The parents seem to have been quite conscientious in remembering the ages of their daughters, and this infers that girls were enjoying considerable attention and probably receiving favorable treatment. Certainly there is no suggestion of female infanticide among the peasants of St. Victor. But as the population aged, so the relative numbers of females declined. Among those peasants of marriage age upwards of fifteen years, there are recorded 127 male bachelors, but only 120 maidens. In losing their numerical preponderance, the girls were, however, simultaneously acquiring a favorable position on the marriage market, as the males would have had to compete for a bride or marry outside the community. Among the married or widowed members of the population, including those adults of unstated status, males still predominate, at a slightly reduced ratio of 104 men to every 100 women. Women thus had permanently lost the numerical advantage they enjoyed as children.

The sex ratio, swinging to favor men as the population aged, implies that women were dying sooner than men. The study of skeletal remains from prehistoric and medieval graveyards shows that in comparable communities women did indeed die younger than the males. A recent study of a late iron-age graveyard in Hungary estimates, for example, that the average age of death for the women buried there was twenty-nine years seven months; and that that of men at death was seven years older.[12]

The survey of the peasants of St. Victor seems to be unique among the Carolingian censuses for the detailed and precise information it offers concerning children. Our second list of Carolingian peasants from Farfa in Italy illustrates the difficulties which are commonly encountered in working with these early surveys. The sex ratio of the population is very high—122.24 men per 100 women, if we exclude the 94 landless slaves who were attached to the manor house at Forcone. But females are especially missing in the ranks of the children. The sex ratio for the adult population, excluding the household slaves, is a reasonable 112. But for the children it is a scarcely creditable 135.54. As a further indication of the erratic reporting of children, the redactors frequently did not name them or state their sex, but only noted that there were *filii* in the family. Unfortunately, the lists from Farfa cannot be used to study how the sex ratio shifted between the various age and status categories.

If children, particularly female children, seem to be underreported in most Carolingian surveys, there is, in contrast, evidence that adult women were carefully reported.[13] The redactors of the survey of St. Victor at one place took pains to point out that "these men from this county have our women." [14] Among the ninety-four household slaves in the Farfa lists, twenty-six are described as children, and of these, sixteen bear a matronymic rather than a patronymic. The descent of these landless slaves was being traced through their mothers, doubtlessly because they passed on their own status to their children. The manorial lords, in other words, had to keep careful account of their adult female slaves and serfs, if they wished to maintain their full rights over the new generation.

Much other evidence shows that women were highly regarded in these rural communities. Among the household slaves at Farfa, women outnumber men by seventy-three to twenty-three. Clearly, the manorial lords favored women more than men as members of their household staffs. Among the laws of the Alamanni, a woman attached to the service of the duke was protected with a wergild—the compensation to be paid in case of her death—three times that of the ordinary woman.[15]

Among the peasants themselves, women were no less valued. The population on the lands of St. Victor included sixty *extranei*, outsiders who had married into the households and the villages; thirty-six are men and twenty-four are women. This means that males were somewhat more likely than females to leave home and village after marriage, and many peasant households sought to keep their married daughters with them. At Farfa too, daughters or younger sisters of the household heads occasionally though not commonly remained in their father's or brother's house after marriage.[16] The retention of daughters in the paternal or fraternal household after marriage, even if not the usual practice, still is notable, particularly because it seems to have been so rare in peasant communities of the later Middle Ages.[17] One is reminded of how Charlemagne himself, according to his biographer Einhard, refused to allow his daughters to depart from his household.[18]

The Germanic codes offer some further, striking inferences concerning the value attached to women in early medieval society. The codes characteristically extended a special protection over women and often assigned them a higher wergild than that allotted to their male counterparts. According to the Laws of the Alamanni, if a person caused a pregnant woman to abort a child, and if the sex of the fetus could be discerned, the one responsible had to pay twelve solidi if the fetus was male, and twenty-four if female.[19] The loss of a baby girl was, in other words, considered twice as grave as the loss of a baby boy. In another equally revealing provision from the Laws of the Alamanni, a free man whose wife had been abducted by another man retained his paternal rights over the children she might bear, even though fathered by another. If those children died, he could claim compensation; the compensation was twice as high for a girl as for a boy.[20] All through her life, still according to the Laws of the Alamanni, women were protected with double fines for any injury done to them. "Fines are always double for their women," the Laws at one place affirm.[21] Perhaps the most extraordinary of all these legal provisions protecting women is the imposition of a double fine even for robbing the grave of a woman.[22] This implies that women were characteristically buried with greater treasure than men, perhaps with the jewelry they had acquired at marriage as gifts from their husbands. At all events, from womb to tomb, the women of the Alamanni enjoyed a privileged status.

The Law of the Salian Franks further show how the social value enjoyed by a woman related to her age. The free girl, before she was old enough to bear children, was worth a wergild of 200 solidi—the same sum which protected free men throughout their lives.[23] But after she began to bear children, her wergild was tripled to 600 solidi, and remained at that high level through all her childbearing years. During the periods she was actually pregnant, the penalty for killing her was 700 solidi.[24] In old age, her wergild reverted to the normal charge for a free person. During her years of young adulthood, even when not actually pregnant, the free woman enjoyed the same protection as that accorded to companions of the king or to Christian bishops.[25]

Early medieval society thus manifests a high appreciation of women. Marriage customs reflect this too. Among the Germans, according to Tacitus, "the dowry is brought by husband to wife, not by wife to husband." [26] This male dowry was often called the *Morgengabe,* the "gift of the morning," given by the groom to his bride after the consummation of their marriage. It frequently appears in the laws and charters of the early Middle Ages. The laws of both the Visigoths and the Alamanni even set limits on the value of the gifts which the bride could receive.[27] Such provisions point to a spirited competition for scarce women, which tended to drive up the costs of acquiring a wife. The shortage of marriageable women, evident among the peasants of St. Victor, seems to have been characteristic of many communities during the early Middle Ages.

Here, however, we encounter a paradox. Women, for all the favor in which they were held, for all the special protection they received in law and custom, were not surviving as well as men. Adult women are conspicuously fewer than men in all our Carolingian surveys, in spite of the value they possessed for their lords and in spite of the care with which they were reported. If the survey of the peasants of St. Victor is typical, the sex ratio tended to swing against women as the population aged. Why were they faring so poorly? We can only indicate some few factors that seem to have diminished their hopes of survival. In a violent society, women seem to have been more usually than men the victims of violence. Why else did the barbarian lawgivers feel compelled to lend them a special protection? The Laws of the Alamanni impose the usual double fine for selling a free woman beyond the frontiers of the province; this seems a clear allusion to a continuing slave trade especially involving women.[28] Moreover, the services which made women so valuable seem simultaneously to have been the burdens which thinned their numbers—childbearing of course, but hard labor too. Among the household slaves at Farfa, thirty women are said to "work well"—a curious but suggestive phrase not applied to the men.[29] Women attached to the manor house had primary responsibility for the *cellarium* or storehouse and the *genitium* or workshop.[30] Probably they also cultivated the gardens and the lands near the house. Among the peasants, women seem to have had chief responsibility for the "inner economy" of the household— baking, brewing, care of the yard animals, and the cultivation of lands close to the house. In Tacitus's famous picture of Germanic society, "the care of house, hearth and fields is left to the women, old men and weaklings of the family." [31] Medieval society was doubtlessly slow to lighten the burden of hard and essential labor traditionally demanded from women. Life was hard and short for women in these peasant communities, and the very scarcity of adult women made them valued.

As almost all historians now recognize, medieval society changed profoundly from approximately the eleventh century. One group in society deeply affected by these changes were women. The intellectual Renaissance of the twelfth and thirteenth centuries also revived interest in the question of human longevity. It is especially interesting to observe how scholars of this central period of medieval history interpreted Aristotle's affirmation that men by nature live longer than women. His tract "On the Length and Shortness of Life" reached the Latin medieval world about 1200 as part of a collection of medical and biological writings entitled the *Parva Naturalia*. Sometime about 1250, Vincent of Beauvais considered the relative longevity of men and women in his scientific encyclopedia, the *Speculum Naturale*. He did no more than repeat Aristotle's opinion; "among men," he wrote, "males live longer than females, because the male is warmer than the female." [32] But there are indications that a different opinion was being formed. The Spanish Muslim philosopher Averroes prepared a synopsis of Aristotle's *Parva Naturalia,* which Michael Scot translated into Latin in the middle thirteenth century. Aristotle's argument was garbled, and the translation reversed the philosopher's conclusion; it affirmed that women live longer than men, because they indulge less frequently in sexual intercourse.[33] But was this a mistake or a correction, attributable to Averroes or his translator? Somewhat later in the thirteenth century, the most prominent biologist of the Middle Ages, Albertus Magnus, offered what is apparently the first extended discussion of the longevity of women.[34] He agreed with Aristotle that men by nature live longer than women, for the reason that they are warmer. He added, however, that *per accidens* women in fact live longer than men. Menstruation purifies their systems and sexual intercourse takes less from them. He especially emphasizes that "[women] work less, and are not so much consumed."

This new opinion seems to have been widely shared in the late Middle Ages, even beyond academic circles. In 1354 the count of Flanders, Louis de Male, declared that crusades and wars had so limited the number of men that many noble women could not find suitable husbands, and that religious houses had therefore to be provided for them.[35] In the 1420s, St. Bernardine of Siena placed the number of girls unable to find husbands at twenty thousand in the city of Milan alone, although he chiefly blamed the reluctance of males to marry.[36] In the early sixteenth century, in a defense of the dignity of women which appears in Castiglione's *Courtier,* one point advanced in their favor is that they live longer than men, and thus fulfill the intention of nature better than the males.[37]

There is, in other words, a body of scattered but consistent comment which indicates that between the early and the late Middle Ages, women had gained a superiority over men in life expectancy which they have since retained. Much other indirect but, I think, compelling evidence supports this conclusion. There is the appearance of what German scholars call the *Frauenfrage* or *Frauenbewegung,* the problem of unmarriageable girls, the irregular social and religious movements associated with them. Such women without cloisters or hearths or a fixed place in society came to be called most commonly "Beguines," a word which may be a corruption of "Albigensian." Appearing even before

1150, this medieval woman's movement gained particular strength from the late twelfth century, especially in the Low Countries, the Rhineland, and other relatively urbanized areas of Europe.[38] Contemporaries several times commented on the extraordinary numbers of pious women in the medieval towns.[39] There can be no doubt that a principal thrust behind the Beguine movement was the difficulty girls were encountering in finding a husband. Changes in age of male marriage and a growing reluctance of males to marry doubtlessly were factors, but so also, as the count of Flanders himself affirmed, was a higher level of male mortality.

At the same time, and for the same reasons, the negotiating position of the medieval girl on the marriage market deteriorated woefully. To judge from Italian charters, the male dowry seems to have retained importance until the middle of the twelfth century.[40] Thereafter the dowry, paid by the bride's family to her husband, replaced the "morning gift" as the dominant economic consideration in the negotiation of a marriage. Moreover, at least from 1200, the sums paid as dowries entered upon an inflationary spiral, as fathers competed to find scarce and reluctant grooms for their daughters. Dante himself lamented how the birth of a daughter struck terror into her father's heart; he and other moralists looked back with nostalgia to simpler, better times, when the marriage of a daughter did not threaten ruin for her family.[41]

In sum, between the Germanic codes of the early Middle Ages and the marriage practices of the thirteenth and later centuries, there had occurred a complete reversal in the flow of property between the bride and groom, or their respective families. It seems certain that in the later Middle Ages, comparatively fewer men than women were reaching the age of marriage.

What do population surveys of the late Middle Ages tell of the comparative numbers of women and men in the community? Those surveys which concern cities, particularly north of the Alps, consistently record a numerical preponderance of women. At Rheims in France in 1422, Fribourg in modern Switzerland in 1444, Nuremberg in Germany in

1449, and other cities, women outnumbered men by ratios of from 109 to over 120 females per 100 males.[42] Even in those cities in which women did not hold an absolute numerical advantage over men, they tended to dominate the older levels of the population.[43] It may of course be that the preponderance of women in cities reflects primarily patterns of immigration rather than longevity: women, clearly, preferred urban to rural life.

One area of Europe in which it is possible to survey an entire community, in both its rural and urban segments, is the province of Tuscany in Italy. In 1427, the commune of Florence undertook to count all the persons under its authority in Florence itself, its subject cities, and in the surrounding rural areas. The grand total of households recorded in this survey, called the Catasto, was nearly sixty thousand, and the persons named totaled two hundred and sixty-four thousand.[44] We shall single out for particular attention here the city of Florence and the rural areas which formed its *contado* or county. This part of the Catasto included one hundred and sixty-four thousand persons, of whom slightly more than thirty-seven thousand were resident in the city of Florence itself. The metropolis, in other words, contained about twenty-three percent of the entire population of its region.

This substantial population of one hundred and sixty-four thousand persons contains more men than women, by a ratio of 111 men for every 100 women. But women are also displaced towards the higher, older levels of the age pyramid. The median age for men, both city dwellers and peasants, is twenty-two years, and it is twenty-four for women. The average age for men is 28.00 and 28.51 for women. If we could assume that the population was closed enough and stable enough to calculate life expectancies, women from birth could expect to live to 29.54 years, and men only to 28.50.[45]

Unfortunately, however, distortions in the data limit the confidence we can place in such gross calculations. The population was not really closed and stable. Immigration and emigration probably has little effect upon the figures, since both urban and rural areas, between which most movement occurred, are included in the survey. However, those persons—and women certainly more than men—who entered the religious life were not included in the count. Moreover, the sex ratio for young children zero to four years of age is a high 124.57; in other words, nearly five little boys appear in the census for every four little girls. Were Florentine families more prone to abandon girls than boys? Did advertent or inadvertent female infanticide, or inferior treatment given to little girls, reduce their numbers? [46] Or were girls simply not reported as carefully as boys? There are difficult questions, for which we cannot as yet offer satisfactory answers. Finally, it appears that older, poorer women in the population were often overlooked, or carelessly reported without a stated age. Within the poorest households—those with no taxable assets—there are present nearly three men for every two women aged sixty and over.[47] These problems in the data, particularly affecting women, make it difficult to trace with precision the entire cycle of their lives. It therefore seems safer to concentrate our attention on that age range during which the population was both relatively stable and for which the reporting was most complete—the ages of adulthood from approximately twenty-five to sixty.

Table 3 in the Appendix provides an overview of the sex ratio of the population at various age levels: twelve years and younger; then by five-year intervals from age thirteen to sixty-two; and for all persons older than sixty-two. Because of the pronounced tendency of the population to report their ages as years exactly divisible by ten and by five, the intervals are selected so that the most favored ages ending in zero or five form the middle year. The sex ratio for the entire population between fifteen and sixty-four is 104.24, which gives assurance of a comprehensive reporting of women. The table shows a marked jump in the sex ratio between the interval centering on age fifteen to the interval centering on age twenty-five. Over these years, the fate of most girls was determined; they either married or were placed in convents, and the latter recourse seems to explain their disappearance from the census. After age twenty-five, when the status of women was relatively fixed, the sex ratio

tends to fall continuously through to age sixty. This indicates that in spite of the risks of childbearing, women
were passing through this span at least of their adult lives
more successfully than men. The contemporary opinion
that women lived longer than men seems to be justified, at
least for the adult ages.

As the population aged, so the residence of women
tended to shift more and more in favor of the city. Women
form a majority of the urban population at Florence from
age forty-three onward, in spite of the need, in an industrial
town, for large numbers of male workers.[48] It seems certain
that the city played a major role in extending to women a
better chance of survival.

What explains this apparent improvement in the relative
longevity of women, between the early and the late Middle
Ages? The curtailment of violence in medieval life aided
them, as it did all the physically weaker members of the
community—children and the aged, as well as women. The
emergence of effective governments assured them greater
personal security and protection against rape, abduction
and enslavement. The slow spread of a Christian ethos also
tempered violence and helped build an orderly society,
which inevitably favored the physically weak. New attitudes
toward warfare had a similar effect. According to Tacitus,
the barbarian woman shared all the dangers faced by her
husband, in peace and war.[49] But the newer ideals of medieval chivalry virtually excluded the woman from direct in-
volvement in the dangerous arts of fighting, and warriors
were urged to defend her. The refinement of manners and
morals, associated with the new courts and the new cities,
probably helped relieve some women of the heavy physical
tasks which earlier medieval society had imposed upon
them.

Fundamental changes in the medieval economy also improve conditions of survival for women. The emergence, in
close association with the city, of an important, non-agricul-
tural economic sector, offered an escape from rural life,
which seems often to have been particularly demanding on
women. Spinning, sewing and other occupations practiced
by women in the towns were less exhausting than planting,

hoeing and harvesting. Albertus Magnus believed that women lived longer than men primarily because they worked less and were not so much consumed. Perhaps he had urban society primarily in mind; perhaps this is a reason why medieval cities strongly attracted women.

There remains, however, this paradox: as her hopes of surviving improved, as her relative numbers grew, so the social position of the medieval woman seems in some ways to have deteriorated. To cite Dante once more, the Florentine father viewed his newborn baby girl with terror in his heart, as he thought how difficult and costly it would be to arrange for her future. Attitudes toward women had departed much from those reflected in the Laws of the Alamanni, in which the loss of a baby girl is reckoned as twice as grave as the death of a baby boy. In the society of the later Middle Ages, particularly in the cities, the contribution of woman in physical labor was less needed than in former times. Her biological function as childbearer and her services as manager of a household remained of course vital to society, but her very numbers assured that many girls would never attain and fulfill those roles. Many women in late medieval society, especially in the cities, were economically superfluous and regarded as a burden by their own families. Many understandably grew alienated from the institutions and the values of society. This surely is why irregular religious movements, such as the Beguines, and full-blown heresies too, had a powerful appeal for women. To its honor, the medieval world over the long course of its history improved conditions of life and lengthened the span of years allotted to women. But it never succeeded in developing for their increased numbers assured and open ways to personal and human fulfillment. That problem it passed on to subsequent generations and subsequent epochs; we face it still today.

Notes

1. The Greek text and an English translation are conveniently available in *Aristotle on the Soul. Parva Naturalia. On Breath*, ed. and trans. W. S. Hett, Loeb Classical Library (London: William Heinemann; Cambridge: Harvard University Press, 1957).

2. Ibid., p. 405.

3. Ibid., p. 403: "The living creature is naturally moist and warm whereas old age is cold and dry, and so is a dead body."

4. See Plini Secundi, *Naturalis Historia*, 7:4, in *Natural History*, ed. H. Rackham, tans. W. H. S. Jones, Loeb Classical Library (Cambridge: Harvard University Press; London: William Heinemann, 1942) 2:530: ". . . feminas clerius gigni quam mares, sicuti celerius senescere. . . ."

5. Galeni comment. III in Hippocratis lib. II Epidemiorum. *Claudii Galeni Opera Omnia* (Leipzig, 1828) 17, pt. 1, p. 445: "Quum autem foeminae quam mares celerius procerentur, hae quoque iuventutem et florem et senectutem citius consequuntur."

6. See especially A. R. Burn, *"Hic Breve Vivitur.* A Study of the Expectation of Life in the Roman Empire," *Past and Present* 4 (1953):2–31.

7. "On the Probable Age Structure of the Roman Population," *Population Studies* 20 (1966–67):245–64.

8. The following discussion is based upon Peter Astbury Brunt, *Italian Manpower, 225* B.C.–A.D. *14* (Oxford: Oxford University Press, Clarendon Press, 1971). See also A. H. M. Jones, "Census Records of the Late Empire," *Journal of Roman Studies* 43 (1953):55–56. Jones describes a fragmentary census of nine peasant households in Asia Minor, dating probably from the early fourth century; in the households men outnumber women by twenty to eleven.

9. M. K. Hopkins, "The Age of Roman Girls at Marriage," *Population Studies* 18 (1964–65):309–27.

10. The "Descriptio mancipiorum ecclesie massiliensis" is published in the *Cartulaire de l'abbaye de Saint-Victor de Marseille*, ed. Benjamin E. C. Guérard, 2 (Paris, 1857), pp. 633–56. For the "De familiis Sanctae Mariae," see *Il Regesto di Farfa compilato da Gregorio di Catino*, ed. Ugo Balzani and I. Giorgi, Societata Romana de Storia Patria (Rome, 1892).

11. For a presentation of the data in tabular form, see Appendix, Table 1, below.

12. E. G. Jerem, "The Late Iron Age Cemetery of Szentlórinc," *Acta Archaeologica Academiae Scientiarum Hungaricae* 19 (1967):159–208. For a survey of studies of skeletal remains from medieval Hungarian graveyards, see Eric Fügedi, "Pour une analyse démographique de la Hongrie médiévale," *Annales-Economies-Sociétés-Civilisations* 24 (1969):1299–1312. The evidence from five sites indicates that men were consistently outliving women by an average of 1.6 years.

13. For further discussion concerning sex ratios in the Caroligian surveys, see Emily R. Coleman, "Medieval Marriage Characteristics: A Neglected Factor in the History of Medieval Serfdom," *The Journal of Interdisciplinary History* 2 (1971):205–19.

14. Benjamin Guérard, *Saint-Victor*, p. 650: "Abent illi homines de illo commite nostras feminas."

15. *Leges Alamannorum*, ed. Karl Lehmann, Monumenta Germaniae Historica, Legum Sectio (Hanover: Hahn, 1888), vol. 5, pt. 1, p. 90: "De feminis, quae in ministerio ducis sunt."

16. Balzani and Giorgi (eds.), *Farfa*, 5:261. The household of "Ursus cum fratre suo anserado" includes two sisters with children. I take the word "affiliatus" used in the survey to mean son-in-law. Cf. ibid., p. 261: "Audefridus cum uxore sua anserada, anteadus affiliatus eius cum uxore sua auta."

17. In the Catasto survey of Florence and its Tuscan possessions, redacted in 1427,

among slightly less than sixty thousand urban and rural households included, there seems to have been not a single instance of two daughters or two sisters with children remaining in their father's or brother's house. Such a situation is found at least once among the less than 300 households of Farfa.

18. *The Life of Charlemagne by Einhard*, trans. Samuel E. Turner, with a foreword by Sidney Painter (Ann Arbor: University of Michigan Press, 1960), chap. 19, p. 44: "Strange to say, although they were very handsome women, and he loved them very dearly, he was never willing to marry any of them to a man of their own nation or to a foreigner, but kept them all at home until his death, saying that he could not dispense with their society."

19. Lehmann, *Leges Alamannorum,* p. 150: "Si quis mulieri pregnanti abortivum fecerit, ita ut iam cognoscere possit, utrum vir an femina fuit, si vir debuit esse, cum 12 solidis componat; si autem femina, cum 24."

20. Ibid., p. 109.

21. Ibid., chap. 68, p. 129: "Feminas autem eorum semper in duplum componat."

22. Ibid., chap. 1, p. 108. The fine was forty solidi for robbing the grave of a free man, and eighty for a free woman. The fine was twelve solidi for robbing the grave of an unfree person of either sex. This implies that the grave of a free woman was especially tempting for robbers.

23. *Pactus Legis Salicae,* ed. K. A. Eckhardt, Monumenta Germaniae Historica, Legum Sectio 1, vol. 4, pt. 1 (Hanover: Hahn, 1962), p. 160.

24. Ibid., pp. 89 and 161.

25. Ibid., p. 154, where those "in truste dominica" or free women are given a wergild of 600 solidi. See the "Capitula legi salicae addita," ibid., p. 273, for reference to the wergild of bishops.

26. *On Britain and Germany. A Translation of the "Agricola" and the "Germania" of Tacitus,* trans. H. Mattingly (Harmondsworth, Middlesex: Penguin Books, 1964), p. 115.

27. *Leges visigothorum,* ed. Karl Zeumer, Monumenta Germaniae Historica, Legum Sectio 1 (Hanover and Leipzig: Hahn, 1892), 1, p. 127. *Leges Alamannorum,* chaps. 55–56, p. 112.

28. *Leges Alamannorum Antiquiores,* pp. 105–6. The penalty for selling a free man who later returned alive was forty solidi, and eighty solidi for a free woman.

29. Balzan, *Farfa,* 5:258: "De manicipiis quae bene laborant. . . ." This is followed by a list of those women slaves "quae mediocriter laborant."

30. See, for example, the *Pactus legis salicae,* p. 261: "ancilla ipsa cellarium aut genitium domini sui tenuerit. . . ." On the economic role of women in the early Middle Ages, see Jutta Barchewitz, *Von der Wirtschaftstätigkeit der Frau in der vorgeschichtlichen Zeit bis zur Entfaltung der Stadtwirtschaft,* Breslauer historische Forschungen, no. 3 (Breslau: Priebatsch, 1937).

31. *Tacitus On Britain and Germany,* p. 113.

32. *Speculum Naturale* (Graz: Akademische Druck- und Verlagsanstalt, 1964), bk. 24, chap. 67 (De vita et morte animalium): "Sed in homine masculini foeminis plus vivunt, quia masculus femina calidior sit."

33. *Averrois cordubensis compendia librorum Aristotelis qui Parva naturalia vocentur,* ed. Aelia Ledyard Shields, with the assistance of Henry Blumberg, Corpus commentariorum Averrois in Aristotelem 7 (Cambridge, Mass.: Mediaeval Academy of

America, 1949), p. 139: "Et propter paucitatem coitus vivit mulus plus quam equus et femine plus quam masculi."

34. *Alberti Magni ordinis fratrum praedicatorum Opera omnia,* vol. 12 (Monasterium Westfalorum, 1955), bk. 15, quaestio. 8, p. 263. Quaestiones super de animalibus. To the question "utrum longioris vitae sit mas aut femina," Albert replied: "Per accidens tamen longioris vitae est femina, tum quia minus laborant propter quod non tantum consumuntur, et magis mundificantur per fluxum menstruorum et etiam minus debitantur per coitum; ideo magis conservantur. Et istae causae accidentales sunt."

35. *Cartulaire du Béguinage de Sainte-Élisabeth à Gand,* ed. Jean B. Béthune de Villers (Bruges, 1883), p. 89.

36. *La prediche volgari,* ed. Ciro Cannarozzi, O.F.M. (Florence: Tipografia E. Rinaldi, 1958), 2:107: ". . . in Milano, quando frate Bernardino tornò, li fu detto che venti milia fanciulle v'erano da maritare, senza le maritate. . . ."

37. *The Book of the Courtier,* trans. Charles S. Singleton (New York: Anchor Books, 1959), p. 219.

38. On the Beguines, see Ernest W. McDonnell, *The Beguines and Beghards in Medieval Culture, with Special Emphasis on the Belgian Scene* (New Brunswick, N.J.: Rutgers University Press, 1954); Herbert Grundmann, *Religiöse Bewegungen im Mittelalter: Untersuchungen über die geschichtlichen Zusammenhänge zwischen der Ketzerei, den Bettelorden und den religiösen Frauenbewegungen im 12. und 13. Jahrhundert und über die geschichtlichen Grundlagen der deutschen Mystik* (Berlin: E. Eberring, 1935; 2nd edition, Hildesheim: Olms, 1961). And Otto Nübel, *Mittelalterliche Beginen und Sozialsiedlungen in den Niederlanden. Ein Beitrag zur Vorgeschichte der Fuggerei* (Tübingen: Mohr, 1970).

39. As early as ca. 1150, the number of women associated with the Premonstratensian religious order in Flanders was said to be ten thousand. See Nübel, *Beginensiedlungen,* p. 15.

40. The marriage contracts recorded in the chartulary of the Genoese notary Giovanni Scriba typically called for a virtually equal exchange of property between bride and groom, or their respective families. For this information I am indebted to Mr. Thomas Mitchell of the University of Wisconsin.

41. *Paradiso* 15, 103–5: "Non faceva nascendo ancor paura / la figlia al padre; chè 'l tempo e la dote / non fuggian quinci e quindi / la misura." See also the *Cronica di Giovanni Villani* (Florence: Magheri, 1823) 2:96. In describing the customs of the Florentines in the days of the Primo Popolo (1250–60), Villani notes ". . . e lire cento era comune dota di moglie, e lire dugento o trecento era a quegli tempi tenuta isfalgorata; e le più delle pulcelle aveano venti o più anni, anzi ch' andassono a marito." Villani himself died in the Black Death of 1348.

42. See Pierre Desportes, "La population de Reims au XVe siècle," *Le Moyen Age. Revue d'histoire et de philologie* 74 (1966):486.

43. The figures are from Desportes, "Reims," p. 486. See also Fritz Rörig, *The Medieval Town* (Berkeley and Los Angeles: University of California Press, 1967), p. 115, for representative sex ratios from German towns in the late Middle Ages.

44. We exclude here additions made to the Catasto of the city of Florence in 1428–29 and 1429–30, which bring the number of the urban population close to 40,000. The exact figure for the urban population without the additions is 37,146

persons. The total population of the Florentine *contado,* including the city, is
164,083; those with ages stated are 161,398.

45. The estimate assumes that the population is stable and closed, without immigration and emigration, and with birth rates exactly equal to death rates. It goes
without saying that it is very crude, but may have some value for comparing the
life expectancies of men and women.

46. Higher mortalities for infant girls than for infant boys are not uncommon in
traditional societies. See the remarks of Peter A. Brunt, *Italian Manpower,* p. 151.

47. The exact ratio of those in the population living in households with no assess-
ment is 144.02.

48. At Bologna, for example, at the end of the fourteenth century, women
formed a majority of those in the population older than fifteen years. See Paolo
Montanari, *Documenti su la popolazione di Bologna alla fine del trecento,* Società Storia
di Bologna-Fonti per 12 storia di Bologna, Testi, 1 (Bologna, 1966), p. 9.

49. *Tacitus on Britain and Germany,* p. 116: "A woman must not imagine herself
. . . immune from the hazards of war. That is why she is reminded, in the very
ceremonies which bless her marriage at its outset, that she is coming to share a
man's toils and dangers, that she is to be his partner in all his sufferings and adventures."

Appendix

Table 1
Sex Ratios among the Peasants of Saint Victor of Marseilles

	Males	Females	Ratio	No Sex Stated *	Totals
Nurslings				29	29
Children	99	106	93.40	126	331
Bachelors	127	120	105.83		247
Adults	212	203	104.43	5	420
Totals	438	430	101.86	159	1027

* Children described only as "filii" with no names or numbers given are counted as two children of uncertain sex.
Source: *Cartulaire de l'abbaye de Saint-Victor de Marseille,* ed. B. Guérard, vol. 2 (Paris, 1857), pp. 633–56.

Table 2
Sex Ratios among the Peasants of Santa Maria of Farfa *

	Males	Females	Ratio	No Sex Stated	Totals
Unmarried Children	328	242	135.54	123	693
Married and Unmarried Adults	352	307	114.66		659
Widowed	18	22	81.82		40
Totals	698	571	122.24	123	1392

* Does not include 22 males and 72 females attached to manor house.
Source: *Il Regesto di Farfa compilato da Gregorio di Catino,* ed. I. Giorgi and U. Balzani, vol. 5 (Rome, 1892), pp. 254–63.

Table 3
Sex Ratios in the Florentine Population, Urban and Rural, 1427

Age Interval	Males	Females	Type I Interval		Type II Interval
0–12	30808	24928		(123.59)	
13–17	6102	6481	94.5		
18–22	6273	5791			108.32
23–27	5329	4531	117.61		
28–32	5487	5172			106.09
33–37	4022	3711	108.38		
38–42	5114	4715			108.46
43–47	3353	3114	107.68		
48–52	3958	4224			93.76
53–57	2421	2294	105.40		
58–62	3495	3830			91.25
63–99	8718	7524		(113.74)	
0–99	85080	76318		(110.87)	

A Type I interval is one centering on a number ending in 5 (15, 25, etc.); a Type II interval is one centering on a number ending in 0 (20, 30, etc.). The intervals are grouped in separate columns in order to show more clearly how the sex ratios shift over time.

Transformations of the Heroine: From Epic Heard to Epic Read

FRANZ H. BÄUML

University of California at Los Angeles

It is not without significance in the context of medieval literature that the two greatest German heroic epics—the *Nibelungenlied* (henceforth *Nl*) and the *Kudrun*—both turn about the figures of two women. In fact, there is something to be said for regarding the *Nl*, among many other things, as essentially a Kriemhild biography, and the *Kudrun* is nothing if not an account of the lives of Hilde and her daughter Kudrun up to the latter's marriage—after which she presumably ceases to be interesting. But however one wishes to characterize the plots of these two poems, in literary-historical terms they are—or were originally—heroic epics. It is precisely the difference between their function before they assumed the form in which they are transmitted and their function in the transmitted form which determines the significance of the protagonists. That this significance extends beyond the boundaries of literary history and criticism is vouched for by the astounding popularity of these poems in the thirteenth century, a fact which assures that the emergence and transformation of a literary symbol found an echo in extra-literary symbolism.[1]

23

In the *Nl* we are immediately introduced in stanza 2 to Kriemhild—the only figure to survive 2375 stanzas, to be dispatched four stanzas from the end. We are told that she was very beautiful, much sought after, and that her polish was exemplary. This description is interrupted briefly by an account of her brothers and the Burgundian court, to resume in the form of an indirect depiction of Kriemhild—indirect because the vehicle is an action: the falcon dream and the ensuing conversation with her mother. Kriemhild had dreamt that a falcon which she had trained had been torn to pieces by two eagles. When her mother interprets the dream as referring to the danger awaiting her future husband, Kriemhild declares that all this is nonsense, she will have nothing to do with love. In fact, she says "I want to remain so beautiful until I die, that I shall never suffer distress because of the love of a man" (15.3-4). These lines have been consistently misinterpreted in direct defiance of the text, in order to avoid a conflict with the traditional view of young Kriemhild as a sort of pre-Goethean proto-Gretchen. In wishing to remain beautiful, however, *so that* she will never have to bear the sorrows attendant upon love, she intends to use her beauty to attract *so that* she can control. Against this, her mother represents the standpoint hallowed by tradition and society: "Don't disparage it," she says, for "if you are ever to enjoy happiness in this world, it will be because of the love of a man" (16.1-3). Kriemhild answers—and this bears out my interpretation of her earlier assertion—that there are examples aplenty of love leading to sorrow, and "I intend to avoid them [love and sorrow] both; thus nothing can ever fail me" (17.4). At this point, therefore, the role of Kriemhild as disruptive, as illustrative—in the terms of Robert Scholes and Robert Kellogg—of one type of disorder in that multifaceted conflict between *ordo* and *inordinatio* which constitutes the *Nl*, is fully prepared.[2] It is of no consequence, in this respect, exactly how the *Nl* is read: conservatively and unhistorically as a double tragedy—the murder of Siegfried and the fall of the Burgundians—or exegetically or pseudo-exegetically as an elucidation of the polarity of *ordo* vs. *inordinatio,* or as an allegorical representation of two types of power, or—related to it—as a symbolic treatment of the conflict between two conceptions of right: might vs. legitimacy. Whatever the case, Kriemhild functions throughout as disruptive and ultimately cataclysmic.[3]

Up to this point we have approached the *Nl* in the usual naive manner: there is a text before us—we shall analyze it; there is a riddle before us—we shall solve it. This approach is not only naive (since it ignores the necessity of a simultaneous analysis of its analytical tools),[4] but is also usually viewed as irreconcilable with, indeed opposed to, a regard for the evolution of the poem. And to the extent that it ignores the development of the object of its analysis, it is unhistorical. It shall be my purpose to suggest that the "historical" or "genetic" approach is not inimical to, but an absolute necessity for any analysis of the epic which is to be defensible on historical and sociological grounds. And furthermore, the historical approach must determine our present critical view and become incorporated in our analytical methodology.

The *Nl*—and we shall concentrate on it for the moment—emanates from the age of the migrations. Its narrative matter is transmitted in various forms in Old Norse as well as in German. As far as the epic proper is concerned, it is transmitted in thirty-four manuscripts or fragments, dating from the thirteenth century or later. In short, around 1200 there began a lively scribal activity around the *Nl*, lively enough to leave behind thirty-four survivors to testify to the poem's popularity. Before 1200, however, there is no evidence of a written tradition of the *Nl* in Germany. Its transmission in Germany appears to have been predominantly or entirely oral. This hypothesis is in agreement with general literary-historical facts as we know them: German vernacular literature was predominantly religious before the end of the twelfth century, and it was only in the latter half of the twelfth century that secular literature began to be written in the vernacular to any appreciable extent. And internal evidence—formulaic diction and thematic composition—also supports our hypothesis that until around 1200, when the *Nl* entered the written tradition, and no doubt for some time after that, it was transmitted orally. Except for this last statement about its formulaic and oral-thematic content, this is the usual literary-historical view, which, when presented in detail, continues to set forth the poem's hypothetical development from concise song to broad epic—the Heuslerian hypothesis. That this hypothesis is untenable in light of our present knowledge of oral composition need not concern us here.[5] Rather, it is of central importance for us to note that the literary-historical fact of the change in medium of transmission from oral to written has profound influences on the perception, and therefore on the significance of the transmitted text. In other words, if the significance of our epic ladies is to be derived from the epic rather than from the creative subconscious of the critic, textual analysis—to repeat an old but often ignored bit of common sense—must be wedded to the historical determinants of that which is to be analyzed. Before we subject them to sociological and anthropological scrutiny, therefore, Kriemhild and Brunhild must curb their epic tempers in the wings while we remove the glasses of twentieth-century literacy and view the nature of their changing native habitats.

Oral poetry is the poetry of the illiterate. Now one thinks of literacy as a rather complicated phenomenon: there are various kinds and degrees of literacy; there are developmental stages; the literacy of the twelfth century was something quite different from modern Western literacy, etc. Illiteracy, however, is usually conceived of simply as an absence of literacy. This is an oversimplification. To begin with, one must distinguish between socially functional illiteracy and illiteracy within a literate society. Socially functional illiteracy prevails in illiterate societies, that is, in societies whose leading strata are illiterate, and in which literacy is the exception and is used only for limited purposes. The society of Homeric Greece is an example, with Linear B used only for very limited, non-discursive communication. To a somewhat lesser extent, some of the tribal societies of the period of the migrations can likewise be considered as being functionally illiterate. In such societies, the knowledge necessary for their social cohesiveness, for their social identity and governance—myth, law, etc.—is transmitted orally.[6] Literate societies depend upon the transmission of such knowledge in writing. This is the case for both modern and medieval society, and has little to do with the actual literacy of individuals. It is immaterial that many noblemen of the twelfth century were illiterate, but it is important that they relied on codified laws and the written doctrine of the Church. That is, whether or not they themselves could read and write, their perception of themselves and the world around them was determined by literacy—even if it was the literacy of others.

In contrast to members of a functionally illiterate society, the illiterates within a literate society—in other words those who do not rely upon writing for the transmission of knowledge—constitute a disadvantaged subgroup. This holds true for the illiterate singers of Yugoslavia investigated by Parry and Lord in the 1930s and 1950s, as well as for the illiterates of Germany in the twelfth and thirteenth centuries. Neither subgroup had occasion to use orally transmitted narrative material in the manner in which it was used within a functionally illiterate society: as a vehicle for the transmission of the knowledge essential for the governance of society. Literate society provided the governance for both groups. Yet these disadvantaged illiterate subgroups did identify with the orally transmitted heroic material as myth. Heroic ages, after all, appear to be born of a need for them by those conscious of their own present disadvantages.[7]

The *Nl* and its women, then—and probably Kudrun and her mother as well—transversed essentially three stages in the social development of the work's poets and its audiences: (1) the stage of its origin—tribal society with its functional illiteracy—or better, preliteracy, (2) the disadvantaged, because illiterate subgroup within literate medieval society, and (3) the literate poet and his public.

In the first stage, identified with preliterate, tribal society, the epic—any epic—fulfilled an encyclopedic role.[8] It was the repository of the knowledge necessary for the function and cohesion of preliterate society. The heroes and their deeds were the vehicles for the illustration of the tribal mores. This essential didactic content, moreover, had no existence independent from the performance, the recitation of the epic. This is one of the most important distinctions between the function of literature in an illiterate, or preliterate society and its function in the context of literacy: a piece of writing has an independent existence; it can be put aside, gone back to, checked and rechecked, and it will not change if it is forgotten; the content of an oral epic lives only in the performance and the memory.[9] The energies of preliterate societies were therefore spent in the effort to *preserve* the continuity of their cultures; only a literate culture can afford, by possessing the means of "freezing" its building-blocks in writing, to innovate on a significant scale.[10] It is therefore safe to assume—to return to Kriemhild for a moment—that her role in the preliterate stage of the epic was quite different from that in the transmitted text. The encyclopedic function of the epic—and it was an epic, not a series of songs—demands that the narrative matter cluster about the culture-hero Siegfried and the issue of revenge for the treachery of Etzel against Kriemhild's brothers. If the narrative matter of an oral epic is to fulfill its function in a preliterate society, if, in short, it is to carry out its function of preserving the group mores, then those who act in it must carry out actions involving the public law and the family law of that society. This is the case with Siegfried and also with Kriemhild as instrument of revenge for Etzel's treachery against her brothers (as transmitted in the *Edda* and the *Völsungasaga*). It is unlikely, to say the least, for a negatively exemplary figure—a villainess—to become the encyclopedic vehicle for the knowledge a preliterate society must preserve. She was not yet what she was to become: she was neither the principal protagonist nor the symbol. And insofar as Kudrun is an anti-Kriemhild, exemplifying wronged womanhood's less ferocious virtues—patience and forgiveness—*Kudrun* must have assumed this relationship to the *Nl* at a later stage, when Kriemhild had already assumed the pejorative function transmitted in the *Nl.* In any case, inasmuch as the transmitted *Kudrun* treats the abduction and servitude of Kudrun as a crime—in distinction to the adventurous abduction of her mother Hilde—Kudrun's pouring of Christian oil upon the troubled waters of heroic revenge is not likely to have formed part of an encyclopedia of preliterate Germanic culture.

Before we follow our ladies into the realm of illiteracy within a literate society, let us look briefly at some of the conditions of their existence in both realms.

The preliterate or illiterate poet does not recite epics from memory; he composes them while he recites. His building blocks are of two kinds: on the lexical level, not words, but formulae. Each formula is a rhythmically organized unit of meaning: "a group of words which is regularly employed under the same metrical conditions to express a given essential idea." [11] The formation of these "semantic formulae" appears to be governed by "syntactic formulae" or "syntactic frames," which are, of course, dependent on the syntax of the language in question.[12] The semantic formulae, however, are part of the oral tradition. Similarly, part of the tradition of oral poetry are the building blocks of the narrative itself: the so-called themes.[13] The recitation of a poem composed in this manner precludes the perception of any part of it as "fixed" in our sense. Each recitation of a given poem by the same poet will differ from each other such recitation—a difference which the poet and his audience may or may not notice. If it is a matter of length, it will be noticed. If it is a matter of the change of words, or of formulae, it is not likely to be noticed unless the narrative itself is changed—and this, of course, is inadmissible since it violates the tradition, which is sacred.[14] The spoken word is as ephemeral as its sound, and it is, moreover, unidentifiable by the illiterate with a visual image of letters on paper. And in addition it is embedded in a rhythmically organized formula. The very element, then, upon which we rely in identifying meaning in a text—the word as form—is unavailable to the illiterate listening to the oral epic.

To continue for a moment with external aspects of oral recitation—for, after all, these externals condition the perception of the poem on the part of the audience. Spoken recitation can be preserved only in the processes of remembrance and repetition, remembrance being dependent on repetition. Repetition, or, better, recitation is dependent for its effect upon one sense: hearing. The material to be recited is therefore cast into forms associable with acoustic laws and rhythm, evoking sympathetic association in the movement of limbs. This use of rhythm is a powerful mnemonic device. Its effectiveness, however, depends on its efficiency in encouraging a psychic merging of perceiver with the matter perceived. This process can be—and in the oral epic demonstrably is—reinforced by the fact that the object of the narrative is action. As Eric Havelock has pointed out: "it is easiest to excite [bodily reflexes of larynx or limbs] through words if the words themselves evoke action and hence if they describe action." [15] The necessity, in oral poetry, of conceiving of any item of knowledge as an event in time, an action rather than a datum frozen into a syntax of general and therefore timeless validity—this necessity itself also reinforces the mnemonic function of oral poetry.[16] The processes of composition and of perception and memory draw upon the same function of paratactic sequences of episodes.

Illiterate subgroups, the disadvantaged in a literate society, had no need of the oral epic as an encyclopedia (which served preliterate society by preserving its socially essential knowledge). But the fact is that it did preserve it and transmit it, just as it was transmitted in preliterate society. The questions therefore arise: why? and what was the relationship of the oral epic so transmitted to the secular epic, written in the vernacular, which began to "surround" it in the late twelfth century? The answer, of course, lies in the restricted function of an illiterate subgroup within a literate society. The oral epic no longer functioned as transmitter of data necessary for the guidance of society, but rather as preserver of the data found useful in the conduct of daily life. To be sure, it had fulfilled this function in preliterary society also. Now, however, among the illiterate disadvantaged, its function was reduced in scope, just as the social function of the illiterates themselves was reduced. Transmitted knowledge cannot be built upon or adapted if its very existence is limited to the process of its preservation. Hence the well-known conservatism of preliterate societies as well as of illiterate subgroups.[17] And this conservatism characterizes attitudes toward the inherited plot of land as well as to myths of general social significance.

The two points of view represented by Kriemhild and her mother respectively regarding Kriemhild's dream of the falcon, for instance, are likely to be understood by the disadvantaged as maternal admonition to play the traditional role of woman and let her fulfillment depend on marriage. And obviously the understanding of this initial scene determines the manner in which the poem is perceived in its entirety: if—as can be expected from an illiterate subgroup of a literate society—this scene is viewed as exemplary of maternal admonition, then the mother is shown to be right in respect to her prophecy that the daughter will marry and like it. I do not suggest that this scene was part of the epic in a preliterate social context—although it can be assumed to have been part of oral transmission in the context of the illiterate subgroup of around 1200 on the basis of its formulaic content. But I do suggest that the common distinction between the Norse and the German traditions—that is, the transformation of Kriemhild from fury avenging the murder of her brothers on her husband to Kriemhild as fury avenging the murder of her first husband on her brothers—I do suggest that this distinction is not one between Norse and German, or pagan and Christian, but rather between preliterate and disadvantaged illiterate. The former is an affair of state, and can only be perceived as an affair of state. Kriemhild, on this level, perpetuates tribal social order. The latter can be perceived as an exemplum of the faithfulness of wife to husband.

Up to this point the philological ice under our feet has admittedly been rather thin in spots. We shall now, however, skate closer to shore. A comparison of the perception of an oral epic by an illiterate public with that of a written epic by a literate audience has the advantage of yielding somewhat surer footing than a comparison of the perception of an oral epic by two types of illiterate audiences.

To begin with, we know that the *Nl,* and the *Kudrun* also, were transmitted orally in virtually the form in which they are transmitted in writing, before and probably still after they were written down. The density of their formulaic con-

tent and their thematic construction testify to that. We also
know that what we have in writing is not merely the written
record of an oral performance. The variations in formulaic
density throughout the text compel the assumption that the
text as transmitted is an adaptation of an oral poem by a literate poet.[18] But apart from all this—and here lies the
point—when words are written down, they are perceived in
a different manner, one which has far-reaching consequences for the perception of their meaning.

The oral poet uses formulae as compositional elements;
the writing poet employs words. The illiterate listener hears
familiar units of meaning (that is, traditional formulae); the
literate reader sees symbolic forms (that is, words), each
form being a semantic unit. The formulae are embedded in
a traditional semantic context; words are isolatable from a
semantically determining context. This makes possible the
perception of verbal irony. We can return to Kriemhild for
an instance: just after her conversation with her mother, we
are told that she did indeed not have anything to do with
love (stanza 18, lines 1–3):

> Kriemhild in ir muote   sich minne gar bewac.
> sît lebte diu vil guote   vil manegen lieben tac,
> daz sine wesse niemen   den minnen wolde ir lîp.

"Diu vil guote" is an oral formula; it means as much as
"she." The context demands a series of formulae such as
these. But what was to the illiterate listener a familiar and
expected epic epithet becomes to the reader a series of
words. This series of words neither is, nor is regarded as
necessarily dependent on tradition. Similarly, these words
are not dependent on a context shaped by and perceived in
terms of a tradition. In fact, the context does not shape the
words; the words shape the meaning of the context. The
relationship between words and context in a written text is
precisely opposite to that between formulae and theme in
oral recitation. It now becomes possible to distinguish between word and meaning—between "wort unde meine"—

and between epithet and action. Now that the word and its meaning are divorced from the passing sound of recitation and are fixed to be seen and weighed, the narrative is no longer perceived simply as a series of actions. That which is said can now be contrasted to that which is done, and without any lexical change an oral formula may become ironic. For now the series of words "diu vil guote" is no longer perceived merely as "she," but rather as comprising the word, and therefore the concept "guot." After the rather heated discussion with her mother about her proper role in life, and in view of the fact that just twelve stanzas previously we are told that her brothers are to meet their death because of the quarrel of two women—Kriemhild and Brunhild—it is obvious that the words "diu vil guote" can be regarded ironically, characterizing Kriemhild as she had not been characterized by the oral recitation of the same words.

The âventiure devoted to the conquest of Brunhild offers several particularly clear examples of the creation of irony through the change in perception from formula to word. The formula "sprach das minneclîche wîp," for instance, or any of its dozens of variations, is applied traditionally in any context in which a woman is denoted as speaking. Any woman, except Kundrie in Parzival, qualifies as a "minneclîche meit"; the formula merely signifies "she said." When Brunhild is told the purpose of Gunther's visit, she makes her athletic stipulations and the consequences of failure unmistakably clear (425):

Den stein sol er werfen   unt springen dar nâch,
den gêr mit mir schiezen.   lât iu niht sîn ze gâch.
ir muget wol hie verliesen   die êre und ouch den lîp,
des bedénket iuch vil ebene,"   sprach daz minniclîche wîp.

The listener hears the familiar formula, "sprach daz minniclîche wîp"; the reader, however, sees a series of words, one of which is "minniclîche," which is called for neither by tradition, nor by context. It might just as well—and far more appropriately—be "griuwelîche." In short, the reader perceives an instance of verbal irony which, due to the function of tradition in oral composition, is not likely to be perceptible to the listener.

But the divorce of word and meaning from the passing sound leads to more than the possibility of perception of verbal irony. In an oral performance, as has been remarked, it is essential—especially in the preliterate society which the oral epic serves as encyclopedia—to make use of all mnemonic devices possible: rhythm, the presentation of all data as events in time, as actions, the use of predominantly visual imagery. The effect of all this—the *desired* effect—is the identification of the hearer with the poem. A written text, as has also been remarked, has an independent existence. It is, moreover, perceived through the eye, which makes it possible to ignore rhythm, and to change or reverse the given sequence of events by perceiving them repeatedly and in different sequences. In the perception of oral poetry, therefore, the poet is identical with the narrator and both are identical with the text. There is no distance between these compositional elements. To the perceiver of a written text, the poet is not present; he is therefore distinct from the text. The narrator frequently enough places distance between himself and the poet, and—as in confessions of ignorance of textual elements (e.g., 10.4), or in repetition of narrative elements for structural purposes (e.g., 18–19)—he sets himself apart from the text. The very aim of the oral poet—to achieve, by means of all sorts of mnemonic devices, an identification of the listener with the poem—is reversed in the written text. The listener to an oral performance ideally merges with that performance, and hence cannot think about it. Only the written text holds still and thus puts the reader at a distance and in a position to think *about* it.

This means that the text also became, in a sense, removed from its subject-matter. But what of this subject-matter? The view of history, or better, the view of the past, of preliterate societies, and of illiterate subgroups within literate societies, is not only conservative: it is homoeostatic. The material transmitting this past—the oral epic—changes as the past is changed by the present, by adapting rather than transforming itself.[19] The past is neither transmitted, nor perceivable as the past. Siegfried receives the training of a twelfth-century knight, yet remains Siegfried, the scourge of dragons and lord of inexhaustible treasures. Kriemhild is the courtly princess, yet remains a "tiuvelinne," and Brunhild is the protocol-conscious twelfth-century queen as well as the preliterate star athlete. In short, an oral poem in an illiterate social environment can never be an anachronism; it is constantly adapted to adhere both to the tradition and to current circumstances, which are conceived as part of the tradition. Oral poetry, after all, only *preserves* tradition; it does not criticize it, or improve upon it. At most, it can adapt the traditional to cultural importations from beyond the tradition it preserves.

The literate, privileged public not only does not share the ahistorical view of its past with the disadvantaged illiterates,[20] it also is freed by the stability of the written text to perceive it, and its meaning, in a different way. "It is the hallmark of a concept or an idea," says Eric Havelock, "that it is more effectively isolated and pondered in silence and with physical immobility. Reenactment and emotional identification have no place in the cogitative process proper." [21] Converted into a cause-and-effect relationship, this can be reversed: it is the hallmark of a written text which can be pondered in silence and analyzed, that it effectively yields concepts or ideas. The written text, in the words of Havelock, makes possible "the separation of the knower from the known." [22] Or, as Franklin Fearing puts it: "as the individual is separated in time or space from the stimulus field, there is opportunity for experiential, attitudinal, or other 'existential substrata' (to quote Robert Merton) to operate. These are the conceptual resources of the individual of which he may or may not be conscious. They are specific for the individual perceiver and the culture in which he lives. In utilizing his repertory of available concepts, he codifies and thus transcends that which is immediately given in experience." [23]

To return, finally, to our ladies. They have crossed the line into literacy, into the socially advantaged audience to whom Wolfram's *Parzival* and Gottfried's *Tristan*—an ironical *tour de force* if ever there was one—were addressed. This audience, confronted by a stable text, was able to "utilize [its] repertory of available concepts" to codify that text, to give it meaning in terms of its "conceptual resources," which themselves rest upon stable texts—the fundaments of its literacy. Given these fundaments, Kriemhild can easily be seen by this audience as emerging through the pattern of her actions—a pattern now perceivable as a stable whole—as exemplary of "falsitatis et vanarum phantasiarum." In the terms of St. Augustine and of a literacy and symbolism directly or indirectly dominated by him, she would be exemplary of The Woman, the perpetual challenge to *sapientia,* that is, order, by which she must be dominated or bring about chaos. The basis of this challenge, of course, is the beauty of Woman, which Kriemhild explicitly emphasizes as a tool in her desire for power—a pattern which may be recognized by the theologically trained reader as reflecting that of a type of tropological analysis of Matthew 5:28, and which, as D. W. Robertson has shown, enjoyed considerable popularity.[24]

But it is that traditional *bête noire* of the traditional woman, the "other woman," who illustrates this point most concisely in the *Nl.* Brunhild is nothing if not the equation of "might equals right" personified. Being conquerable only by Siegfried, she characterizes him as the ultimate example of this equation. She is the proof, as it were, that Siegfried is Siegfried. As such, she is a threat to the order which Gunther, Hagen, and Dancwart represent before her defeat at the hands of Siegfried: she is Woman seeking to dominate. With her defeat, however, and her subordination to her supposed vanquisher, Gunther, her role becomes constructive. It is now she—Brunhild—who, in the famous quarrel between the two women, defends *ordo* against the challenge of the *inordinatio* of Kriemhild.[25] This *inordinatio* reaches its apex in the second part of the epic, when Kriemhild—in demanding the source of Siegfried's power, his treasure—explicitly wants to *be* Siegfried.

Kudrun, we have seen, cannot have functioned as an anti-Kriemhild on the preliterate level. On the level of the illiterate disadvantaged, however, the heroine was probably per-

ceived as a long-suffering Christian antidote to the perception of Kriemhild on the same level. On the literate level,
likewise, Kudrun could be perceived as anti-Kriemhild. She
is not in this context an example of steadfastness in adver-
sity and Christian forgiveness, but is rather representative
of the concept of the *patientia,* the submission proper to the
symbolic Woman in any well-ordered hierarchy. And any
well-ordered hierarchy may, in medieval terms, be thought
of as a "marriage," [26]—a concept emphasized by Kudrun
throughout her captivity and finally by the quadruple marriage in which the epic culminates. In both cases—in the *Nl*
and the *Kudrun*—literate perception, ironically enough, repeats the preliterate perception of the narrative as a matter
of political significance. The sociological reasons are obvious
enough: just as in preliterate society, it is again perceived by
a socio-politically conscious and effective public. A second
and no less important reason, however, lies in the concep-
tualization of the narrative matter made possible only by literacy. This, in turn, causes the transformation of the
former preservative function of the narrative into a method
of elucidation and criticism. The preliterate Kriemhild, a
positive figure, preserving tribal social order by taking revenge on its subverter, is now transformed by the circumstances of literacy into a negative figure, subverting social
order by her lust for domination. By being "frozen" into a
stable text—a text moreover, which reflects the anachronisms of its prior oral tansmission—she is transformed into
a symbol. Only by refraction through a symbol can these
anachronisms be resolved. The function and significance of
this symbol is determined by the social and political function as well as by the conceptual resources of its perceivers;
in this case the privileged stratum of society, that is, literate
and politically active courtly society, comprising both secular and clerical cultural determinants. In short, this type of
conceptual interpretation of the text is possible only in the
context of literacy. Indeed, literacy in the cultural context
of the thirteenth century entails an interpretation of this
sort.

   On the basis of these three types of transmission—the
preliterate, the illiterate disadvantaged, and the literate—

one can perhaps clarify the descent of our ladies in other works, such as the *Rosengärten* and the *Klage,* as dependent on one or the other level of illiterate or literate transmission. The literate transmission thus bears within itself its ancestral illiterate transmissions, which must be seen not simply through the glasses of literate perception in the manner of Heusler and the nineteenth century, but through the types of perception posited by the sociological, historical and anthropological facts. And each of our epic ladies thus emerges not as one woman, but as an example of G. K. Chesterton's dictum that "variability is one of the virtues of a woman. It obviates the crude requirements of polygamy. If you have one good wife you are sure to have a spiritual harem."

Notes

1. The popularity of the *Nl* is testified to by the number of surviving manuscripts, and is beyond question. The popularity of the *Kudrun* is a different matter: it is transmitted in a unique and very late manuscript, written between 1504 and 1516, and is therefore regarded as not very popular. The conclusion scarcely follows from the premise. Paucity of transmission does not necessarily presuppose lack of popularity, particularly if—as in the case of the *Kudrun*—references to the narrative in other works are plentiful, quite apart from a reference in the text (288, 2–4) to other versions of the narrative. In addition, it is a methodological error to base an assumption of lack of popularity of an epic with relatively high oral-formulaic content on paucity of written transmission.

2. Robert Scholes and Robert Kellogg, *The Nature of Narrative* (London, Oxford, New York: Oxford University Press, 1968).

3. Cf., e.g., Bert Nagel, *"Das Nibelungenlied": Stoff, Form, Ethos* (Frankfurt a. Main: Hirschgraben Verlag, 1965). Bernard Willson, *"Ordo* et *Inordinatio* in the *Nibelungenlied,"* *PBB* (West) 85 (1963): 83–101, 325–51; W. J. Schroeder, "Das Nibelungenlied. Versuch einer Deutung," Beiträge zur Geschichte der deutschen Sprache und Literatur 67 (1954):56–143; Siegfried Beyschlag, "Das Motiv der Macht bei Siegfrieds Tod," *Zur Germanisch-Deutschen Heldensage* ed. Karl Hauck, Wege der Forschung, vol. 14 (Darmstadt: Wissenschaftliche Buchgesellschaft, 1961), pp. 195–213.

4. For this methodological standpoint, see Frederic Jameson, "Metacommentary," *PMLA* 86 (1971):9–18.

5. "Franz H. Bäuml and Donald J. Ward, "Zur mündlichen Überlieferung des Nibelungenliedes," *Deutsche Vierteljahrsschrift* 41 (1967):351–90; Franz H. Bäuml, "Der Übergang mündlicher zur artes-bestimmten Literatur des Mittelalters: Gedanken und Bedenken," *Fachliteratur des Mittelalters. Festschrift für Gerhard*

Eis, ed. Gundolf Keil, Rainer Rudolf et al. (Stuttgart: Metzler, 1968), pp. 1–10; also Franz H. Bäuml and Agnes M. Bruno, "Weiteres zur mündlichen Überlieferung des Nibelungenliedes." *DVjs* 46 (1972):479–93.

6. Eric Havelock, *Preface to Plato* (Cambridge, Mass.: University Press, 1963) offers an excellent treatment of the functions and implications of oral poetry in preliterate society.

7. Cecil M. Bowra, *In General and in Particular* (London: Weidenfeld and Nicolson, 1964), pp. 63–84.

8. Havelock, pp. 61–86.

9. Havelock, pp. 36–60.

10. Havelock, pp. 91, 165–214.

11. Milman Parry, "Studies in the Epic Technique of Oral Verse-Making 1," *Harvard Studies in Classical Philology* 41 (1930):80.

12. Godfrey L. Gattiker, "The Syntactic Basis of the Poetic Formula in *Beowulf*" (Ph.D. diss., University of Wisconsin, 1962).

13. For the role of tradition in the mechanics of oral composition, see the fundamental work on oral epic poetry as a whole: Albert B. Lord, *The Singer of Tales* (Cambridge, Mass.: Harvard University Press, 1964).

14. Themes can, of course, be expanded or contracted, and occasionally rearranged where the narrative will permit it, but they cannot be altered in nature. Havelock, pp. 88–89, describes the oral poet's relationship to the traditional themes admirably: "Let us think of him . . . as a man living in a large house crowded with furniture, both necessary and elaborate. His task is to thread his way through the house, touching and feeling the furniture as he goes and reporting its shape and texture. He chooses a winding and leisurely route which shall in the course of a day's recital allow him to touch and handle most of what is in the house. The route that he picks will have its own design. This becomes his story, and represents the nearest that he can approach to sheer invention. This house, these rooms, and the furniture he did not himself fashion: he must continually and affectionately recall them to us. But as he touches or handles he may do a little refurbishing, a little dusting off, and perhaps make small rearrangements of his own, though never major ones."

15. Ibid., p. 167.

16. Ibid., pp. 171 ff.

17. Howard Becker and Harry Elmer Barnes, *Social Thought from Lore to Science,* 3d ed. (New York: Dover, 1961), 1:5.

18. If it were merely a matter of written transmission or an oral performance recorded in writing, the formulaic density could be assumed to be relatively stable throughout the text. In the *Nl* it varies, however, from less than twenty-five percent to eighty percent per stanza.

19. See Becker and Barnes, 1:9ff., on preliterate conservatism. On homoeostasis in the oral tradition, see Rüdiger Schott, "Das Geschichtsbewusstsein schriftloser Völker," *Archiv für Begriffsgeschichte* 12 (1968):184, 197.

20. This does not, of course, imply that the medieval reader's concept of history was in any way similar to the modern, post-Herderian historicism.

21. Havelock, p. 167.

22. Havelock, chap. 11, pp. 197–214.

23. "An Examination of the Conceptions of Benjamin Whorf in the Light of

Theories of Perception and Cognition," *Language in Culture,* ed. Harry Hoijer (Chicago: University of Chicago Press, 1954), p. 73.

24. D. W. Robertson, Jr., *A Preface to Chaucer: Studies in Medieval Perspectives* (Princeton: Princeton University Press, 1962), pp. 71–73.

25. I use the formula *ordo* and *inordinatio* since it aptly defines the problem treated by the *Nl.* I cannot, however, subscribe to the interpretation of Bernard Willson (see n. 2 above).

26. Robertson, p. 375.

Isolt and Guenevere:
Two Twelfth-Century Views
of Woman

GERARD J. BRAULT

The Pennsylvania State University

The medieval view of woman was far more complex and varied than is often realized.[1] What has generally been emphasized is that men, especially clerks, tended to regard the opposite sex with the open hostility associated with certain Church Fathers; women were, in other words, considered to be depraved and treacherous daughters of Eve.[2] It is notorious, too, that feudal economics viewed marriage contracts primarily as arrangements calculated to increase or at least to consolidate familial wealth and power, women in these transactions often being treated as mere chattels.[3]

While there is no denying these salient and repugnant facts of medieval life, a more balanced view takes numerous other factors into consideration. Important changes came about in the status of women, for instance, in the second feudal age.[4] Each social class, then as now, had its own vastly different attitudes, economic pressures, and values.[5]

Also, it is grossly misleading to reduce the role of the
Church, which introduced far-reaching liberalizing influences with regard to the position of woman in society, to
that of a promoter of antifeminism and misogyny.[6]

So far as discussions of twelfth-century literary manifesta-
tions are concerned, so-called courtly love has certainly held
the stage.[7] While this much-debated question is doubtless a
very important one, it is hardly the only lens through which
to view leading female characters. In our analysis, attention
will be focused on two important figures, Isolt in Thomas's
romance and Guenevere in Chrétien de Troyes's *Chevalier
de la Charrette,* poems written in the second half of the
twelfth century.[8] Many fine studies have appeared in recent
years presenting in some detail the divergent psychological
motivations of these characters.[9] However, I propose to
show that in each case the personage may also be analyzed
in terms of the narrative itself. In other words, Isolt and
Guenevere will be approached as artistic creations reflecting
the concern on the part of each poet to be consistent in
character, structure, and theme.

Three constants may be observed in virtually all discussions of Isolt and Guenevere in the works in question.The
first concerns the poet's intention in portraying the adulterous relationship between the wife and lover. Some scholars
point out that Thomas and Chrétien sympathize to such an
extent with the lovers that each in his own way is glorifying
illicit love.[10] However, other scholars maintain that Thomas
and Chrétien wrote in the ironic mode; that is, while seem-
ing to praise adultery they were actually condemning it.[11]

In addition to being riveted on the author's intention,
scholarly concern has also focused on whether or not the
love depicted in these two romances reflects a historical reality. There has been much debate on whether Chrétien's
romance is a fictional portrayal of ideas, and even practices,
associated with the court of Countess Marie of Champagne,[12] and the suggestion has also been made that
Thomas's romance is a reflection on the personal life of the
poet's patroness, Eleanor of Aquitaine, Marie's mother.[13]

A third factor governing most interpretations of the roles
of Isolt and Guenevere has been the relevance of Celtic

sources. It is generally agreed that *Tristan and Isolt* and the *Chevalier de la Charrette* are reworkings of Celtic themes and motifs.[14] Scholars may differ as to the extent and exact nature of the archetypal material, but the assumption is clearly that one of the best ways to approach these twelfth-century tales and the characters in them is to compare the presumed prototype with the corresponding forms found in Thomas and Chrétien de Troyes.

I do not question the considerable merits of these approaches and I value the impressive findings amassed over the years by specialists since the end of the nineteenth century. However, two points need to be made. First, the discussions centering on the dominant morality of the twelfth century, the emergence of a new ethos (that of courtly love), and the pertinence of Celtic material, are all products of the comparative-historical method, considered by its early proponents to be the only scientific approach. The answers provided over the years have been many and diverse, but the questions have tended to be those first posed a century ago. To put it another way, what we think of Isolt and Guenevere is very much conditioned by old philologic and positivistic concerns. Valid as these questions may be, they are not the only ones we can or should ask ourselves.

Let me cite a paragraph about *Tristan and Isolt* written by an eminent critic:

Dans ce drame, tumultueux, profond et changeant comme la mer, la mer est sans cesse en vue ou en action: elle y joue presque le rôle d'un acteur passionné; elle le berce tout entier. A chaque instant reviennent des vers comme ceux-ci:

A grant espleit s'en vont par l'onde,
Trenchant s'en vont la mer parfonde.

C'est en venant par mer de son pays natal que Tristan, enlevé par des pirates norvégiens, aborde pour la première fois le rivage de Cornouaille. C'est la mer qui amène le Morhout dans la même contrée pour y réclamer le tribut accoutumé, et qui, après le combat de l'île Saint-Samson (une des Sorlingues), le remmène en Irlande, portant dans son crâne le morceau brisé du glaive de Tristan. Tristan, blessé et désespérant de guérir, se fait mettre dans une barque sans mât, sans rame et sans gouvernail, et s'en va ainsi au hasard, cherchant un sauveur, n'emportant que sa harpe, dont il fait retentir les accords sur les flots mouvants. C'est dans la traversée qu'ils font d'Irlande en Cornouaille qu'Iseut et Tristan boivent le fatal breuvage qui cause leurs amours et leur mort. Tristan, banni, passe l'Océan pour aller vivre dans la Bretagne armoricaine. Et quelle part elle prend à l'action, cette mer immense et incertaine, quand elle ramène Iseut auprès du héros mourant, qu'elle manque l'engloutir devant le port même, et qu'Iseut la supplie de lui laisser revoir une dernière fois celui auquel elle l'a jadis fiancée!

These lines, written in 1894 by Gaston Paris,[15] evince a laudable sensitivity to thematic considerations. Yet the French scholar's main purpose was to present an argument in favor of the Celtic origins of the Tristan story, for, he continues: "Qui ne sent que ces tableaux sont nés dans l'âme d'un peuple maritime, dont les tribus étaient disséminées sur les rivages de Cambrie, de Cornouaille et d'Armorique, et à qui la mer était un chemin constant et sans cesse parcouru?" [16]

Joseph Bédier's reaction to his master's words is characteristic: "cette page sur la mer est vraiment admirable; mais G. Paris s'y montre plus poète que tous nos anciens poètes de Tristan réunis." [17] The scholars of that generation, reacting very strongly to the lyrical excesses of commentators of an earlier day, were doubtless right in scrutinizing analyses of this type very carefully, as does Bédier in the sharp critique which follows the quotation from Gaston Paris, but in the process they tended to be far too negative in their appraisal of imaginative reactions to poetry.

The second point I should like to make about the three constants in earlier discussions is that they often approach the text from without. Naturally, we should avail ourselves of any outside information at our disposal when analyzing texts or characters and we must always test our hypotheses against established facts. However, in what follows, I have endeavored to let the text of Thomas's *Tristan* and Chrétien's *Charrette* assume a more preponderant place in interpreting the roles of Isolt and Guenevere than is frequently the case.

As we read Thomas's version of *Tristan and Isolt,* we cannot help but be struck by the recurrence of several themes which give the poem a remarkable consistency. We have already mentioned the sea. Another major theme is that of sorrow and suffering in love. An overwhelming sadness pervades Thomas's poem from beginning to end and gives it its characteristic tone and mood.[18] The hero's very name, while it may be of Pictish origin and have been associated with the Welsh triads, is explicitly linked by the poet to the adjective *triste* 'sad'.[19] Tristan was so named, says Thomas, because of the sorrow surrounding his birth. The child was sired by the suffering Rivalen and conceived by the distressful Blancheflor.[20] Moreover, the hero's father is slain in battle and the heartbroken mother dies in childbirth. The baby is christened "Tristan", then, to commemorate these tragic circumstances.[21] But, the poet adds, the name also prophesied the manner of his life and of his death.[22] "Yea," says Thomas, "those who hear this tale to the end will understand how well he was named."[23]

No medieval romance can boast more lamenting, suffering, and weeping than *Tristan and Isolt.* The sorrowful nature of the poem is best epitomized in the celebrated passage where Thomas speaks of the paradoxical relationship between Mark, Isolt, Tristan, and Isolt of the White Hands, a 123-verse discourse which begins:

> Entre aus quatre ot estrange amor:
> Tut en ourent painne e dolor,
> E un e autre en tristur vit;
> En nul d'aus nen i a deduit.[24]

The theme of the sea and that of sorrow fuse constantly as, for example, when Isolt, in her anguish at not being able to reach her dying lover, calls for him to come drown with her in the becalmed sea.[25] The most significant intersection of these themes, however, is in the famous triple pun on the word *amer* in the love potion scene: *l'amer,* Anglo-Norman for 'love'; *l'amer* 'bitterness, sorrow'; and *la mer* 'the sea'. Right after partaking of the fatal drink, Isolt moans: "*L'amer* is my torment; *l'amer* oppresses my soul; *l'amer* is grieving me." Tristan questions Isolt on the meaning of her

lament, acutely aware that *l'amer* can mean 'love' but daring
not to suggest this in his query. "I believe, fair Isolt," he
says, "that the sea and sickness are the cause of your distress; you feel the sea and the wind; the sea and the wind
are making you ill." "No, my lord, no," replies Isolt, "what
are you talking about? Neither one is grieving me; I suffer
from neither the wind nor the waves. Only *l'amer* torments
me." Tristan, having grasped her meaning, speaks softly
and discreetly: "In truth, beautiful lady, I feel the same
way: love and you are my torment." [26]

Gaston Paris saw that the play on words here is "in-
timement mêlé à l'action et la fait avancer à un de ses moments les plus critiques." [27] Characteristically, however, his
chief purpose in mentioning the subject and the only use he
made of it was to argue the precedence of Thomas's *Tristan*
over Chrétien's *Cligés* where the same pun is attested but is
used less effectively.[28]

Another important structural component in Thomas's romance is the intricate family relationship which exists
among the principal characters and also the echoing names
of several individuals. Tristan's mother Blancheflor is King
Mark's sister. The hero slays the giant Morholt, who is
Queen Isolt's brother. The latter is the mother of and bears
the same name as Tristan's mistress Isolt, and Tristan mar-
ries yet another person having the same name, Isolt of the
White Hands. We have earlier noted the retrospective and
prophetic significance which the poet attaches to the name
Tristan. Thomas also asserts that Tristan fell in love with
his future wife partly because of her beauty but partly also
because of her name, which reminded him of his mistress.[29]
A character named Tristan the Dwarf seeks and finds the
hero.[30] Finally, as Tristan lies on his deathbed, he repeats
three times in the presence of his spouse the ambiguous
words: "Amie Ysolt." [31]

While the sea, sadness, and family and name relationships
all play an important role in this romance, the poet's concept of Isolt depends mostly on a motif whose significance
has thus far been completely overlooked by commentators.

After the Life in the Forest episode, when the lovers must
part, Isolt gives Tristan a ring as a pledge of her undying

love, as a consolation, and as a reminder of their separation.[32] Henceforth the ring becomes a crucial element in the
story. It constantly puts Tristan in mind of his absent
mistress and of his promise to remain faithful to her. Thus,
on the night of his wedding to Isolt of the White Hands, he
gazes at the ring, then decides to turn away from his new
bride, his love for his mistress having overcome his sexual
desire for his spouse.[33] In the Hall of Statues episode, Isolt
is depicted with a ring in her hand and the ring is also used
as a secret signal between the lovers.[34] Finally, when Tristan
is about to die, he sends the ring back to Isolt [35] with the
message that this time she is to keep it.[36]

The ring also has structural implications in Thomas's
poem. While the story may ultimately be derived from the
linear idea of an elopement,[37] Thomas's version is circular,
that is, ring-like, in that it tells over and over again of the
union of the lovers followed by a separation, then a new
union followed by another separation, a third meeting then
another separation, and so on. The lovers are together for a
time but are continually being forced apart, the path of
their wanderings away from each other curving like a pa-
renthesis, the lines always converging anew. The lovers'
meetings occur at different times and different places as the
story moves to its inevitable conclusion, that is until the ring
is permanently closed when Isolt dies with her dead lover in
the circle of her arms. The Norse *Saga*, which is probably
following Thomas here, states that Isolt of the White Hands
caused the lovers to be buried on different sides of a church
so that they would at least be separate in death. But two oak
trees grew next to each grave and their branches became in-
tertwined.[38] Even the satellite poems in Thomas's wake conform to this ring pattern as they tell over and over again of
Tristan being separated from his mistress but succeeding in
meeting her in one disguise or another, only to be forced
once again to leave her side.[39] There is an interesting parallel, finally, in Marie de France's *Chèvrefeuille*, where the
looping of the honeysuckle vine around the hazel branch
gives the lay its title and is also the central metaphor.[40]

The giving and wearing of rings was an important part of
medieval life as it remains today, for that matter, and the

custom, of course, dates back to Antiquity. In the Middle Ages, the ring symbolized eternity and union.[41] A ring was used to seal the marriage vow and could also be part of symbolic wedding ceremonies, as when Eleanor's son Richard was installed as Duke of Aquitaine at Poitiers in 1170. The placing of St. Valérie's ring on Richard's finger marked his union with the vassals of Aquitaine.[42] In courtly literature beginning with Provençal poetry, the ring is a pledge of faithfulness in love and of its acceptance, often in secret.[43] The giving of a ring by Isolt is a kind of investiture, that is the feudal rite consisting in handing over an object intended to symbolize the act of concession.[44] When Tristan returns the ring, he is, consequently, divesting himself of a fief,[45] but this divestiture is not to be viewed as a renunciation but as a sign that he has faithfully kept his word to the very end. The return of the ring thus corresponds exactly to Roland's dying gesture as he lifts his gauntlet to God, signifying that he has been true to his Lord to his last breath.[46]

Professor Jonin has suggested that the ring in Thomas's *Tristan* is a chastity symbol, Tristan, by accepting this token, vowing to abstain from having sexual intercourse with anyone else.[47] We have seen how, on his wedding night, Tristan gazes at his ring, then decides to turn away from his wife. Jonin compares this to the custom of wearing a ring as a sign of mystical betrothal to the Blessed Virgin. He cites the historical example of St. Edmund of Canterbury as well as several similar occurrences in early hagiographic literature.[48] However, even in such profoundly religious practices, Jonin notes a connection with the popular custom of carrying talismans. The wearing of a ring by Tristan, Jonin is saying then, implies a belief in magic. In this instance, the ring is worn to ward off temptations of the flesh.[49]

While not eliminating any of the meanings which the ring may very well suggest in Thomas's poem, I feel that the magical element needs to be emphasized more than it has until now in order better to grasp Isolt's essential role. The point is repeatedly made by Thomas that whenever Tristan or Isolt gaze upon the ring they immediately feel sad.[50] The ring, then, is closely related to the Petit Crû motif found only in Thomas.[51] Petit Crû is a little dog with strange coloring given to Tristan by a friend to divert him in his sadness. The dog is of fairy origin and wears a little bell around its neck. When Petit Crû shakes itself, the tinkling of the bell casts a spell over the hero, makes him forget his sorrow, and fills him with joy. Tristan gives the dog to Isolt to free her from her grief, but she does not wish to be happy when her lover is sad, so she tears the bell from the dog's neck, thus breaking its spell. While the ring has exactly the opposite effect on the lovers, causing them to be sad (whereas Petit Crû's bell makes them happy), its power is clearly much the same and at least quasi-magical.

Rings often have supernatural power in medieval romances, notably in Chrétien de Troyes. In the *Charrette,* for example, the hero wears a magic ring given to him by his fairy foster-mother. Merely gazing upon the ring undoes any spell cast over the hero, an effect very close to that exerted by Tristan's ring.[52] In the romance which bears his name, Yvain is given a ring by Lunete which makes him invisible [53] and another by Laudine which, so long as he is a true lover, preserves him from prison and from loss of blood.[54] When, a year later, the latter ring is snatched from his finger, Yvain goes mad—only to be cured by the Lady of Norison with a magic ointment given to her by Morgan le Fay.[55]

Now magic and healing, as is evident in the case of Laudine's ring, were intimately associated in the Middle Ages and we come now to what I regard to be the key to Thomas's concept of Isolt. Throughout Thomas's poem but particularly at the beginning and at the end, Isolt is a healer. Initially, the wounds Tristan receives from the poison in Morholt's sword, then from the dragon, are cured by Isolt's mother, but the daughter is always in attendance.[56] Like magic, leechcraft was held in awe by the people of the Middle Ages, but the line between medicine and the black art was often blurred. Thus it is quite in character for Isolt's mother, a healer, to brew the magic love potion destined for King Mark and his bride, but consumed through a fatal error by the lovers. At the end of the poem, the stricken Tristan sends for Isolt and she comes to him, out of devotion, of course, but first and foremost as a healer.[57]

Derived in part perhaps from Ovid's conception of love as a sickness,[58] but amplified and greatly altered, love in Thomas's *Tristan and Isolt* is something which must be healed. In several romances of the twelfth century, there are female healers who tend the hero's wounds.[59] These ubiquitous ministering angels—fairies usually—often seem to exist solely for the purpose of throwing themselves into the arms of knights errant [60] (this is, of course, the eternal male erotic fantasy) or of treating their wounds. They frequently do both, and one gets the distinct impression that it amounts to the same thing. Following the encounter with Isolt in which the hero disguises himself as a leper, Tristan hides under the steps of an abandoned palace in the courtyard. Sick unto death as a result of his constant fasting and waking and because of his sorrow over the absent Isolt, he is accidently discovered by the porter's wife and eventually brought to his mistress's marble chamber. After a night of lovemaking with Isolt, Tristan returns to Brittany, evidently cured of his infirmity.[61] Thomas's Isolt is plainly related to the passionate healers of literary tradition but she transcends them all because (1.) her tragic role forces her into infidelity either to her husband or to her lover and because (2.) healing Tristan becomes more important to her than her own life.[62] Her pathetic last wish is that she arrive in time to heal her lover or that at least they die together of one anguish.[63]

Isolt represents different things to different people. In the Middle Ages, she was admired as an ideal lover. Thus she is depicted on countless marriage caskets, combs, mirrors, murals, and tapestries, as well as in poetry.[64] But she was also reviled by others because of her unfaithfulness. Astonishing as this notion may seem to us today, in Chrétien's *Cligés* Isolt is scorned for being unfaithful to her husband (because she lived in constant adultery), but also for being untrue to her lover (because she continually gave Mark her body).[65] Depending on one's point of view, Isolt is either a summit of courtliness or of antifeminism. But Isolt is also woman viewed as a healer, a healer who ultimately fails in her role.

Thomas's *Tristan and Isolt* concludes with the following words:

> Tumas fine ci sun escrit:
> A tuz amanz saluz i dit,
> As pensis e as amerus,
> As emvius, as desirus,
> As enveisiez e as purvers,
> A tuz cels ki orunt ces vers.
> Si dit n'ai a tuz lor voleir,
> Le milz ai dit a mun poeir,
> E dit ai tute la verur,
> Si cum jo pramis al primur.
> E diz e vers i ai retrait:
> Pur essemple l'ai issi fait
> E pur l'estorie embelir,
> Que as amanz deive plaisir,
> E que par lieus poissent trover
> Chose u se puissent recorder:
> Aveir em poissent grant confort,
> Encuntre change, encontre tort,
> Encuntre paine, encuntre plur,
> Encuntre tuiz engins d'amur![66]

Thomas was clearly mindful in this passage of Horace's precept that good literature should combine the useful and the agreeable (*utile dulci*), although there may also be an echo of Romans 15:4 ("These things have been written for our instruction so that through the consolation offered by the Scriptures we may have hope"). However, to give comfort or consolation also suggests a cure, a healing.[67] Thus, in the end, while Isolt may fail as a healer, her story is designed to heal the lovesick and the lovelorn.

Chrétien de Troyes was influenced by a great many things in his poetic career but one of his most significant re-actions was to the legend of Tristan and Isolt and to

Thomas's poem.[68] He informs us that he himself composed a work on the subject of King Mark and Fair Isolt; [69] there are important allusions to the story in the *Erec,* the *Cligés,* and the *Yvain;* and the second of these romances is generally held to be a specific reply to Thomas's *Tristan.*[70] What interests us particularly here is the fact that in the *Chevalier de la Charrette,* Chrétien again borrowed a number of motifs from Thomas, notably the matter of the bloodstained sheets and the ambiguous oath.[71]

Chrétien's concept of Guenevere does bear a certain relationship to Thomas's depiction of Isolt in that both are complex beings, part tenderness, part cruelty; part symbol of undying devotion and loyalty in love, part symbol of marital deceit and infidelity. But Guenevere is no healer and there is also a fundamental difference arising from the fact that Thomas's tale involves a magic potion compelling the lovers to be forever drawn together, whereas Chrétien's lovers are voluntarily adulterous.

In the case of Thomas, we found that viewing Isolt as a healer had the advantage of relating the heroine to the ring motif, to the theme of sadness, and to the structure and meaning of the story. Proceeding in similar fashion, we shall endeavor now to define Guenevere in terms of Chrétien's narrative.

One of the most curious passages in Chrétien's *Chevalier de la Charrette,* but again one that has received scant attention from scholars, is the Comb episode.[72] Queen Guenevere has been abducted by the treacherous Meleagant and Lancelot is rushing to her rescue. The hero must overcome several obstacles to gain the cooperation of the only individuals, it would appear, who can show him the way. He meets a dwarf who agrees to take him to Guenevere if he mounts a cart, an act universally regarded as disgraceful. Later he encounters a maiden who provides additional information in exchange for a promise of service, a pledge quickly redeemed when Lancelot is asked to spare a knight defending a ford, whom he defeats.[73] Another damsel offers him lodging if he will sleep with her. Lancelot consents but, in a scene reminiscent of Tristan's wedding night, remains true to his mistress.[74] The following day, the same damsel asks to accompany him on his voyage, reminding him of the custom of Logres about escorting maidens. The two are riding along when they see a fountain in a meadow. On the well's stone slab someone has left a gilded ivory comb behind, but this object is not seen at first by the pair. For a reason not initially made clear—it later develops that she is trying to avoid an importunate suitor who evidently frequents this place—the maiden tries to lead Lancelot down another path. Lancelot, lost in his thoughts about Guenevere, suddenly comes to his senses and insists on following the most direct route, which leads them to the well and the comb.

The comb is an extraordinarily beautiful object and several strands of golden hair are tangled in its teeth. The maiden asks Lancelot to give her the comb and he promptly accedes to her request. But as he holds it in his grasp, he becomes fascinated and even tortured by it. When the maiden reveals that the comb and hair are Guenevere's, the hero swoons. Then, having removed the strands of hair before giving the comb to his companion, he proceeds to adore (aorer) [75] the hair by touching it a thousand times to his eyes, his lips, his forehead, and his whole face. Then he places the precious lock of hair next to his heart and ecstatically continues on his way where, in quick succession, he encounters, among other things, a group of carolers (that is dancers),[76] and, finally, a cemetery containing the graves of several of Arthur's knights, including Lancelot's.[77]

I have taken pains to describe in detail the Comb episode—which critics are wont to dismiss as a mere digression or as of marginal interest at best [78]—because something important happens here. It marks the transition in this romance from love described in Ovidian terms—that is, as a sickness causing sleeplessness, swoons, and the like—to love described in Christian terms. As we shall see, this has a direct bearing on the concept of Guenevere in Chrétien's romance.

Most scholars recognize in the Cemetery of the Future scene a strong connection with Holy Scripture. Lancelot finds a tomb bearing an inscription prophesying that whoever raises its lid will free all who are imprisoned in the kingdom from which no one returns. Cross and Nitze see in the fact that the hero succeeds in raising the lid a clear allusion to John 20:1 which relates how, on the first Easter, Mary Magdalene came to the sepulchre and found the lid removed from Christ's tomb.[79] Frappier is not so specific but does state that "the adventure of the tomb conferred the aspect of a Messiah [on Lancelot]."[80] Moshé Lazar links the scene to Christ's Resurrection but also to the Harrowing of Hell.[81] However, no one, to my knowledge, has seen anything religious about the comb, the well, and the carol which precede this incident.

So far as Guenevere's comb is concerned, our initial impression, of course, is that it is a kind of extension of her body and that caressing and kissing this object and the strands of hair is a way of cherishing the absent Queen herself. It is a little difficult for people today to consider a common and even at times a repulsive toilet article like a comb with any degree of reverence. As a matter of fact, in twentieth-century American culture the comb has become the symbol of adolescent *male* vanity! However, Chrétien insists a good deal on the beauty of the comb and we can get a better idea of what he means by considering the remarkable ivory combs which have survived from this period, some of which are veritable treasures.[82]

Yet the notion of vanity is present here, not the conceit we consider harmless—though perhaps silly—and to which I have just alluded, but the vanity which the Middle Ages associated with the vice of Pride. A mirror and comb were the familiar attributes of Luxuria (Lechery) and the Whore of Babylon, not to mention sirens.[83] In each case, the unholy female character conjured up an image of sinful lasciviousness.

D. W. Robertson, Jr., followed by John V. Fleming, has identified the personage of Oiseuse (Idleness), who greets the Dreamer with mirror and comb in hand in the *Romance of the Rose*, as a Lechery figure.[84] I do not believe it has been noticed before that there is a resemblance between certain initial adventures of the Dreamer in the *Romance of the Rose* and those which befall Lancelot. I refer specifically to the comb-Oiseuse parallel, the well, and the carol. The fountain in Guillaume de Lorris's poem is identified by the author himself as Narcisssus's well, which Robertson explains as a symbol of the dangers of self-love and idolatry.[85] In a similar vein, Fleming interprets the carol incident in the same romance as a metaphor of the "frenetic enslavement of man's higher faculties by his animal passions" made more explicit, for example, in Pierre Michault's fifteenth-century *Dance aux aveugles.*[86] It is worth noting, at this juncture, that a mosaic in the Cathedral of Otranto, Italy, dated about 1165—that is, roughly contemporary with the *Charrette*—depicts a figure with a scepter or club in his hand astride a goat. The illustration is labeled "Rex Arturus" and the goat has been identified as another Lechery symbol.[87] Rita Lejeune has recently linked the Otranto mosaic with sculptures in the twelfth-century tower known as La Ghirlandina facing the Cathedral of Modena with its famous Arthurian archivolt featuring a Guenevere rescue. The tower basreliefs include a figure of Guenevere, on the one hand, and a male personage astride a goat—which the Belgian scholar believes is Arthur—on the other.[88]

I suggest that the comb, the well, and the carol in Chrétien's *Charrette* have religious overtones—like the Raising of the Tomb and the Arthurian figures at Otranto and Modena. Whether or not the use of such emblems by Chrétien and Guillaume de Lorris was deliberately moralistic is a problem which may never be resolved to everyone's satisfaction. I hesitate to take a position on the *sens* involved here but I submit that there is a possibility that the *matière* is of a religious nature and that, consequently, it has a bearing on Chrétien's concept of Guenevere. For henceforth what characterizes the love of Lancelot for Guenevere is the blasphemous notion of adoration and sacrament. As we have seen, her hair becomes a precious relic worthy of veneration. But it is in the Night of Love episode that we find the boldest and most elaborate description of profane love as a mystical experience. Lancelot enters his lady's chamber like a chapel:

> Et puis vint au lit la reïne,
> Si l'aore et se li ancline,
> Car an nul cors saint ne croit tant.[89]

When the time comes to tear himself away from his mistress, the hero is *droiz martirs* and suffers *grant martire*.[90] Finally:

> Au departir a sploié
> A la chanbre, et fet tot autel
> Con s'il fust devant un autel.[91]

Critics have noted the brazenness of these expressions and aptly characterized Lancelot's love as a kind of religion.[92] The hero's attitude parallels that of Tristan in the Hall of Statues. Forced to live apart from his mistress, Tristan fashioned a beautiful life-size statue of Isolt which he placed on a pedestal in a vaulted chamber carved out of rock.[93] The image of Isolt crushes with its foot the evil dwarf who had accused her before King Mark. This is, of course, the traditional manner of portraying the triumph of an individual over his persecutor, an iconographic stereotype dating back to Antiquity but probably familiar to Thomas in its Virtue-over-Vice form.[94] More significant here, though, is the fact that Tristan, like Pygmalion, engages in simulated love-making, fondling and kissing the statue he has made.[95] The part of the *Romance of the Rose* written by Jean de Meun also has a Pygmalion episode and Robertson, again followed by Fleming, has argued that it constitutes a condemnation of sexual idolatry.[96]

What concerns us here is not the decision which Robertsonian critics would have us make about the moralistic intentions of Jean de Meun or, by implication, of Thomas and Chrétien. I cite the connection merely to place Guenevere in her proper setting as an object of religious cult. Whatever we think of Guenevere's character or morality, it must be recognized that Chrétien has defined her in religious terms. One of her most important attributes is that she is the inspirer of prowess. It is germane to our discussion to stress here that viewing woman as an inspiration is part of a distinctly religious tradition. The biblical heroine not infrequently functions as the instiller of courage in man. She pushes him to action and, at times, shows him what must be done through personal example. Offsetting the image of women as perfidious daughters of Eve in the Middle Ages is that of women in the line of Esther, Judith, Rebecca, Ruth, and the mother of the seven brethren Maccabees.[97]

Chrétien was not the first medieval author to conceive of a heroine in religious terms. The Provençal poets preceded him and, as we have seen, he is ever aware of Thomas's *Tristan and Isolt*.[98] The fact remains, however, that Chrétien succeeded in creating in Guenevere the most enduring incarnation of woman viewed in this fashion.

Lancelot pauses a moment before mounting the cart and much in the romance hinges on this seemingly trivial hiatus in the hero's otherwise unhesitating devotion to his lady. Like God, Guenevere is forgiving, but God, by definition, is also just. Thus, before granting him the delights of Paradise, Guenevere must first insist that he go through Purgatory even for such a minor infraction.

I have stated that I hesitate to commit myself as to precisely what meaning Chrétien had in mind when he imagined his story and created a character like Guenevere. The logic of my argument that the comb, the well, and the carol have a religious background invites the conclusion that Chrétien was suggesting the evil which ensues when sensuality subverts reason.[99] However, I have shown elsewhere that the metaphor of the eye and the heart, which has important structural implications in Chrétien's *Charrette* and also has religious overtones, consistently casts Lancelot in the role of Good triumphing over Evil in the person of Meleagant.[100]

Perhaps the solution to this dilemma lies in the Augustinian doctrine that the same symbol at times has two contradictory meanings.[101] In other words, Lancelot—and Guenevere, too, then—may be viewed alternatively *in bono* and *in malo*. Another way out of our dilemma is suggested in a recent article by Norris J. Lacy, who argues that ambivalent situations, such as we find in Béroul's *Tristan*, establish an esthetic distance between the reader and the text.[102] In other words the author, by creating apparently contradictory themes, encourages the audience to view the story with detachment.

Most writers of profane literature in the Middle Ages including, no doubt, Thomas and Chrétien, were primarily concerned with telling stories as imaginatively as they could, and their appropriation of such concepts as Woman as Healer or Woman as Object of Religious Cult for their own esthetic ends, does not necessarily imply a didactic purpose. Many people in the Middle Ages—churchmen mostly—concerned themselves with the moral aspect of such poems, some being shocked at their pagan ethos, others reading them allegorically and judging them to be in conformity with prevailing morality. Here, however, as in so many other spheres of medieval activity—art, ethics, heraldry, law, what have you—the theory and practice of literature all too frequently did not converge.

While each poet offers a distinct perspective on woman, the one conditioned by popular notions of magic, the other influenced by Christian beliefs, Thomas and Chrétien are alike in that they plumb the wellsprings of human experience and its greatest mysteries: life, love, death, and femininity. In the final analysis, each view of woman is interesting not so much for its realism—that is, for what it tells us of medieval woman—as for the information it imparts about male clerical fantasies about woman in the second half of the twelfth century. But fantasies tell us quite a bit about the thought processes of human beings and cultures generally. And that, I believe, is a subject about which we would all like to know a good deal more.

Notes

1. On the numerous forces which combined to produce medieval satire and defense of women, consult Francis Lee Utley, *The Crooked Rib: An Analytical Index to the Argument about Women in English and Scots Literature to the End of the Year 1568* (Columbus, Ohio: Ohio State University Press, 1944), pp. 3–38.

2. The pertinent biblical and patristic texts are conveniently summarized in Katherine M. Rogers, *The Troublesome Helpmate: A History of Misogyny in Literature* (Seattle and London: University of Washington Press, 1966), pp. 3–22.

3. Margaret Adlum Gist, *Love and War in the Middle English Romances* (Philadelphia: University of Pennsylvania Press, and London: Oxford University Press, 1947), p. 17.

4. John F. Benton, "Clio and Venus: An Historical View of Medieval Love," in *The Meaning of Courtly Love: Papers of the First Annual Conference of the Center for Medieval and Early Renaissance Studies, State University of New York at Binghamton, March*

17–18, 1967, ed. F. X. Newman (Albany: State University of New York Press, 1968), pp. 19–42.

5. Doris Mary Stenton, *The English Woman in History* (London: George Allen & Unwin; New York: Macmillan, 1957), chaps. 1, 2, 3, and 5. See also Andrée Lehmann, *Le Rôle de la femme dans l'histoire de France au moyen âge* (Paris: Berger-Levrault, 1952); Friedrich Heer, *The Medieval World: Europe 1100–1350,* trans. Janet Sondheimer (New York and Toronto: New American Library; London: New English Library, 1961), pp. 317–23.

6. See W. B. Faherty, "Woman," in the *New Catholic Encyclopedia* (1967), 14:993–95.

7. For "A Selected Bibliography of the Theory of Courtly Love," see *The Meaning of Courtly Love,* pp. 97–102.

8. All textual references are to Joseph Bédier, ed., *Le Roman de Tristan par Thomas. Poème du XIIe siècle,* Société des Anciens Textes Français, 2 vols. (Paris: Firmin Didot, 1892–95), and to Mario Roques, ed., *Les Romans de Chrétien de Troyes,* vol. 3, *Le Chevalier de la Charrete,* Classiques Français du Moyen Age, vol. 86 (Paris: Champion, 1958).

9. Notably by Pierre Jonin, *Les Personnages féminins dans les romans français de Tristan au XIIe siècle: Etude des influences contemporaines,* Publication des Annales de la Faculté des lettres, Aix-en-Provence, n.s., vol. 22 (Gap: Ophrys, 1958), for Isolt; and by Jean Frappier, *Chrétien de Troyes,* Connaissance des lettres, vol. 50 (Paris: Hatier, 1957), pp. 142–46, and by F. Douglas Kelly, *Sens and conjointure in the Chevalier de la Charrette,* Studies in French Literature, vol. 2 (The Hague and Paris: Mouton, 1966), pp. 54–61, 213–17, for Guenevere.

10. For Thomas, see Gaston Paris, "Tristan et Iseut," *La Revue de Paris* 1 (April 1894): 174–75; Bédier in his edition of Thomas, 2:51; John H. Fisher, "Tristan and Courtly Adultery," *Comparative Literature* 9 (1957): 150–64; Frederick Whitehead in *Arthurian Literature in the Middle Ages,* ed. Roger Sherman Loomis (Oxford: Oxford University Press, Clarendon Press, 1961), pp. 142–43; Moshé Lazar, *Amour courtois et "fin' amors" dans la littérature du XIIe siècle,* Bibliothèque française et romane, series C, vol. 8 (Paris: Klincksieck, 1964), pp. 160–73; for Chrétien, see Reto R. Bezzola, *Le Sens de l'aventure et de l'amour (Chrétien de Troyes)* (Paris: La Jeune Parque, 1947), p. 44; Kelly, pp. 69–85.

11. D. W. Robertson, Jr., *A Preface to Chaucer: Studies in Medieval Perspectives* (Princeton: Princeton University Press, 1962), p. 462; John F. Benton, "The Court of Champagne as a Literary Center," *Speculum* 36 (1961): 562–63, 587; Benton, "Clio and Venus," in *The Meaning of Courtly Love,* p. 28. The majority of scholars are of the opinion that Chrétien agreed to write the *Charrette* for Countess Marie, contrary to his own inclination (see Kelly, chap. 1).

12. Gaston Paris, "Etudes sur les romans de la table ronde. Lancelot du lac: II. Le Conte de la Charrette," *Romania* 12 (1883): 459–534. For a contrary view, see Benton, "The Court of Champagne," pp. 562–63.

13. Rita Lejeune, "Rôle littéraire d'Aliénor d'Aquitaine et de sa famille," *Cultura Neolatina* 14 (1954):32–35; Heer, *The Medieval World: Europe 1100–1350,* p. 167. Benton, "The Court of Champagne," p. 581, believes that some of the decisions ascribed to Eleanor by Andreas Capellanus may be ironic comments on her behavior.

14. The best studies are Gertrude Schoepperle [Loomis], *Tristan and Isolt: A Study*

of the Sources of the Romance (1913; rpt. New York: Burt Franklin, 1960), chap. 6, and Tom Peete Cross and William A. Nitze, *Lancelot and Guenevere: A Study of the Origins of Courtly Love,* The Modern Philology Monographs (Chicago: University of Chicago Press, 1930), chap. 2.

15. Gaston Paris, "Tristan et Iseut," pp. 144–45. The verses cited by Paris are not from Thomas; see *La Folie Tristan d'Oxford,* ed. Ernest Hoepffner, 2nd ed., Publications de la Faculté des lettres de l'Université de Strasbourg, Textes d'étude, vol. 8 (Rodez: P. Carrère, 1943), p. 50, vv. 87–88.

16. "Tristan et Iseut," p. 145.

17. Bédier in his edition of Thomas, 2:145.

18. In the fragments of Thomas which have been preserved, the word *amur* rhymes with *dolur* no fewer than twenty-three times; Isolt's relationship with Mark is similarly characterized six times by the rhymes *dolur/seignur.*

19. For the name, see Schoepperle, 2:313 (bibliography in n. 3) and Helaine Newstead in *Arthurian Literature in the Middle Ages,* p. 125 (bibliography in notes 2–6), for the connection with *triste,* see Bédier in his edition of Thomas, 2:194; Schoepperle, 2:100.

20. Thomas, 1:19.

21. Ibid., 1:25, 26–27.

22. Ibid., 1:27.

23. Ibid. For medieval allusions to this explanation, see Bédier in his edition of Thomas, 2:400.

24. Thomas, 2:317–18, vv. 1011–14.

25. Ibid., 1:408.

26. Ibid., 1:146.

27. "Cligés," *Journal des savants* (1902): 355–56. For other uses of the same pun, see Bédier in his edition of Thomas, 1:146, n. 1; *Les Fragments du roman de Tristan, poème du XIIe siècle par Thomas,* ed. Bartina H. Wind (Leiden: E. J. Brill, 1950), pp. 14, 15.

28. See also Bédier in his edition of Thomas, 2:53–55.

29. Thomas, 1:258.

30. Ibid., 1:379ff., vv. 2179ff.

31. Ibid., 1:412, vv. 3041–42: " 'Amie Ysolt' treis fez a dit, / A la quarte rent l'espirit."

32. Thomas, 1:250: ". . . qu'il vous tienne lieu de bref, de sceau et de serment, qu'il vous console et vous remémore notre amour et cette séparation!" This is Bédier's translation of a passage from the Old Norse *Saga* based on Thomas's poem. The gift of the ring is also found in Béroul (see Jonin, *Les Personnages féminins,* p. 220) and in the Berne *Folie* immediately after the Life in the Forest episode. Thomas invents a garden episode here; see Bédier in his edition of Thomas, 2:258; Schoepperle, 1:81 (and n. 1). For Blancheflor's ring, see Thomas, 1:24. Isolt's ring is alluded to in *Escoufle,* v. 4616; see Bédier in his edition of Thomas, 2:399–400.

33. Thomas, 1:278–279, vv. 443–62. On this scene, see Jean-Charles Payen, *Le Motif du repentir dans la littérature française médiévale (Des Origines à 1230),* Publications romanes et françaises, vol. 98 (Geneva: Droz, 1968), pp. 357–58.

34. Thomas, 1:311, 337 (see also 338, 339). According to the *Saga,* the ring often traveled between the lovers, borne by messengers (Thomas, 1:337, note to v.

1264). In the scene where Tristan, disguised as a leper, manages to see his mistress, Isolt attempts to drop her ring into his hanap (1:367, vv. 1830–50) but is prevented from doing so by Bringvain. For the ring as a signal between the lovers in Eilhart, see Schoepperle, 1:43, 52, 59.

35. Thomas, 1:390 (v. 2457), 392 (vv. 2515–2517), 399, 401. The motif of a ring as a sign of impending death is associated with King Edward the Confessor in a legend attested for the first time in 1163; see Louis Réau, *Iconographie de l'art chrétien,* vol. 3, part 1 (Paris: Presses Universitaires de France, 1958), p. 412.

36. On the significance of this divestiture, see below.

37. Schoepperle, 2:471: "The romance of Tristan [has as its nucleus] a Celtic elopement story."

38. Thomas, 1:416, note to v. 3124.

39. Schoepperle, 1:227–41. The twelfth-century marriage casket preserved at Vannes features two such episodes (Tristan the Minstrel and Tristan the Monk); see Gerard J. Brault, "Le Coffret de Vannes et la légende de Tristan au XIIᵉ siècle" in *Mélanges offerts à Rita Lejeune,* vol. 1 (Gembloux: J. Duculot, 1969), pp. 666–67.

40. *Les Lais de Marie de France,* ed. Jean Rychner, Classiques Français du Moyen Age, vol. 93 (Paris: Champion, 1966), pp. 151–54; Schoepperle, 1:138–47.

41. For the ring as a symbol of eternity, see Robertson, pp. 78–79.

42. Réau, *Iconographie,* vol. 3, part 3, (1959), p. 1305; Heer, p. 170.

43. Lazar, p. 120 (see also pp. 69, 126, 157, 165, 245, 250). For an allusion to this custom in the *Perceval,* see *Chrétien de Troyes, Le Roman de Perceval ou Le Conte du Graal,* ed. William Roach, 2nd ed., Textes Littéraires Français, vol. 71 (Geneva and Paris: Droz, 1959), vv. 550–56, 710–33.

44. F. L. Ganshof, *Feudalism,* trans. Philip Grierson, 2nd ed. (New York: Harper & Bros., 1961), p. 126. Jean Marx, "Observations sur un épisode de la légende de Tristan" in *Recueil de travaux offerts à M. Clovis Brunel* (Paris: Société de l'Ecole des Chartes, 1955), 2:265–73, has suggested that in Béroul following the discovery of the lovers in the forest, King Mark's substitution of his own sword, ring, and glove represents a kind of investiture asserting his right to the lovers' loyalty.

45. Ganshof, p. 128.

46. Roland's gesture is often described as a symbol of homage but this is manifestly an error, as the latter was accompanied by *immixtio manuum,* "the name given to the rite in which the vassal, generally kneeling, bareheaded and weaponless, placed his clasped hands between the hands of his lord, who closed his own hands over them" (Ganshof, pp. 72–73).

47. Jonin, p. 415. For another interpretation, see Anthime Fourrier, *Le Courant réaliste dans le roman courtois en France au moyen âge. I. Les Débuts (XIIᵉ siècle)* (Paris: Nizet, 1960), p. 102.

48. Jonin, p. 412 and n. 1.

49. Jonin, p. 412, n. 1.

50. Thomas, 1:278–79 (vv. 443–62), 311, 316–17 (vv. 975–84), 399 (vv. 2697–98). This in spite of the fact that the ring is supposed to give comfort (1:250, passage quoted above in n. 32).

51. Thomas, 1:217–31; Schoepperle, 2:320–25.

52. *Charrette,* vv. 2336–55, 3124–25; see Cross and Nitze, pp. 10 (n. 1), and 74.

53. *Les Romans de Chrétien de Troyes. IV. Le Chevalier au Lion (Yvain),* ed. Mario Roques, Classiques Français du Moyen Age, vol. 89 (Paris: Champion, 1971), vv.

1026–37. See Cross and Nitze, p. 10, n. 1; Roger Sherman Loomis, *Arthurian Tradition and Chrétien de Troyes* (New York: Columbia University Press, 1949), pp. 294, 300; Philippe Ménard, *Le Rire et le sourire dans le roman courtois en France au moyen âge (1150–1250)*, Publications romanes et françaises, vol. 105 (Geneva: Droz, 1969), pp. 408–9 (bibliography on p. 408, n. 99).

54. *Yvain*, vv. 2602–15; Loomis, *Arthurian Tradition*, pp. 239, 296–97, 301, 304–5.

55. *Yvain*, vv. 2772, 2779, 2948–49; Loomis, *Arthurian Tradition*, pp. 309–10.

56. Schoepperle, 1:84–89, 194–97.

57. In Thomas, 1:394, v. 2559, Isolt is referred to as a *miriesce* 'female healer' (var. *mire;* see also *mire*, v. 2634). Bédier in his edition of Thomas (2:211–12) has suggested that the name which Tristan assumes in an episode in Eilhart (*Pro* of *Iemsetir*) may be an anagram for *Iset por mire*.

58. Edmond Faral, *Recherches sur les sources latines des contes et romans courtois du moyen âge* (Paris, 1913), pp. 133–43; Ménard, p. 194 (bibliography in n. 47).

59. Loomis, *Arthurian Tradition*, pp. 102, 139, 143–45, 179, 183, 205, 260, 262, 296, 309, 428. Loomis generally associates the type with Morgan le Fay.

60. Ménard, pp. 286–92.

61. Thomas, 1:368–73, vv. 1855–2002.

62. Ibid., 1:409, vv. 2947–50.

63. Ibid., 1:410, vv. 2964–66.

64. See Bédier in Thomas, 1:397–398; Roger Sherman Loomis and Gertrude Schoepperle Loomis, *Arthurian Legends in Medieval Art* (London: Oxford University Press; New York: Modern Language Association of America, 1938).

65. *Les Romans de Chrétien de Troyes. II. Cligés*, ed. Alexandre Micha, Classiques Français du Moyen Age, vol. 84 (Paris: Champion, 1970), vv. 3105–36, 5200–5211, 5249–69. See Micha, "Tristan et Cligès," *Neophilologus* 36 (1952):1–10.

66. Thomas, 1:416–17, vv. 3125–44.

67. *Confort* and *conforter* are frequently associated with healing in Thomas, notably in the passages involving the pun on *salu* 'greeting' and 'healing' (1:390 [v. 2474], 391 [vv. 2478, 2485], 393 [v. 2537], 400 [v. 2715]); see also 1:370 (vv. 1937, 1940), 372 (v. 1974), 412 (v. 3020). *Confort* rhymes with *mort* in two of these passages and in fourteen other couplets.

68. See Micha in the introduction to his edition of *Cligés*, p. x.

69. *Cligés*, v. 5.

70. Jean Frappier in *Arthurian Literature in the Middle Ages*, pp. 171–72.

71. Schoepperle, 1:213–26; Cross and Nitze, pp. 16, 78 (for other possible borrowings, see pp. 8, n. 2; 30; 50, n. 1; 52, n. 4; 73; 76).

72. *Charrette*, vv. 1344–1499.

73. Cross and Nitze, p. 7. Two different maidens may actually be involved here; see Kelly, p. 115, n. 22.

74. *Charrette*, vv. 931–1280. On the nameless damsels in the *Charrette*, see Moshé Lazar, "Lancelot et la 'mulier mediatrix'. La Quête de soi à travers la femme," *L'Esprit Créateur* 9 (1969):243–56.

75. *Charrette*, v. 1462. Gerald of Barry, writing about 1217, states that when Guenevere's body was exhumed at Glastonbury in 1191 a lock of her yellow hair was still intact but crumbled away on being touched; see Robert Huntington Fletcher, *The Arthurian Material in the Chronicles Especially Those of Great Britain and France* (1906; rpt. New York: Burt Franklin, 1958), p. 190.

76. *Charrette*, vv. 1634–1828. This episode also involves an encounter with the damsel's suitor who is restrained from fighting Lancelot by his father, a motif paralleling the Baudemagus-Meleagant relationship.

77. *Charrette*, vv. 1837–1954.

78. Cross and Nitze, pp. 8, 72–73 ("also a reminiscence of *Cligés*" [vv. 1621–1622, where Chrétien mocks the hero for kissing the strand of golden hair sewn in Soredamor's shirt]; see also Ménard, pp. 241–42); Kelly p. 119, n. 28: "This entire episode, including the fountain and the later encounter with the maiden's suitor, is the application of one of the forms of *digressio* taught in the medieval arts of poetry as a means of amplification of the narrative." Ménard, p. 242, considers the episode to be comic.

79. Cross and Nitze, p. 72.

80. Frappier in *Arthurian Literature in the Middle Ages*, p. 180; see also his *Chrétien de Troyes*, p. 146.

81. Lazar, "Lancelot et la 'mulier mediatrix'," pp. 248–49.

82. Alfred Maskell, *Ivories* (1905; rpt. Rutland, Vt. and Tokyo: Charles E. Tuttle, 1966), pp. 269–76, 281–82 (liturgical combs), 304–6 (domestic combs); Raymond Koechlin, *Les Ivoires gothiques français* (1924; rpt. Paris: F. de Nobele, 1968), 1:423–28 (reference to *Charrette* episode, p. 425); 2:411–15.

83. Réau, *Iconographie*, vol. 2, pt. 2 (1957), pp. 715–17; Robertson, *Preface to Chaucer*, pp. 92–93; Florence McCulloch, *Mediaeval Latin and French Bestiaries*, University of North Carolina Studies in the Romance Languages and Literatures, vol. 33 (Chapel Hill: University of North Carolina Press, 1962), p. 169 and plate viii, 3; John V. Fleming, *The Roman de la Rose. A Study in Allegory and Iconography* (Princeton: Princeton University Press, 1969), pp. 75–79. For an episode involving an encounter with a damsel with mirror and comb sitting on a bed in a red tent by a well, see *Durmart le Galois. Roman arthurien du treizième siècle*, ed. Joseph Gildea, O.S.A., vol. 1 (Villanova: Villanova Press, 1965), vv. 3055–96.

84. Robertson, *Preface to Chaucer*, pp. 92–93; Fleming, *Roman*, pp. 75–81.

85. Robertson, pp. 93–94; see also Fleming, pp. 95–98.

86. Fleming, pp. 82–89. For other commentaries on the enchanted carol motif, see Loomis, *Arthurian Literature in the Middle Ages*, p. 301, n. 1; Ménard, p. 411.

87. Loomis, *Arthurian Legends in Medieval Art*, p. 36; Jacques Stiennon and Rita Lejeune, "La Légende arthurienne dans la sculpture de la cathédrale de Modène," *Cahiers de Civilisation Médiévale*, 6 (1963): 294–95 and plate xi, fig. 24; Rita Lejeune and Jacques Stiennon, *La Légende de Roland dans l'art du moyen âge* (Brussels: Arcade, 1967), 1:104.

88. Stiennon and Lejeune, "La Légende arthurienne," pp. 294–95.

89. *Charrette*, vv. 4651–53.

90. *Charrette*, vv. 4689, 4691.

91. *Charrette*, vv. 4716–18. Cligés kisses the strand of hair in Soredamor's shirt (see above, note 78) but (as Chrétien makes quite clear) stops short of actually worshipping it (*Cligés*, vv. 1597–99). Cf. Lancelot's "monkish" attitude in bed with the maiden at the second castle (*Charrette*, v. 1218). On the hero's supine posture, see Ménard, p. 287, n. 496.

92. Especially Frappier, *Chrétien de Troyes*, pp. 145–46; Lazar, *Amour courtois*, p. 238.

93. Thomas, 1:309–12.

94. Adolf Katzenellenbogen, *Allegories of the Virtues and Vices in Mediaeval Art,* trans. Allan J. P. Crick (New York: Norton, 1964), pp. 14–21.

95. Thomas, 1:313–15. For the comparison with Pygmalion, see Frederick Whitehead in *Arthurian Literature in the Middle Ages,* p. 143. Other literary examples of statue-fondling are cited by Ménard, p. 192.

96. Robertson, pp. 101–3; Fleming, pp. 85–86, 91, 228–41.

97. *Dictionnaire de spiritualité ascétique et mystique. Doctrine et histoire,* vol. 5 (Paris: Beauchesne, 1964), col. 135. In a paper entitled "The Magdalene Tradition: A New Medieval View of Women" read on 1 May 1972 at the Seventh Conference on Medieval Studies at Western Michigan University, Kalamazoo, Michigan, Professor Robert W. Frank, Jr. described a comparable idealistic view of women derived from the "faithful women" who remained with Christ in His last hours (see the mimeographed Conference abstracts, p. 21).

98. Lazar, *Amour courtois,* pp. 67–70. Cf. also the religious concepts in the views of woman found in the writings of Hrotsvitha of Gandersheim and Heloise, wife of Abelard; see Grace Frank, *The Medieval French Drama* (Oxford: Clarendon Press, 1954), p. 10; Heer, p. 114.

99. Robertson, *Preface to Chaucer,* p. 452.

100. Gerard J. Brault, "Chrétien de Troyes' *Lancelot:* The Eye and the Heart," *Bibliographical Bulletin of the International Arthurian Society* 33 (1972), 142–53.

101. Robertson, pp. 297–98.

102. Norris J. Lacy, "Irony and Distance in Béroul's Tristan," *The French Review,* vol. 45, Special Issue, No. 3 (1971), 21–29.

Petrarch's Laura:
The Convolutions of
a Humanistic Mind

ALDO S. BERNARDO

State University of New York, Binghamton

Never so much as in the Middle Ages was woman viewed as a creature of extremes.* As a figure of Eve or of the Virgin Mary (Ave-Eva) she was regarded as a potential source of both sin and salvation. Though considered strictly inferior to man physically and sociologically, she more than compensated for such inferiority through her role as the moving agent in the inescapable and central human drama of love, the human passion which, more than any other, was conceived as the essential cause of all good and of all evil and which, from the twelfth to the fifteenth century, was the principal theme for writers in the newly evolving vernaculars. In moving from France to Italy this drama assumed deeply spiritual and mystical characteristics. Italy's three greatest early writers, Dante, Pe-

* A brief Italian version of this paper, in its embryonic form, was read at the first International Conference held in Arquà, Italy (Petrarch's place of burial) in November 1970, in commemoration of the six-hundredth anniversary of Petrarch's death in 1974.

trarch and Boccaccio, were literally haunted by the female figure. For Dante, Beatrice was nothing less than Revelation itself. Boccaccio was tormented by his Fiammetta (Little Flame) who seemed to ignite his passions in mysteriously primitive ways. But Petrarch found in his Laura a veritable divine *furor* that drove him to near-despair in his seemingly endless attempts to redefine her in poem after poem throughout his life. Never before or after Laura has a single woman so completely haunted the entire psychological, emotional and intellectual life of a highly learned and lyric poet. The purpose of this paper is to indicate the extent to which the famous love drama was really the drama of a mind on the threshold of the Renaissance.

There is no disputing the fact that throughout Petrarch's life the two most consistent sources of inspiration for his poetry were Scipio Africanus, the great military commander and savior of Rome, and Laura, his beautiful beloved. In these two personages Petrarch apparently saw the kind of foundations on which he felt that true poetry should rest. In my book *Petrarch, Scipio and the "Africa"* [1] I have analyzed Scipio's role in Petrarch's poetic imagination. In this paper I wish to do the same very briefly with Laura in an attempt to show that the two are really complementary.

In his abortive epic on Scipio's African campaigns Petrarch attempted a fusion of Livy, Cicero and Virgil in the hope of producing a distinctive work which enclosed the inherent values of history and philosophy in the glittering wrappings of poetry, without clashing with Christian ideals. In his *Canzoniere* and *Triumphs* Petrarch sought to sing and fuse within a nebulous Christian aura the concomitant human ideals of glory, virtue and beauty, starting with a highly personal vision, and to apply it to mankind generally. Fortunately the vision never quite gelled in the *Canzoniere*, whence, in my opinion, its true poetic power. It almost did in the *Triumphs*, whence their lack of such power.

Down through the ages, commentators and critics of Petrarch's Italian works have dealt with Laura in a great vari-

ety of ways. Generally speaking, the very earliest commentators showed concern either for her identity or for her
allegorical significance. Following the biography by the
Abbé De Sade in the eighteenth century,[2] interest in Laura's
exact identity began to wane. Nineteenth-century Petrarchan criticism became primarily biographical-aesthetic,
and Laura was viewed basically as a beloved whose beauty
had moved Petrarch to lyrical song throughout most of his
life. In keeping with the evolution of literary criticism since
then, subsequent critics have tended to disregard all the bio-
graphical implications of Laura, stressing rather her role as
a persistent psychological stimulus of a complex love drama.
As yet, no one, with the possible exception of Carlo Calcaterra (*Nella selva del Petrarca*) has undertaken a truly comprehensive study showing the evolution or even the vicissi-
tudes of Laura as a purely poetic image either in the
chronological succession of individual poems as Petrarch
wrote them, or as they appear in the *Canzoniere,* or in the
ordering of the poems as the *Canzoniere* progressed from
one form to the next. Nor, for that matter, has anyone attempted to indicate in any extensive degree the distinction
or connection between the Laura of the *Canzoniere* and the
Laura of the *Triumphs.* Since, however, previous criticism
has afforded some insights into the problem, it might be
well first to examine very briefly the views of those major
critics who seemed to have had most to say on the subject of
Laura in the *Canzoniere.*

In his *Saggio critico sul Petrarca,* De Sanctis distinguishes
between the accomplishments of Petrarch the man of letters
and Petrarch the poet by noting that "his scholarly labors
have acquired for him a truly distinguished place among
the great men of letters; but the glory and fame of a great
man came to him because of his poetry. He has reached us
accompanied by Laura." [3] In tracing the particular directions taken by love poetry in Italy, De Sanctis states, "The
fundamental concept is love religiously called spiritual
friendship and philosophically called Platonic, which sup-

poses an honest beloved and a courteous and noble lover; a love which is a source of virtue, and, as Petrarch himself says, 'Of soulful attractiveness,' that is, such as would give life to appealing works." Each love poet, furthermore, had his own personal world, "more or less vast," in which he believed and which influenced his imagination. Petrarch's world was Laura.

The fact that Petrarch's love remains unrequited throughout prompts De Sanctis to pose the problem of how best to define Laura. He concludes that "Laura is a goddess, she is not yet a woman . . . she is the species, the female." She has not yet assumed human form nor entered the stream of human events. She is rather man's ideal in life's journey, his star, the beacon that marks his ultimate destination. As with preceding conventional types, she is an exemplar of perfection that directs the soul to the contemplation of heavenly things: "She is a ladder to the Creator, her eyes indicate the road that leads to heaven, from her derived virtue and holiness." And yet, as with Dante, Petrarch's Platonic-Christian tendencies prompted him to imply such super-human traits without losing sight of the beloved's earthly body. It was always Laura's physical beauties that provide the jumping off point. Indeed, for De Sanctis "Laura is the most beautiful creature of the Middle Ages, she has no other companion than Beatrice. The poet has made a glorious transfiguration of her."

De Sanctis's critical acumen emerges full force in his attempt to define this transfiguration. Laura, he says, is like an actress before the play starts. She is not yet mother, bride or mistress; nor is she any particular woman in any particular situation. She is like a closed book and almost like inert, spiritless nature. "Whence that calmness of appearance which is typical of nature and which expresses the absence of movement and of passion. . . ." She is in the middle of events and yet remains outside of them; she is in contact with passions and yet keeps herself above them; she is on earth and yet no human misery touches her. One almost feels that she is beyond death.

For Benedetto Croce also Petrarch's love represents a complicated experience, not so much because it roared into his life like a blinding hurricane, but because it penetrated all of his being completely and forever and became its center and its fulcrum.[4] Since this love caused the poet to dare "bargain with death," it followed that the very soul of that love was indeed a passion and not a religious, moral, political or other ideal. While it is true that the poet does call upon the Christian God and the Virgin for support, "His God or Goddess, his ethos, his overwhelming politics was called Laura." This pervasive love is highly human, entailing, as it does, "exchange and possession," and the poet's perennial hope resulting from the adamancy of the beloved. When the poet asserts that his love raises him to the Eternal Good and teaches him the straight path to heaven, it is a mere manner of speaking, for basically he himself does not believe it. His happiness resides not in heaven but in Laura, who is no ladder to something else, but is rather herself all, the beginning and end. When, finally, the lover's hopes become dashed by the death of his beloved, he transfers and tenaciously continues his love in heaven, where Laura is as human as ever. Following Laura's death, Petrarch passes from a beautiful dream of profane love "to a dream of a kind of humanizing and secularizing of paradise."

It is Carlo Calcaterra, however, who gives the most intriguing analysis of what Laura meant to Petrarch. In his series of studies that appeared in 1942 under the significant title of *Nella selva del Petrarca*,[5] Carlo Calcaterra undertook to trace the evolution of Petrarch's spiritual and artistic development by analyzing the changing aspects of Laura's image as she appears in Petrarch's poetry. In his interpretation of Petrarch's love of Laura, Calcaterra starts off: "In the radiant days of his youth, when Laura's face appeared to him as the beauty of life, and the art of writing and glory as the purpose and goal of his actions, he personally confesses that he was overcome by such a pagan and Apollonian intoxication that he almost saw in those fascinating images the purpose of life and indeed the apex of happiness." But he was also plagued by a sense of the transitoriness of all things. It is within this context that Petrarch has St. Augustine remind him in the *Secretum* of the in-

timate religion of his early youth and has him express the
fear that "that unseasonal flower might be shaken and
struck by the strong winds of springtime and that if it had
remained whole and intact, it would in time have produced
a remarkable fruit." For Calcaterra, the "springtime of
strong winds" fell between 1327 and 1342 when the poet's
passion for Laura and desire for glory led him into a
"splendid abyss" from which he managed to extricate himself following the spiritual crisis of 1335–42, in which the
Christian religion had played a central role. The poet's spiritual state at this time could best be described by a phrase
appearing in the *Secretum* with its clear Augustinian ring:
"Sentio inexpletum quoddam in praecordiis meis semper."
This, for Calcaterra, is not the *inexpletum* of a Leopardi or
of an Amiel, but of a Christian wayfarer who had been
bewitched by an evanescent earthly beauty, had consequently found himself trapped in a splendid abyss, and
who tries desperately to rise above it.

In Calcaterra's view, the "splendid abyss" resulted from
the inspiration provided by the myth of *Parnasia laurus,* in
which the poet saw the correspondence between his love for
the fleeing Laura and the myth of Daphne. "Daphne had
appeared to him the immortal fantasy of earthly love which,
fleeing the senses, becomes pure beauty in art." Petrarch
thus focussed his earliest poems on the name of Laura and
on the green laurel, "the symbol of poetry inspired by un-
seizable love, since Laura, as Daphne for Apollo, could be
nothing but poetry for him." As a result, this earliest poetry,
best represented in the canzone "Nel dolce tempo della
prima etade" (no. 23), is essentially literary, academic and
Parnassian, as are all subsequent poems that repeat this
same motif. They all have as their primary focus the spell-
binding contemplation of a beautiful image.

In the *Secretum* Petrarch condemns this early bent for
pure imagery as "delirationes." Yet he could not turn his
back upon it, and came to regard it as an example of his
"primo giovenile errore," and of his "vario . . . stile." Already in 1338 he had admitted that he had become "the
prey of unclean spirits and the laughing stock of the raven-
ous dogs of passions." In time his poetic horizons widened

beyond the Daphnean. The irreproachable conduct of
Laura inspired him to superimpose a Christian sense over
his love poetry and to feel the applicability of the Christian
view of woman to his beloved. He thus began to endow his
image of Laura with the characteristics necessary to convert
her into a lady-guide to the Christian heaven. Later, indeed,
he anchored the entire architecture of the *Canzoniere* on the
spiritual contrast between the two configurations of Laura-
Daphne and Laura-guide-to-heaven with the ultimate victory of the latter, and even referred to the region where his
love had evolved as ". . . il mio Parnaso." The general architecture of the *Canzoniere* is consequently not only aesthetic but moral and religious in its attempts to reflect this
"redenzione interiore." The structure emerges from the al-
ternating of the two basic themes of the "Parnasia laurus,"
with its Apollonian contemplation, and the "dì sesto
d'aprile" with its implication of Christian redemption. For
Calcaterra, the true beauty of the *Canzoniere* emerges when
the two themes of Laura-Daphne and Laura-guide-to-
heaven are complemented by an imaginative handling of
the *inexpletum quoddam.*

The prevailing Daphne theme of the earlier poems ended
with the writing of the *Secretum* and of the poem on glory
(no. 119). From that moment the poet's search turned to
the laurel of virtue, having assimilated the Ciceronean-
Senecan concept that virtue possesses a loftier moral value
than glory. This new direction is also symbolized in the
"Triumph of Chastity" when Laura solemnly places her
crown and Cupid's spoils in the Temple of Chastity in
Rome. Calcaterra finds it significant that in sestina 142,
which presumably closed the first form of the *Canzoniere,*
the two concepts are juxtaposed as if calling for a choice,
and that in the second part of the poem the poet turns to a
"new love" and a "new tree" which is the Christian God and
heaven. Yet, the perennial wavering recurs shortly thereafter, in no. 148, where the traditional laurel appears once
again. Indeed, in the final form of the *Canzoniere,* the very
last poem on Laurel alive, no. 263, is a hymn to the laurel.

Following Laura's death, the image of the earthly laurel
breaks (no. 269). The poet's attempt to sanctify the laurel in

no. 228 is never followed through, but in his ordering of
the poems so as to "make a near lyrical poem of his youthful error and purification," a point of juncture is reached in
the tercets of no. 269 which express the conviction that the
poet had procured a justifiable glory for his beloved inasmuch as she had "operato virtute" in him. In such wise does
the poet fuse the two themes of the "donna lauro" and the
Laura *inexpugnabilis et firma* who *iuvenilem eius animum ab
omni turpitudine revocaverat.* By the time we reach poem no.
318 we learn that "Quel vivo lauro," though now in heaven,
had left deep roots in the poet's heart.

In another chapter of his book Calcaterra analyzes Petrarch's coronation oration, focussing upon the central
image of the laurel and the Horatian phrase *Sub lauro mea*
which stands "come gemma nel discorso." This "birth
certificate of Humanism" as Calcaterra calls the oration,
reflects a large network of connections in Petrarch's mind
between his Latin and Italian works, between his concept of
poetic glory and Laura, and between the laurel crown of old
and the one that is being bestowed upon him. So taken was
Petrarch with the implications of the laurel and its connection with the name of his beloved that "At certain moments
the poet would, in a state of ecstasy, actually dive into a
wood of laurels . . ."

Having once analyzed the essential nature of Petrarch's
poetics and his basic inspiration, Calcaterra, in still another
chapter, elaborates further on the Christian superstructure
that seemed to pervade all Petrarch's thinking. The theme of
the chapter is Petrarch's obvious concern to place his two
most important poetic works, the *Africa* and the *Canzoniere,*
within the framework of the Christian ethic by emphasizing
the role played by the drama of Holy Week in both the bio-
graphical and artistic textures of the works. In a thorough
and scientific way, Calcaterra shows how for Petrarch the
date of 6 April (*feria sexta aprilis*) represented the true fixed
day of Christ's passion without regard to the moveable recurrence of Good Friday. This explains the puzzling problem of how Petrarch was able to set his first meeting with
Laura as well as her death on the day of Christ's passion
despite the fact that neither in 1327 nor in 1348 did Good

Friday fall on 6 April. In fact, 6 April was also traditionally considered the day on which man was created and Adam sinned. This finds its importance in the fact that Petrarch accepted fully St. Augustine's view that "omnis homo Adam et omnis homo Christus." By connecting his love of Laura to all these spiritual events, Petrarch was consciously implying a connection with the Christian drama of the redemption.

The extent to which these connections permeated Petrarch's thinking can be seen in his attempts to link them with other important events in his life. Not only did he presumably start the *Africa* on 6 April, but he actually arranged for his coronation to take place within the same period. Following his qualifying examination by King Robert, he set out for Rome on 4 April 1341, arrived in the Holy City on 6 April, and was crowned on Easter Sunday. Within this context, even the poet's depositing of his crown on the altar of St. Peter assumes truly symbolic proportions. Thus, there is also a conscious connection between the *Africa* and the theme of the redemption of mankind. Calcaterra sees still further ramifications in the death and burial of Laura taking place on 6 April 1348. Since in that year Easter Sunday happened to fall on 6 April, the poet was clearly implying both Laura's enjoyment of divine grace and her resurrection in Christ. This is why the poet could view that date as marking his liberation from all earthly passion and his preparation for a resurrection in Christ.

In trying to summarize how Petrarch had organized his personal life around the date of 6 April, Calcaterra points out that love had first smitten the poet on that day as he observed the rites of Holy Week, whence the poet's assertion that it was born at a time of "comune dolor." Eleven years later, in 1338, while again meditating during his observance of Holy Week, he was inspired to write his *Africa*. Ten years later, in 1348, Laura died on Easter Sunday. Laura had thus captured him on the day of Christ's passion and had freed him on the day of the resurrection. In fact, even the number 21, which Petrarch felt surrounding all these events, found symbolic meaning in the significance of the digits 7 and 3 in medieval numerology. In short, as is the case with the *Divine Comedy,* the poet naturally expected his readers to feel the additional dimensions of meaning provided by this superstructure both in the *Africa* and in the two parts of the *Canzoniere.* For Calcaterra the full force of these various dimensions can even be felt in such individual verses as "Era de l'anno e di mia etate aprile."

In his famous *Saggio d'un commento alle correzioni del Petrarca volgare,* Gianfranco Contini uses a particularly happy phrase to define the manner in which Petrarch's poetic imagination viewed nature. In his analysis of poem no. 188 of the *Canzoniere* he first summarizes Calcaterra's position regarding Petrarch's attitude toward classical mythology and toward the history of mankind. Having granted that there is some justification for viewing the poem as an example of a baroque Petrarch, especially in the opening quatrains, he proceeds to show how suddenly the reader is confronted with an unexpected development: ". . . the laurel, slightly shaded initially, gradually occupies the central position, its branches replace the light, its life becomes vegetation. . . . The comparison of the lady to the laurel, of the laurel to Apollo-Sun binds the substances, establishes a system of universal interpenetration of nature." [6] Similarly in no. 34 when the poet, in inviting Apollo the sun God to contemplate his beloved Laura-laurel with him, changes the original form "branches" to the later form "arms" in his reference to Laura's pose, we have another example of "quell'amorosa compenetrazione." The extent of such "interpenetration" may be seen in the amazing fact that the poet often sees himself assuming the same forms assumed by Laura, such as the phoenix in no. 135, or the laurel in no. 23.

In 1946 Umberto Bosco set the tone of the most recent direction of Petrarchan criticism in his highly perceptive *Francesco Petrarca.* [7] The premise of the book takes the position that there is no true evolution of Petrarch's thought or works, for practically all of his works resulted from life-long revisions that ended only with the poet's health. As a result every page of the poet that has come down to us reflects "all of Petrarch: immobile, in his perplexity, from the beginning to the end." The purpose of the book, therefore, is to try to untie the knot which holds together Petrarch's thought and poetry. By means of a thorough analysis of all the works of Petrarch which Bosco considers a single block, the book seeks to identify "the individualizing of the spiritual center of Petrarch for the one and only purpose of understanding as deeply as possible its poetry."

The book opens with a brief glance at Laura's role in Petrarch's works. After tracing the various approaches followed by commentators and critics down through the centuries in trying to define the role, Bosco concludes that while it is true that in Petrarch's life his love of Laura is but a single episode, it is "an episode that the lyric poet wishes to represent for us as central and deterministic; an episode transformed into poetic 'myth.'" Whether Laua is historically real or not is basically unimportant. It is, however, important to define "the essence of the larger hope and despair that it pleased the poet to sing under the guise of his own hope and despair of love."

Bosco opens the following section, entitled "Amore e contemplazione" by minimizing the resemblance of Laura to Dante's Beatrice. Thus, in a poem such as no. 119 in which the figure of Glory recalls Laura, we do not have Laura becoming a symbol or an allegory. It is rather the symbol or allegory that assumes Laura's characteristics. What we really have in this poem, therefore, is an example of how the poet's love for Laura serves as a means for making concrete lyrically the poet's complex sentiments.

In 1962 Adelia Noferi published a book entitled *L'esperienza poetica del Petrarca* [8] consisting of a series of studies that she had completed and published separately over a number of years. Noferi starts with the assumption that in order to penetrate to the depths of Petrarch's poetry one must constantly keep all of his works in mind and that there is very little evolution in his love poetry, representing as it does, a series of new starts to achieve perfection of expression. In fact each poem is a kind of nucleus around which there develops "a complete system of referrals, connections, allusions," thereby making the poems "live centers of energy."

Noferi does, however, see a kind of evolution in the figure of Laura as Petrarch's inspiration. Starting with the poet's well-known cry in *Familiari* 2.9, "Simulatio esset

utinam, et non furor!", she proceeds to show how Laura
evolves from a representative and evocative figure to one
possessing clearly Platonic overtones, to one reflecting first
the nature of an "apology," and then the nature of a
legend. By then appearing to be both remote and close, the
essentially distant mirage takes on the qualities of a "myth."
Petrarch's poetry achieves its greatest purity when he makes
"all his liveliest themes coincide in the fabled name of
Laura, and redeems them in that innocence, to the point of
a perfect confluence. . . . Therefore [it is] not a diary of
love, and, to one side political, religious, moral, and philosophical concerns, but all these elements consummated to
their extreme essence, . . . in the fable of that love"
(pp. 7–9).

    In 1969 Walter Binni collected in one volume a series of
essays on the Renaissance by Raffaello Ramat, essays that
had previously appeared in a variety of publications. The
first of these deals with Laura and first appeared in the late
1950s.[9] In it Ramat develops the thesis that Laura was essentially the central reflection of Petrarch's endless idealiza-
tion of himself. As the unifying image of this process she
acquires an increasingly complex significance. All that Petrarch had dreamed, enjoyed and suffered at the hands of
love becomes fused in the single image of Laura, the Lady:
all the possibilities, whether Christian, religious or literary,
offered to a man for his salvation or damnation. "It is an
exceptional love of an exceptional man for an exceptional
woman, not an episode but a fixed moment around which
revolves the entire life of the poet . . . like an inexhaustible
source of vital flux or energy." Laura thus becomes the dy-
namic essence of things, their active and dramatic beauty.
How to reconcile such dynamism with the static condition of
perfection and divinity was the lifelong quest of Petrarch
and, one might add, of the Renaissance.

    From De Sanctis's "mysterious and deathless goddess," to
Croce's "center and fulcrum," to Calcaterra's "Parnassus
and Calvary," to Contini's "universal interpretation of na-

ture," to Bosco's "larger hope and despair," to Noferi's
"perfect confluence," and to Ramat's "vital flux or energy,"
Laura's image in Petrarch's poetry certainly assumes complex proportions. But for all of these critics, Laura's image
emerges from the final form of the *Canzoniere* as we know it
today—a form that required the better part of Petrarch's
lifetime to assume its present physiognomy, a form, furthermore, that contains not only 366 poems (implying total
immersion throughout the calendar year) but one which
opens with a recantation, proceeds to a roughly chronological history of the poet's overwhelming passion within the
framework of other distracting tensions, is neatly divided
into the life and death of the hauntingly beautiful beloved,
and ends with a hymn to the Virgin Mary.

What would happen if it were possible to follow the evolution of Laura's image as the poet structured the collection
through the several forms that we know the *Canzoniere* to
have undergone? Would the analysis of how the poet pro-
ceeded to add blocks of poems to the original nucleus of
poems provide any insight in support of or against the position of the critics with respect to the evolution of Laura's
image? As is generally known, Petrarch stands almost alone
among writers of his day to have had not only autographs
but actual worksheets come down to present times in relatively large quantities. As a result, it has been possible to
recreate the almost step by step development of the *Canzoniere*. Consequently, it should also be possible to analyze
the evolution of Laura's poetic image as the collection progressed from form to form throughout the poet's life.

The full story of the process whereby Petrarch selected
poems from the worksheets on which they had been composed and began building his collection has been remark-
ably told by the late Ernest H. Wilkins.[10] Since, however,
Wilkins identifies no fewer than thirteen forms and sub-
forms undergone by the collection, we shall confine ourselves only to the first five, which bring us to the beginning
of Petrarch's own first definitive version as it now exists in
the famous Vatican MS *Vat. Lat.* 3195. We can, by considering in some detail only the first five forms, arrive at certain
conclusions that show Calcaterra's approach as being essen-

tially correct, although not complete. Since a full analysis would be too lengthy, we shall present only the general conclusions that would emerge were one to analyze Laura's image as it evolves from form to form.

For our purposes it will be necessary first to repeat succinctly the conclusions reached by Wilkins on the chronology of the process whereby the collection reached its final form, and then to examine the qualities or nature of the contents of each of the stages to see whether there is any distinct evolution in the image of Laura. It is essential to keep in mind that we are here speaking of the *order* which Petrarch gave his individual poems and not of their moment of composition.

The first form of the collection. It was not until 1342 that Petrarch began to think in terms of making a selective and ordered collection of his Italian lyrics (which he had begun writing at least as early as 1327).[11] Between 1342 and no later than 1347 he selected from the worksheets on which he had composed his poems a number of lyrics that had been written quite early. Of these, only fourteen are assignable with any degree of certainty (nos. 34–36, 41–46, 49, 58, 60, 64, 69). Which and how many other poems written before 1342 were included in this form is difficult to determine, but all evidence points to the very strong possibility that no. 34 was the opening poem.[12]

Accepting Wilkins's arguments on the identification of these fourteen poems as part of the first form of the *Canzoniere* and on the appropriateness of no. 34 as the opening poem, we can draw certain general and tentative conclusions about the contents of this first form with respect to the image of Laura. If there is any dominant theme it is that of Apollo and Daphne and the identification of the name Laura with the laurel. In fact no. 34, which presumably was intended to set the tone, opens with the name of Apollo and is an invocation to the classical God of light pleading that he clear the atmosphere of the inclemencies that are harmful to the laurel. Three other poems are heavily involved with the theme of Apollo and Daphne (nos. 41–43), while four others (nos. 44–46, 49) make reference to David, Caesar, Narcissus, and Medusa in projecting Laura's image.

It would therefore seem safe to say that in the very first form of the *Canzoniere* Laura's image is projected against a complex background of classical mythology and history reflecting a wide spectrum of meaning symbolized primarily in the drama of Apollo and Daphne. In other words, there is little question that when Petrarch first began to select poems with which to initiate an ordered collection, his concept of Laura was impregnated with classical overtones that were clearly Platonic in nature, but that contained what Calcaterra calls "a pagan and Apollonian intoxication." The argument that we do not know what other poems were also included in this first form of the collection in no way detracts from the conclusion that when Petrarch first undertook to give form to the *Canzoniere,* he sought as his setting a kind of classical poetic paradise in which Laura reigned as queen.

The second form of the collection. According to Professor Wilkins, the only facts known with any certainty concerning the contents of this form are that it was begun in or before 1347, that it for the first time divided the collection into two parts, and that no. 1 opened Part 1 and no. 264 opened Part 2. Wilkins also adduces evidence to support the contention that both no. 1 and no. 264 were written in 1347, the year before Laura's death. Finally, he indicates that "the total number of poems contained in the second form was somewhat less than 150." [13]

As is generally known, Petrarch underwent a spiritual crisis between 1335 and 1342, resulting from a more intimate knowledge of the Church fathers, especially St. Augustine. The *Secretum,* begun in 1342, is commonly viewed as the work in which the poet's crisis is resolved. This resolution, however, lies rather in the definition of the principal elements of the crisis rather than in the discovery of ultimate answers. This is also reflected clearly in the two poems that open the two parts of the collection in this second form. To put it as briefly as possible, one year before Laura's death Petrarch had written two poems intended to set the tone of a collection that had now undergone a kind of dichotomy. The first poem was to introduce the collection as a whole to the reader as a series of vain experiences

which the poet now recants. No. 264, on the other hand,
was to introduce a Part 2, in which the recantation is defined as practically impossible for the poet. The image of
Laura has thus assumed an even greater complexity in that
the poet feels both its serious dangers and its inescapable
fascination and appeal.

The third form of the collection. This form is generally considered the first "official" form of the *Canzoniere* since it is
known that Petrarch had it prepared for Azzo da Cor-
reggio.[14] As Wilkins has shown, it was started in 1356 (almost ten years after the start of the second form), was completed in 1357–58, contained about 170 poems, and
retained the division into two parts. Part 1 contained about
142 poems and Part 2 about 29 poems. Furthermore, each
part indicates real artistic concern in the arrangement of
the poems to secure both variety in form and variety in content.[15]

The single most significant event that had happened in
Petrarch's life between the inception of the second form in
1347 and of the third in 1356 was, of course, the death of
Laura, during the plague of 1348, which had also caused
the death of many acquaintances and friends dear to the
poet. That the awesome power of the Great Reaper was
truly brought home to the poet during that terrible year
and contributed greatly to his sense of the transitoriness
and instability of all things human can hardly be disputed.[16]
On the other hand, what we find happening in the poems
added by the poet in this form is a reinforcement of the
themes appearing in poem no. 264 rather than the recantation found in poem no. 1. In other words, as was the case
with the *Secretum,* the voice of St. Augustine was once again
muffled by the doubts and convictions of the poet-
humanist, who simply could not accept the idea that all
earthly striving was in vain.

It was this moment that Calcaterra refers to as the spiritual transformation of Laura. The poet began to endow her
poetic image with the characteristics necessary to convert
her into a lady-guide to the Christian heaven; the theme of
"Parnasia laurus" thus became enmeshed with that of the
"dì sesto d'aprile." Accepting Wilkins's argument that Part 1

of the third form of the collection ended with no. 142, and recalling Petrarch's view of the artistic importance of the opening and closing moments of a literary work,[17] we find in poem no. 142 clear evidence of the transformation. Through an extensive analysis of his lifelong relationship with the laurel, "la pianta più gradita in cielo," and through a description of his utter devotion to the "belle frondi," the poet summarizes, in the first part of the poem, the effects wrought upon him by the image of the Daphnean Laura. In the second part he describes how age and the passage of time is beginning to teach him another road to heaven, one that offers true fruit, "non pur fior' et frondi." As a result, he is beginning to seek "Altr'amor, altre frondi et altro lume . . . et altri rami." While on the surface it appears as though this poem is implying a clear turning away from the image of Laura-laurel and toward the Christian God and the Christian heaven, the fact that the latter are still described in terms of *frondi* and *rami* indicates a blurring and modification of the original Laura image rather than its abandonment. If, as Wilkins indicates, this poem was also written just before the death of Laura,[18] the fact that the poet decided to use it as the concluding poem of Part 1 for a form which was begun about ten years after the death of Laura when Laura's new role as lady-guide to heaven had already been conceived, shows an almost deliberate attempt to provide a bridge between the two images, as well as a note of finality. As Wilkins has observed, the poem "served admirably to close a Part 1 which was in the intent of the author to have been followed by a Part 2 beginning with "I' vo pensando." [19] Some of the poems known to have been included in the second part of this form likewise provide evidence to support some of the above conclusions.[20]

Thus, in the third form of the collection we see Petrarch on the verge of having Laura's image undergo a clear conversion from one reflecting the Daphnean myth of earthly beauty, love and art to one implying a lady-guide to the Christian God and the Christian heaven. The vision remains blurred, however, and achieves focus only in the fourth or "Chigi" form of the *Canzoniere*.

The fourth form of the collection. This form was prepared in

the years 1359–62 and represents the first extant form of
the *Canzoniere* that has come down to us. According to Wilkins, the poems added to the third form to make this form
number 33 in Part 1, and 12 in Part 2.[21]

A brief glance at these additions indicates further evolution in the image of Laura. No. 143 indeed shows the poet
viewing his beloved in an entirely new perspective: she is no
longer turning away from him but toward him. Not only is
her beauty as striking as it ever was, but it was the sweetness
of a song of love that prompted the poet to return willingly
to a consideration of Laura's qualities. Poems 144–56, also
added at this time, concentrate on Laura's unusual virtues
and beauty to the point of incapacitating the poet to follow
the "too steep path," since Laura has the same effect on him
as she has on the grass and other plants, which take on new
life as she treads on them.

The final series of poems added to Part 1 of the fourth
form (nos. 176–78, 184–85) continue to shroud Laura in
mystery; she is depicted first as the guiding light which
leads the poet back from the dark and distant shores and
then as a Phoenix in all its oriental splendor. The form
concludes with a poem reflecting the poet's panic as he loses
sight of Laura's guiding light. (no. 189)

The bulk of the poems added to Part 2 of this form focus
upon Laura as a guide to heaven. She is called a "noble mir-
acle" and is pictured in heaven receiving the laurel crown
and the palm for her pursuit of the Good, for her great virtue, and for exposing his madness. In the fourth form,
then, we sense a spiritualizing of Laura in the theme of the
lady-guide to heaven, but there is also present a heaven
where human qualities are not looked upon disparagingly.

The fifth form of the collection. As Wilkins has shown, this
form for all intents and purposes might be considered the
final form of the collection, inasmuch as it eventually became *Vat. Lat.* 3195 which represents Petrarch's own definitive version of the *Canzoniere.* Wilkins refers to the first version of this form as the Johannine form, from the name of
the scribe whom Petrarch employed in 1366 to start the
transcription of the final form. When in the spring of 1367

the scribe inexplicably decided to leave Petrarch's employ, Petrarch personally continued transcribing poems into the two parts until the very year of his death.[22] Despite the fact that this form represents a process of final transcription of poems from worksheets or from what Wilkins calls "reference collections," it is possible to discern even in this form the continued evolution of Laura's image as it emerges from the addition of various blocks of poems to each of the parts.

The result of the scribe's work of transcription in the years 1366–67 was a series of sheets containing, in addition to the poems of the fourth or Chigi form, a number of new poems, fifteen in Part 1 and four in Part 2.[23] It might be well to recall here a rather obvious but essential point. With this form we have reached a moment almost twenty years since the death of Laura. While it may be true, as Wilkins asserts, that there is no clear evidence "that Petrarch ever thought of 263 as a terminal poem for Part 1, or that he was ever concerned to bring the total number of poems in the *Canzoniere* to three hundred and sixty-six," [24] the fact does remain that the poet conceived of Part 1 as containing only poems pertaining to a "live" Laura, and Part 2, except for the three introductory poems, as containing only poems pertaining to a "dead" Laura. Thus, almost twenty years after Laura's death we find Petrarch still trying to decide which poems (mostly written before Laura's death) to include in Part 1, and in what order, while at the same time working on a desired expansion of Part 2. It would seem to follow that the writing and ordering of the poems in Part 2 in which a "new" Laura seemed to be developing must have had some influence in the selection of poems for Part 1. Furthermore, if, as seems to be the case, the inception of *Vat. Lat.* 3195 reflects Petrarch's determination to give his collection a final form, we must assume that perhaps in some vague fashion Petrarch had by this fifth form arrived at some outline of how he wanted the collection to evolve.

The most interesting observation to be made regarding the start of the fifth form is that Petrarch did not ask his scribe simply to transcribe all of the poems contained in the fourth, or Chigi, form. Instead, he had him reorder and add a number of poems in the fourth form before going on.

As a result, classical echoes appear once again in Part 1. There is one poem (no. 166) that expresses the poet's regret for not having remained at Apollo's cave on Parnassus, which would have made him vie with the great classical poets. Instead he has turned to vernacular poetry which he doubts can lead to true greatness without the grace of God. In the following poem (no. 167) Laura's singing is compared to the effect of the sirens' song upon Ulysses, while in still another poem (no. 168) Laura's look is compared to Medusa's. These are followed by another series in which we see the poet returning to his "aurea fronde" (no. 180), describing the trap set by Cupid under the "arbor sempre verde" to catch him forever (no. 181), and finally indulging in an almost orgiastic panegyric as he compares Laura to such ancient heroes as Aeneas, Achilles, Ulysses, Augustus, Agamemnon and Scipio, adding that she is much more worthy of such poets as Virgil, Homer and Orpheus. The concluding poems added to Part 1 return to the mythical dimensions of Laura, as in one (no. 188) the poet invites Apollo (sun) to contemplate with him "quella fronde ch'io sola amo, tu prima amasti," and which is without equal since the birth of Eve. Similarly no. 189, with its sense of despair and fear, is followed by the concluding poem added to Part 1, no. 190, which continues the atmosphere of mystery and classical allusion. In it Laura appears to the poet as a "candida cerva . . . con duo corna d'oro" between two rivers in the shade of a laurel at a spring sunrise. The poet undertakes immediate pursuit, but at high noon realizes that the deer wears around its neck a tag of diamonds and topaz declaring her untouchable because her "Caesar" intended to make her free.

The block of poems that Petrarch gave to his scribe for transcription into Part 2 seem not only to reflect the same tendency to restore some of her classical aura to Laura, but to inject a new factor into the relationship between lover and beloved. The image of the lady-guide continues, but the poet begins to decry Laura's untimely death because it came at a time when age was cooling his passion and when love could easily have been controlled by chastity. But let us restrict ourself to the very last poem added to this form—no. 318.

With this last poem we get a distinct new movement in the evolution of Laura's image. The old, "live" laurel that death had overthrown is replaced by a new one to which the poet feels attached not only through Love but through the muses. It takes its life from roots left in the poet's heart by the old one. Unlike the former one, however, in whose branches the poet's "alti penseri . . . solean far nido," this one provides an outlet only for "chi chiami, et non . . . chi responda."

The poet has thus, in a sense, come full circle. His Laura is now a new laurel with its roots implanted firmly in his heart. She has now become part of his very being, and works as an internal rather than as an external stimulus. In short, she has become real spirit rather than flesh. But this spirit partakes of classical elements as much as it does of Christian ones. The dead Laura now enjoys the eternal sight of the Christian God, but what she has left behind in the poet's heart are the roots of the first laurel defined as ideals and aspirations: *Fama, Honor, Vertute, Leggiadria, casta bellezza in habito celeste.* In short, her image is one which "Amor obiecto scelse, subiecto in me Calliope et Euterpe." The poet is as much a victim of the classical muses as he is of Cupid—all within a framework of Christian salvation.

If we now look at the very last forms of the collection put together by the poet in the very last four years of his life, we find an interesting development. According to Wilkins the poet added about sixty-eight poems to the collection from 1370 to his death, thirty-five in the first part and thirty-three in the second. Recalling that Laura presumably died in 1348, almost thirty years earlier, the additions that the poet makes in the first part are rather interesting, in that we see in them Laura as alive as ever. From a series of poems that reveal Laura almost as pure passion (nos. 235–38, 199, 239–42, 121, 245) we come to the very last series added in the very last month of the poet's life, and there we find an unexpected change in direction. First there is no. 228, in which the image of Laura-laurel seems to return with new force. This is the poem in which the roots of the noble plant had been defined as "fame, honor, virtue, gracefulness, chaste beauty in heavenly dress." The additions following this poem begin naturally to express the poet's fear that Laura may be about to die (nos. 248–54). But in this series we find Laura's image again undergoing the influences of classical mythology as the poet first compares her to Calisto (no. 254) and then returns to the Laura-laurel motif (no. 255), this time expressed in terms of the poet's preference for the day over the night because during the day he can see "two suns." In this sonnet (no. 255) Laura is a sun like Apollo, as well as a woman like Daphne and Calisto; but the poet, if he must choose, prefers the Apollo metaphor (because it "quiets him"), and not the woman metaphor (which "brings him suffering and sorrow.)" As though wanting to underpin this figure the poet adds an earlier poem (no. 246) beginning "L'aura che 'l verde lauro et l'aureo crino," which enhances the Apollonian image of Laura. The final poems added to Part 1 move in a clearly Platonic direction to the very last one before the second part, no. 263. In this poem Laura is first defined as a Daphnean figure with ramifications that go far beyond the contemplative life of the poet to the active life of the warrior king. The poem alludes to Laura as "the victorious triumphant tree, honor of emperors and poets." This is quickly modified in terms of a woman whose only concern seems to be "honor" and who does not care about the workings of Cupid. Finally she even scorns "nobility of blood" and "beauty without chastity."

Surprisingly, a similar movement seems to mark the very last poems added to Part 2 during this last period of Petrarch's life. The first series of poems added (no. 335–36, 350, 355, 351, 352, 354, 353, 366) include the very last poem, no. 366, of the collection which is the famous Hymn to the Virgin. As is well known, this controversial concluding poem clearly enumerates the essential qualities of Mary in terms that seem to reflect everywhere the beauties of Laura. Upon adding the second series of poems however, one senses a return to the Laura-Daphne-Goddess image with the addition of no. 337, a clear recollection of what might be called the classical qualities of Laura in no. 338, and a confession by the poet that after so many poems he had still not defined the true Laura but instead had barely revealed what he refers to as a mere "distillation of infinite abysses." (No. 339).

In a supplementary series of poems subsequently added we find no. 359, in which the poet describes a vision of Laura who crowns him not only with a laurel crown but with a palm branch, symbols of triumph and of victory over worldly matters. The very last poem added by the poet to the second part and to the collection was a poem which found its place in an earlier position, no. 327. In this poem the Laura-Daphne image emerges full force. In it the poet not only complains of the disappearance of "L'aura et l'odore, e 'l refrigerio et l'ombra/del dolce lauro et sua vista fiorita," but inserts a clear allusion to Apollo and finally a declaration which curiously recalls both the last words of Dante's *Vita Nuova* and of Petrarch's *Africa*. These words are: "and if my poems are capable of anything, it will be the eternal memory of your name consecrated among noble intellects."

It is clear therefore that up to the very last moments in the formation of the *Canzoniere*, Petrarch was tormented by the Daphnean image of Laura. His song never loses that classical tone that includes the imprint of mythical mysteries. In fact it could be said that the poetry seems constantly to express the enchantment felt by a Christian Apollo for a Christian Daphne. But the very terms were too contradictory. The Christian heaven could never admit of the purely humanistic dimensions of the pagan myth. Consequently, the poet's vain and endless attempt to reconcile the two dimensions in the figure of Laura is what endows his book of songs with a poetic power that goes far beyond the mere singing of a passionate love for a beautiful lady. What confronts us are veritable convolutions of a humanistic mind intent on showing that Mount Parnassus and Mount Calvary are not *necessarily* contradictory. At the summit of each is something too beautifully human and too beautifully divine to be mutually exclusive. And this something is the power of creativity for which man is crowned with a crown of laurel and God with a crown of thorns. This explains Petrarch's near-obsession with Good Friday and Christ's Passion, which remain constantly in the background of all his accomplishments so nebulously that a reader hardly takes notice. As a result, critics through the century have found it much more convenient to ascribe Petrarch's poetic power to his sensitive insight into the movements of the heart overpowered by an unbridled love. Instead, I would hold that by the time the *Canzoniere* had begun to assume the form of a balanced collection, Petrarch viewed his love of Laura as not much different from God's love of creation, an unselfish movement toward the Good for its own sake and one desirous of uniting with that Good. But as Petrarch has St. Augustine point out in the *Secretum,* his fundamental error lay in placing the creature before the Creator. Consequently the relationship between the laurel crown and the crown of thorns must remain a dilemma as long as the poet's angle of vision is from the bottom up rather than from the top down.

Laura's image thus becomes almost a pure Platonic Form with all its beauties, but incomplete since subject to almost uncontrollable feelings. It remains essentially an intellectual construct which, though based on a vast store of learning, is incapable of shaking off the shackles of an overpowering earthly beauty and passion. This is why the love romance continues to attract the attention of readers; and why Petrarch called his love poems *mere trifles* and yet tried for so long to redefine Laura in his *Triumphs.* Thus, Petrarch's humanism, conceived as the conviction that the learning and culture of classical times can be justified even before the Christian God, emerges even in the very process of selection of poems for admission into the *Canzoniere.* Calcaterra was indeed right when he described as "near ecstasy" the spirit with which Petrarch would engulf himself in his "forest of laurel." This is a far cry from Dante's desperate attempts to *emerge* from his *selva* in the opening moments of the *Divine Comedy.* We are indeed on the threshold of the Renaissance. And it was a female *figura nova* that showed the way.

Notes

1. *The Birth of Humanism's Dream* (Baltimore: The Johns Hopkins Press, 1962).

2. Jacques F. P. A. de Sade, *Mémoires pour la vie de Francois Pétrarque, tirés de ses oeuvres et des auteurs contemporains, avec des notes ou dissertations et les pieces justificatives,* 3 vols. (Amsterdam and Avignon: Arskée and Mercus, 1764–67).

3. Francesco de Sanctis, *Saggio critico sul Petrarca* (1869; Torino, 1952), pp. 80–91.

4. "La poesia del Petrarca," in *Poesia popolare e poesia d'arte* (Bari, 1946), pp. 65–80.

5. (Bologna: L. Cappelli), pp. 8–18, 32–80, 103–4, 210–237.

6. (Firenze: G. C. Sansoni, 1943), pp. 22–23.

7. See Bosco, *Francesco Petrarca* (Turin: 1946; Bari: 1961), pp. 7–11, 15–22.

8. (Firenze: F. Le Monnier, 1962), pp. 1–9.

9. See Raffaello Ramat, *Saggi sul Rinascimento,* ed. Walter Binni (Firenze, 1969), pp. 1–32.

10. *The Making of the 'Canzoniere' and other Petrarchan Studies,* Storia e Letteratura, No. 38 (Rome, 1951), chaps. 4–9, 22.

11. Ibid., p. 287.

12. Ibid., pp. 146–50.

13. Ibid., pp. 150–53.

14. Ibid., p. 154.

15. See Ruth S. Phelps, *The Earlier and Later Forms of Petrarch's Canzoniere* (Chicago: University of Chicago Press, 1925).

16. See Francesco Petrarca, *Le Familiari,* ed. Vittorio Rosse, 4 vols. (Florence: G. C. Sansoni, 1933–42), 8:7–8. The fourth volume was edited by Umberto Bosco.

17. See Petrarca, *Familiari,* 1.1.46, where Petrarch explains how he had organized his *Familiares* so that the beginning and end were strong, the middle weak. See also *Sen.* 17:3, where he explains to Boccaccio how this same principle had led to his decision to translate into Latin the last tale of the *Decameron.*

18. Wilkins, *The Making of the 'Canzoniere,'* p. 352.

19. Ibid., p. 97.

20. The specific poems are analyzed in my forthcoming book, *Petrarch, Laura, and the 'Triumphs'* (Albany: State University of New York Press, 1974).

21. Nos. 143–56, 159–65, 169–73, 176–78, 184–85, 189, 293–304. Wilkins, p. 365.

22. Ibid.

23. Nos. 157–58, 166–68, 174–75, 180–83, 186–88, and 190 in Part 1; 305–18 in Part 2.

24. Wilkins, pp. 186–87.

A Fifteenth-Century View of Women's Role in Medieval Society: Christine de Pizan's *Livre des Trois Vertus*

CHARITY CANNON WILLARD

Ladycliff College

It is no doubt significant that on this program devoted to the role of women in the Middle Ages there is only one woman speaker and that a relatively small portion of the subject matter concerns itself with real women—as opposed to literary figures—or with women's own view of their place in medieval society. This is not entirely the fault of the program committee for, as Simone de Beauvoir pointed out some years ago in *Le Deuxième Sexe*, women's history has traditionally been written by men.[1] Among the exceptions to this rule, women who have themselves had something to say on the subject, she cites Christine de Pizan, along with Sappho and Mary Wollstonescraft. A rather strange company, one would say, but important to consider, for contemporary writers on "Women's Lib" seem to draw their "stereotypes" almost entirely from the nineteenth century or after. The time is certainly ripe to look farther back into history.

For this reason, among others, it is rewarding to be able to turn to such a writer as Christine de Pizan, who expressed at considerable length her views on women's role in the society which was familiar to her, which is to say France just before and after 1400, dwelling not only on the scene as she observed it, but offering a whole program of suggestions for improving the situation.

Although Christine wrote extensively on the necessity of respecting the dignity of women, and even undertook to defend her sex against the slander which characterized a whole section of medieval literature, and especially the *Romance of the Rose,* the subject of the quarrel in which she engaged with several of the early Parisian humanists, the work which sets forth her ideas on the subject most completely, is the *Livre des Trois Vertus,* written in 1405 and last printed in 1536. The book was, to be sure, the subject of a rather superficial study by Mathilde Laigle,[2] but even so it does not seem to be very well known, a circumstance which has not prevented certain scholars from writing at length on Christine's educational ideas, or her feminism, without even mentioning this important text.[3]

One reason why it is essential to know this text, and to read it closely, is that Christine has sometimes been used to support ideas that she did not really express, notably by the feminists who flourished around the beginning of the twentieth century: Rose Rigaud, for instance in "Les idées féministes de Christine de Pizan," a thesis presented at the University of Neuchâtel in 1911, which concludes on the following note:

Car si Christine n'a pas pu concevoir dans son esprit ce type de femme "qui aurait les qualités d'un honnête homme," elle l'a réalisé avec une admirable inconscience. Elle a été spontanée jusqu'à l'abandon; sincère jusqu'à la naïveté; courageuse jusqu'à la combativité. . . . Sa généreuse nature l'a emporté bien au-dessus de l'être édulcoré du *Livre des trois vertus,* puisqu'elle seule, dit M. Robineau, sut avoir à une époque de lâcheté et de basses intrigues "des qualités viriles et des sentiments français." [4]

There was also Lula M. Richardson's *The Forerunners of Feminism in French Literature of the Renaissance,* with the first chapter devoted to Christine, and Mathilde Kastemberg's "Die Stellung der Frau in den Dichtungen der Christine de Pizan." [5] Therefore, before we succumb again to the temptation of interpreting Christine's words to suit our purposes, in the name of Women's Lib, let us try to understand what she really did say and consider it in the light of what we know about the society which surrounded her.

It would be prudent to begin, however, by calling to mind a few of the facts of Christine's life as we know them. She was born in Venice, presumably in 1364, a time when her father was an official of the city government, a "conseillier salarié" as she called it. Her maternal grandfather had held a similar appointment, and both men had been educated at the University of Bologna during a significant period in its history. Christine's father's training was in medicine, in those days closely related to astrology, though the University of Bologna was also noted for its studies of the classics. It must also have been at about this same period that Coluccio Salutati was attending the Notorial School in Bologna, not far from the University. The education of a young man in Bologna in the middle of the fourteenth century could scarcely have been limited to the books he studied. In Venice, Thomas de Pizan would undoubtedly have had some sort of contact with Petrarch, although perhaps only as one of the medical men to whom the great humanist paid his disrespects in his *De suis ipsius et multorum ignorantia,* where he took issue with the sort of education offered by the University of Bologna. He could also have encountered Philippe de Mézières on his way back to France from the Middle East; at least it is certain that Christine was in contact with him in Paris after her father's death, when she sold him some property she owned near Melun. The important point to be established, however, is that Christine owed her basic education, as she herself explained, to a father who had spent his life in centers of considerable intellectual ferment, where contacts were possible with many sorts of people. If the daughter's formal education was limited by the conventions of the time in which she lived, it was nonetheless given a broader scope than might have been assumed from the fact that she lived most of her own life in Paris.[6]

The extent of her father's contacts is demonstrated by the fact that shortly after her birth he was invited to both the courts of France and of Hungary. Choosing the former opportunity, he eventually established his family in Paris, where he enjoyed the favor of Charles V. In due course, when Christine was about fifteen, he married her to a young man who showed promise of a good career in official circles, Etienne du Castel, who was a notary from a solid Picard family and was eventually appointed one of the king's secretaries.[7] The marriage was certainly a very happy one, and doubtlessly the basis for all of Christine's pleas in favor of marriage in succeeding years. Unfortunately her happiness was of short duration. In 1389, in his capacity as king's secretary, Etienne du Castel accompanied Charles VI to Beauvais, where he unexpectedly died in an epidemic raging there. Even earlier, Thomas de Pizan, who had lost the royal favor with the disappearance of Charles V, had died in what would be called today "reduced circumstances." Thus Christine, at the age of twenty-five, found herself a widow, and charged with the support of her mother as well as of her three young children. Her brothers returned to Italy to claim family property in the region of Bologna, leaving behind a niece for Christine to marry off in France. We find a trace of her in a gift from the Duke of Burgundy intended to provide a dowry for her. Christine's own children created a more serious problem. One of them died in childhood; the daughter, possibly through royal favor, was able to enter the royal Abbey of Poissy. Her presence there is recorded in Le Dit de Poissy, written in 1403, which recounts a visit Christine paid her there, one of the writer's most charming evocations of a contemporary scene. The older son was sent to England, presumably at the time of Isabel of France's marriage to Richard II. With the disgrace of the unfortunate king, Henry of Lancaster expressed an interest in keeping the young man in England, and even made overtures to Christine to join her son there. Christine seems to have dissembled long enough to ensure her son's safe return to France, with the wry comment "et

de mes oeuvres cousta." [8] It seems evident that she hoped to
place this son at the court of Louis of Orleans, the king's
brother, whose wife, Valentine Visconti, was of course a
compatriot of Christine's. This ambition apparently met
with no success whatsoever, in spite of the fact that Christine dedicated to the prince several early works, notably the
Epistre Othéa and the *Preudommie de l'homme* (which she later
revised as the *Livre de Prudence,* without the original dedication). It was in the household of the Duke of Burgundy that
the young man was finally given a place, a turn of events
which may be related to the dedication of the *Livre des Trois
Vertus* to a Burgundian princess.

During the years when Christine was faced by innumerable problems of maintaining her household, without much
help or guidance in solving them, she can scarcely be said to
have suffered in silence. From her earliest poems, which
lament her widowhood, to longer, largely autobiographical
works such as the *Chemin de long estude,* the *Livre de l'Avision,*
and the *Mutacion de Fortune,* she described her troubles in
almost excessive detail. She tells how she was beset by law-
suits when she tried to claim money due her husband, how
some of her property was seized, and we know that she was
obliged to sell more of it. However, when she says in *l'Avision* that she was obliged to assume the role of the man in
her family, she does not make it clear just how she con-
trived to do this. Although it is evident that she began to
write poetry, some of it on command, about five years after
the advent of her widowhood, it scarcely seems possible that
this would have furnished more than a pittance. There
would have been a period of about ten years before her first
literary success of any magnitude, her *Epistre Othéa* written,
or at least first copied, around 1402. How did she manage
to keep body and soul together in the meantime? The most
reasonable explanation would be that she was a copyist, first
of all possibly for officials at the Châtelet, where she speaks
of going frequently, and under very distasteful circumstances.[9] She might also have been a sort of editor for an
atelier which copied literary manuscripts. There is evidence
of her connection with the workshop which put into circula-
tion the first Boccaccio manuscripts, for instance, which be-

came popular shortly after 1400. Such a position would account for her access to certain texts she used as sources for her own writings and could account for the miniatures of Christine writing which are to be found in some of the earliest manuscripts containing her poetry. Although these are an obvious imitation of humanistic representations of literary people, they could represent Christine copying as well as composing. It also seems evident that Christine was in close contact with some of the artists who illuminated manuscripts, especially the two whom Millard Meiss has baptized the *Cité des Dames* Master and the *Epître d'Othéa* Master; Christine herself speaks in the *Cité des Dames* of the woman artist Anastaise, whose work was so greatly admired in Paris. There are many problems in this realm which remain to be solved, in spite of the excellent leads which have been given by Meiss in his *French Painting in the Time of Jean de Berry.*[10]

It is also to be expected that she would have maintained some sort of relations with her husband's former colleagues at the royal chancery. It was with some of these, Jean de Montreuil and Pierre and Gontier Col, that she became involved in the humanistic literary quarrel over the merits of the *Romance of the Rose* and from there, in the dispute over the traditional literary abuse of women. It has even been suggested that she started the discussion herself with her *Epître au Dieu d'Amour* (1399) in which she was already raising the question of the double standard represented by all the talk of chivalry and the popularity of Courts of Love in a society where women really had a very tenuous place, as she had learned through much bitter experience. She was willing to admit that the French might have played an honorable role in the cultivation of chivalry in the past, but insisted that times had changed to a shocking degree.

This poem and possibly the *Dit de la Rose* (1403) certainly belong logically with the series of letters which she exchanged with Gontier Col and Jean de Montreuil over the literary and moral values represented by the *Romance of the Rose,* even though we have no way of knowing whether the connection was intended or fortuitious. It was perhaps inevitable that the question of the slanderous attitude towards

women expressed by Jean de Meung should arise, although
it is less certain that this is the basic premise of the quarrel.
It is indeed surprising that Christine should have been willing to take on professional men of letters, whose remarks to
her were, in some instances, considerably less than gallant,
but it seems probable that she would already have known
them in the days when her husband was their colleague in
the royal chancery. In any case, the affair gained for Christine the backing of the celebrated chancellor of the University of Paris, Jean Gerson, and no doubt attracted a considerable amount of attention in Parisian literary circles. A
good deal has been made of this quarrel by more modern
writers who have wanted to show that Christine was the
forerunner of modern feminists in her defense of women's
rights. Unfortunately, a careful reading of the letters does
not bear out this view. Christine was at most merely pointing out flaws in Jean de Meung's logic in his censure of
women, and she was objecting to his vocabulary, insisting
that there was no literary merit in using such crude language, even though she, a doctor's daughter and the
mother of three children, was not shocked by such words
used in a suitable context.

Probably a good deal of the zest generated by the quarrel
came from the fact that it was a sort of humanistic exercise,
a debate carried on between the daughter of an Italian intellectual and a group of Frenchmen who were in close contact with Italian intellectuals of their own day. The predominantly literary nature of the quarrel has been well
characterized by Gilbert Ouy in his article entitled "Paris,
l'un des principaux foyers de l'humanisme en Europe au
début du XVe siècle" [11] where he says:

> Que cette 'querelle'—à vrai dire peu envenimété avant
> tout une joute littéraire, on pourrait en voir une preuve dans la
> curieuse epître 161 de Jean de Montreuil. Devenu soudain plus
> feministe que Christine de Pisan, le prévôt de Lille, compose,
> non sans faire quelques emprunts à Plaute, Terence, Virgile,
> Cicéron et Pétrarque, le discours que pourrait tenir à son mari
> la femme de Gontier Col, se plaignant de l'injustice de son sort:
> c'est un texte fort sérieux, en dépit de quelques passages plai-
> sants, et qui rend un son tout nouveau.[12]

It seems certain, in any case, that her role in the quarrel was an important stimulus to Christine to pursue the idea of pointing out the merits of women in their historic role, a project which must have been given further impetus by the first French translation of Boccaccio's *De Claris Mulieribus* (1402), a principal source for Christine's *Cité des Dames* (1405), although she also made use of the *Decameron,* which was not translated into French until nearly ten years later.[13] In addition to the examples drawn from the past, or from Italy, Christine had the excellent idea of adding a certain number of cases from French history, even from fairly recent times, a device which undoubtedly greatly increased the popularity of her book among French ladies.

Then, as she herself explains, when she had constructed the City of Ladies under the guidance of three supernatural creatures, Raison, Droitture and Justice, the same three goddesses directed her to write a guide for contemporary women to make them worthy to dwell in the city. She undertook this task as soon as she had completed the *Cité des Dames,* and finished it before the end of the year, probably in the course of the late spring and summer. It is sometimes called the *Trésor de la Cité des Dames.*

The three virtues—who are often shown appearing to Christine in a vision in the manuscripts of both works— recall the representations of allegorical figures in Italian frescoes and murals—the Chapel of the Palazzo Pubblico in Siena, for instance. The important point, however, is that they are secular rather than theological virtues, and as such indicate a new approach to educational precepts.

Such then is the poetic genesis of the book. The historical explanation is perhaps even more interesting. It was dedicated to, possibly even commissioned for, Margaret of Burgundy, when she was about to be married to the French dauphin, Louis of Guyenne, in August 1404. According to the custom of the day, the contracting parties were mere children. Margaret was twelve, but had already been betrothed to Charles, the former dauphin who had died in 1401, before the marriage could take place. The second betrothal, like the first, marked a final political triumph for the princess's grandfather, Philip the Bold, in his politics of advantageous marriages, which he had pursued indefatigably since his own marriage with Margaret of Flanders had brought about his succession to the vast lands of Flanders as well as the Duchy of Burgundy. By the marriage of his oldest granddaughter he had hoped to reinforce his influence over his nephew, the frail and mentally unstable Charles VI, by assuring himself that the next Queen of France would be a member of his family. At the same time a match was arranged between Michelle of France and the Duke's only grandson, the future Philip the Good. It was his intention to counterbalance once and for all the drive for power undertaken by the mad king's brother, and the Duke of Burgundy's chief rival, Louis of Orleans. The old duke was an astute politician, but he had not counted on one factor, his own sudden death in 1404, before either projected marriage could be celebrated. Posterity has continued to be reminded of that unfortunate turn of events by the remarkable funeral procession which winds eternally around his tomb in his Burgundian capital, Dijon.

Margaret was the oldest of six daughters in the family of John the Fearless. These Burgundian princesses were reared in what appears to have been an affectionate family atmosphere in the various ducal residences of Burgundy, Rouvres, or Montbard, or near the dowager duchess in Artois. It is understandable that there might have been some concern about sending a young daughter to the French court in Paris, dominated as it was by the frivolous and greedy Isabeau de Bavière. It is not known who suggested to Christine that a book on the education of princesses would be welcomed by the duke's family, but it might have been John the Fearless himself, for he made a substantial gift to the author soon after the presentation of the book.

John the Fearless has traditionally been presented in a very bad light by historians, many of them writing in Paris where he has usually been regarded as an arch-enemy. What is less often recognized is that he represents a new idea in government, the demagogue who depends more on popular appeal than on the support of the nobility. It was a model familiar in Italy, but less known or favored in the North. Probably some of his advanced ideas came as the result of his youthful adventures far removed from the conventions of French courtly life, for he had been a captive of the Turks after the disastrous Battle of Nicopolis (1396), and upon his release from captivity he had been given the opportunity to visit several foreign lands on his way back to France. Thus he had not only seen Hungary and experienced the rigors of a Turkish prison, but had also visited Rhodes and Venice, so gaining a much broader view of the world than any prince of the French royal family since Saint Louis. Furthermore, his close contacts with the Rapondi family, the Italian silk merchants and bankers, would also have broadened this view as Dino Rapondi arranged for the payment of the enormous ransom demanded by the Turks through business contacts which extended from Bruges to Pera, while Jacques Rapondi provided the ducal library with a fine copy of Livy as well as the first French manuscripts of Boccaccio. Such contacts with Italy may well have given Christine's own Italian heritage a special appeal to the duke, in addition to the fact that his father, Philip the Bold, had already commissioned her to write the official biography of the late king, *Les Faits et bonnes moeurs de Charles V*. At the same time it should be realized that women in the Burgundian ducal family were expected to play a significant part in the scheme of things. Such had been the case with the duke's mother, Margaret of Flanders, as well as with his wife, Margaret of Bavaria, who acted as his representative in the North and then in Burgundy while he pursued his political ambitions in Paris. No doubt there was the expectation that Margaret of Burgundy would play a significant role, first as Duchess of Guyenne and then as Queen of France. The object of Christine's treatise was, first of all, to prepare her for her future duties.

So, though the reproach has sometimes been made that Christine concerns herself unduly with the education of princesses and noble ladies at the expense of the lower classes, the original intent must be borne in mind. It is true that about half the treatise is devoted to this section of society. But in addition to the dedication to Margaret, it must not be forgotten that it was the kings and noblemen who possessed most of the libraries of the day and provided the chief patronage for literary and artistic activities. Furthermore, it

is true that the book belongs, at least in a general way, to the
humanistic texts which concern themselves with the formation of "the perfect prince," a problem to which Christine
devoted herself more directly in the *Corps de policie* and the
Livre de la paix. Paul Oscar Kristeller has called attention to
the great popularity of this sort of literature in both the
later Middle Ages and the early Renaissance, observing that
the tone is more secular than religious and that the promised reward for a good life is everlasting fame rather than
the blessings of a future life, although it must be said that
Christine is inclined to hold out both rewards.[14] It must also
be considered an innovation on Christine's part to have
devoted even a part of the book to the lower social orders, a
point of view which corresponds to the introduction of artisans in the illustrations of that celebrated manuscript, the
Très Riches Heures de Jean de Berry at Chantilly, or indeed, in
the early Boccaccio manuscripts.[15]

The *Livre des Trois Vertus,* then, is divided into three parts.
The first is devoted to the education of princesses and noble
ladies, and the second to women who live at court as well as
to members of the lesser nobility who live on their lands in
the country, and who in the absence of their husbands may
be called upon to manage their estates; the third part describes the role of middle-class women, the wives of merchants and artisans living in towns, and also the wives of ag-
ricultural laborers who share the toil of their mates in the
fields. No such comprehensive description of women in
these sections of society had been attempted previously, although slightly later evidence for the accuracy of Christine's
classification is to be found in Martial d'Auvergne's *Danse
Macabre des femmes,* and for the early sixteenth century, in
the margins of a Book of Hours published in Paris by Philippe Pigouchet for the bookseller Simon Vostre.

There is no question of the didactic intention of Christine's treatise. She was convinced that women had a serious
role to play in society, whether the fact might be recognized
by the early Parisian humanists or not, and that women
should be up to assuming their responsibilities, princesses
even more than others because they were more frequently
in public view and thus had the duty of setting a good ex-

ample for their humbler sisters. Christine's pedagogical in-
stincts, here as elsewhere, are strong and this could have
made her writing tiresome if her theorizing were not interspersed with lively sketches of the life of her contemporaries. Indeed, some of the situations she describes, because
they should be avoided, recall the *Quinze Joyes de Mariage,* as
we shall have occasion to notice. It is also curious to observe
that in her discussion of country life on a large estate, she
warns against the same sort of dishonest practices on the
part of shepherds that characterize the shepherd Agnelet in
the *Farce de Maistre Pierre Pathelin.*

There are innumerable observations on late medieval life
which deserve comment if space permitted, but suffice it to
point out here that throughout the book there are certain
recurring themes which mark themselves as particular concerns of the writer. They appear not only here but in other
of her writings as well. There is, to begin with, (1) the sorry
plight of widows, which Christine knew all too well from
personal experience, and her resulting insistence that
women should have sufficient education or training to be
able to manage their own affairs should experience require
them to do so; (2) as a related theme there are constant references to women's relative insecurity in a society where
they are almost completely lacking in civil rights, with the
resulting need to remain in the good graces of husband,
family and friends who could turn against them, and especially to avoid making enemies who could do them serious
harm; (3) there are repeated attacks on indolence, envy and
extravagance, along with the overweening desire to appear
to be more than one really is, all of which give women a bad
name; (4) there is also the repeated admonition to perform
well the duties expected of women, the running of a household according to the needs of the husband, the rearing of
children, perhaps the management of an estate, a business,
or even a country in the husband's absence, and to carry out
these duties with such grace and dignity as to belie the evil
tongues, masculine as well as feminine, which will wag at
the slightest provocation. Finally, (5) there is perhaps Christine's greatest innovation, her constant attack on the hypoc-
risy and the deceptions which are the unpleasant reality of

the outworn ideal of courtly love. While admitting that it might have been a noble ideal in the past, Christine multiplies warnings as to the price which must almost inevitably be paid by the woman who gives in to an illicit love affair. In contrast to most of her contemporaries in France, she extols the joys of married love, as she knew them from experience, and the pleasures of a well-organized family life. In this she reflects the ideal which was taking shape in Italy, as seen, for example in Giovannini Dominici's *Regola del governo di cura familiare,* but which was new to French letters. Both the intent and the atmosphere of such French works as *Le Chevalier de la Tour Landry* and *Le Menagier de Paris* are different. In both of these late fourteenth-century treatises on the education of women—specific women in both cases—the purpose is to form a wife according to a man's whim and pleasures. There is little if any interest in the question of the education of women in general, nor in furthering a dignified and satisfying role for women in society, both of which were important to Christine.

Let us now examine in some detail what the *Trois Vertus* has to say about these five problems. The situation of widows was not only the first, but also one of the most original of the themes to be found in Christine's writings. Very probably she spoke so eloquently because it lay so close to her own experience. Although "Seulete suy et seulete vueil estre" is undoubtedly the best known of her lyric poems, it is only one of several, beginning with the very first of the *Cent Balades* which, as she herself explained in *L'Avision,* she wrote for her own consolation. She mentioned 1399 as the beginning of her literary career, but Balade IX would seem to have been written in 1394, the fifth anniversary of her husband's death.[16] In addition to several other *balades,* four of her *Rondeaux* (I, III, IV, XXIV) and one of her *Autres Balades* (VI) take up the theme. This last poem is of particular interest because there Christine begins to depart from her own personal affliction and to speak of the sorry lot of widows in general.[17]

In case one should be tempted to see Christine's complaint as all too subjective, one must take into account the chivalric order of the *Escu vert à la Dame Blanche,* founded at

Easter 1399 by the Maréchal Boucicaut and twelve of his knightly companions, all of whom swore to defend women, and especially "poor widows." There is no evidence to show whether or not the order ever really existed, but the statutes are set forth in the *Livre des faits du Maréchal Boucicaut,* written by one of his admirers some ten years later.[18] One of Christine's *Autres Balades* honors the thirteen knights (XII).

Christine took up the theme of the dispossessed widow again in the *Mutacion de Fortune* (1404). Even though Suzanne Solente, in her admirable edition of the long poem, sees in the passage no more than the reflection of Christine's personal experience, taken together with all the references in other writings, it seems equally possible to observe there one more stage in the writer's evolution from the personal tone of the early *balades* to the generalized and highly practical consideration of widows' problems in the *Livre des Trois Vertus.*[19]

In the latter composition, Christine devotes two chapters (Part I, xxii–xxiii) to widowed princesses, whereas in Part III (iv) she turns to the problem as it applies to women from other classes of society. In the case of the princesses, she speaks of the precarious situation of the widow who must maintain a regency for a young heir, a problem which could be well understood in either France or England. Although the Duke of Guyenne was scarcely an orphan, his father's insanity created the need for a regency, thus putting a considerable amount of power into the hands of Isabeau de Bavière, to the misfortune of the country; England would soon be confronted with a similar problem during the minority of Henry VI, grandson of the unfortunate Charles VI. As for widows of lesser status, the advice turns on the dangers of law-suits, where it is essential to have both good legal counsel and considerable financial backing. Christine's own financial problems had been complicated by lengthy legal entanglements, as we know, but to show that there were other ways in which widows were exploited, we can turn to the Burgundian Archives and see how one of Philip the Good's most successful bureaucrats made his fortune from exploiting a susceptible widow. There is no reason to suppose these examples unique; indeed Christine warns against the ultimate folly, that of the elderly widow who is taken in by the blandishments of a young man.[20] Less humorous is her reference to friends who cease to be faithful after the loss of a husband, a grief already mentioned in the *Mutacion de Fortune*.[21]

Nevertheless, Christine does not limit herself to practical advice in the *Trois Vertus;* she also reveals her true compassion for the sorrow of these women; she speaks, for instance, of their need to express grief, but admonishes them not to retire from life so long as to injure their health. Bearing in mind Aliénor de Poitiers's allusion, in *Les Honneurs de la Cour*,[22] to the fifteenth-century customs of mourning, which required a royal widow to spend a full year in a darkened room, one grasps Christine's independence of thought. These admonitions against unduly prolonged periods of grief do not exactly conform to Johann Huizinga's generalization about such mourning customs, where he says: "the general instability of the soul, the extreme horror of death, the fervour of family attachment and loyalty, all contributed to make the decease of a king or a prince an afflicting event."[23] How much more normal is Christine's humane and reasonable suggestion that in due course the widow should give thought to her health, her children, and the duties incumbent upon her, and that she should thus turn her thoughts back to the problems of the living.

Although it is in the *Trois Vertus* that Christine devotes herself at greatest length to the trials of widows, she returns to the theme some ten years later in the *Epistre de Prison de vie humaine,* where she addresses to Marie de Berry, daughter of Jean de Berry and wife of the Duke of Bourbon, one of the victims of Agincourt, her sympathy not only for her in particular (she has lost both father and husband), but also for all women who have suffered from the military disaster and from other sorrows in the difficult times.[24] In spite of the separation between Christine and the modern reader due to her antiquated language and prolix style, one can scarcely fail to be touched by the note of sincerity in her effort to think if her own experience of sorrow could possibly bring comfort to others in affliction. This attitude also marks an interesting psychological evolution from the self-pity of the sorrowing widow of twenty-five to the seasoned and philosophical writer of more than fifty years of age who projects her sympathy into the sorrows of others.

The sense of insecurity which comes to light repeatedly in the course of the advice to widows as well as in recommendations for maintaining good relations with the living, seems to mark a profound difference between Christine's contemporaries and our own, in spite of the troubled society in which we live. Not only was medieval life uncertain because of the political upheavals brought on by recurring war between the French and English, the threat of civil war in France was on the horizon in 1405 (the first show of arms between the partisans of Burgundy and Orleans occurred in the early fall of that year when the Queen and the Duke of Orleans attempted to kidnap the Dauphin and his bride, the Margaret to whom the *Trois Vertus* was dedicated, with the intention of removing them from the Burgundian sphere of influence).[25] The uncertainty was heightened by the mortality from epidemics and other forms of illness which were beyond the reach of the medical knowledge of the day. Christine's own father, it should be recalled, practised medicine based on astrology, and even where faith in the stars was subject to question, it was replaced by other practices equally dubious. To be sure, the fifteenth century seemed to revel in the idea of the *Danse Macabre* and the corruption of the body, but what emanates from the *Trois Vertus* is something more subtle stemming primarily from women's situation in society, first under the tutelage of their fathers, then as property of their husbands. The widows were in a certain sense better off than the wives and daughters, but even so, Christine warns against the danger of entering into any new marriage without the approval and advice of family and friends. In such a precarious situation it was important for a wife to get on as well as she could with even a difficult and unreasonable husband, of which plenty of examples were known to all, as Christine admitted. It was also important to cultivate his family and friends, and most especially any of them who might be real or potential enemies, for any of these might be capable of gossiping about her, or bearing tales to her husband which could do her serious harm. If this suggestion seems far-fetched, one has only to think of the case of Margaret of Burgundy's sister, Catherine, who in 1410, at the age of eleven, was sent to marry Louis of Anjou, son of the King of Sicily, who needed the dowry money for an expedition into Italy. In the late summer of 1413, when John the Fearless lost his political dominance in Paris, the marriage was broken off and the princess, now fourteen, was sent home as the House of Anjou changed sides in the civil war. Catherine was proposed in the following year as a possible bride for Henry V of England, but she did not survive long enough to be accepted or rejected, the victim, according to some, of the disgrace she had suffered.[26] Three generations later Margaret of Austria was sent home from the French court when it was decided that there would be greater advantage to France in marrying the future Charles VIII to Anne of Brittany. Margaret's humiliation was such that she had not forgotten it years later when, as regent of the Netherlands for her nephew the Emperor Charles V, she negotiated the *Paix des Dames* at Cambrai with the mother and sister of Francis the First. Margaret of Burgundy, the Duchess of Guyenne, was herself to be sent away from the French court in the summer of 1413 when her father was forced to flee for his life from Paris. The Armagnacs saw fit to replace her at her husband's side by a favorite mistress, La Cassinelle, although it is doubtful if even under happier circumstances the vain, pleasure-loving Louis would have been a very satisfactory husband.[27]

The same sense of insecurity pervades the *Enseignements d'Anne de France,* written by Louis XI's daughter for her daughter Suzanne de Bourbon in 1504, nearly a hundred years after the composition of the *Trois Vertus.* Anne de France speaks not only of the omnipresence of death, but of the dangers of life in this world, saying: "Je vous conseille plus le doute que la sûreté . . . les assauts et les aiguillons de ce monde sont forts à passer, si ce n'est pas par l'aide de Dieu." [28] Anne de France, Margaret of Austria, like the Duchess of Guyenne, had copies of Christine's *Trois Vertus* in their libraries. All of them bore witness to the truth of Christine's words.

If one should be left, at this point, with the impression that wives were generally victimized by cruel or unfaithful husbands, such a view must be modified by Christine's numerous references to the idleness and extravagance of certain women from nearly every section of society. Here she is frequently in accord with *Les Quinze Joyes de Mariage* and with the preachers of her day. Early in the book she gives a marvelous sketch of a vain and lazy princess who lies abed most of the morning and thinks only of how to get the better of her social rivals. One cannot fail to think of the reputation of the French queen, though Christine would scarcely have dared to make the resemblance too obvious. She speaks of the excesses in dress, of the desire to outdo one's neighbors, however, in terms which remind one of the machinations of the wife, in the First Joy of Marriage, to get a new dress which her husband cannot afford. Christine also mentions people who go into debt to buy the latest fashion, comparing them unfavorably with the greater moderation of Italian women, who do not change fashions so often.[29] If the upper classes are extravagant, the artisans suffer from not being paid for their work. In Part III, Christine cautions the artisans' wives to prevent their husbands from accepting commissions from nobles who will not pay them promptly or, perhaps, ever.

Two other aspects of society which Christine chooses for comment are amusing because they correspond to the vituperations of other medieval writers. One of these is the habit of going on pilgrimages, especially in the spring of the year. Of course the suppression of this custom would have cost the world one of its literary masterpieces, but it is evident that the Wife of Bath had sisters in many countries. Huizinga mentions extensive criticism of the habit, citing among others Nicolas de Clamanges and the Chevalier de la Tour Landry, who classifies pilgrimages along with jousts as profane pleasures. He also speaks of the pilgrimage, described by Froissart, which was the pretext for presenting Isabeau de Bavière to Charles VI, with a view to bringing about their marriage. Even better known is the Eighth Joy of Marriage, where the wife pretends that her young baby is ill so that she can get away from home in the company of her friends on the pretext of fulfilling a vow made at the time of the child's birth.[30] Christine accuses certain women of running from church to church all year long, expressing her disapproval of using God as an umbrella for less than spiritual purposes.[31]

The other custom to which Christine alludes with disapproval is the pretention of a commoner to have a lying-in which rivals the grandeur to which only her betters are entitled. As Huizinga pointed out, the ceremonial of the lying-in chamber equalled mourning as an opportunity for differentiation in society. Green, for instance, could be used only by royalty. Aliénor de Poitiers in *Les Honneurs de la Cour* describes Isabelle de Bourbon's lying-in at the birth of Mary of Burgundy, on which occasion there were five state beds, all hung with green, not to mention a great display of silver vessels on several sideboards.[32] A comparable display is documented by the Burgundian accounts detailing expenditures for the elaborate preparations for the lying-in of Jeanne de Saint-Pol, wife of Philip the Bold's second son, Antoine, in 1403.[33] The affair described in the Third Joy of Marriage is, to be sure, at the other end of the social scale, but there, too, the *commères* who flock to attend the birth of the child all but eat the poor husband out of house and home.[34]

The merchant's wife described by Christine, who created such a scandal by having a lying-in to rival the queen's, can be judged by the fact that her arrangements seem scarcely less sumptuous than those prepared for the Duke of Burgundy's daughter-in-law. She had hangings embroidered with her crest in gold thread, even if she had only three state beds rather than five. She did not go so far as to appropriate the royal green, but she lay in a bed hung in scarlet silk with matching pillows ornamented with pearl buttons. The display of silver on the dressers gave every indication of being worthy of a queen and led Christine to exclaim: "For without fail the pride and pretentions from great to small were never so outrageous as they are now,

and one can judge this by the chronicles and ancient history. . . ." [35] Her final comment on the useless expense of
such a display is as heartfelt as that of the poor man in the
eel-basket, the husband in *Les Quinze Joyes de Mariage.*

This is not to say that Christine found nothing to praise
in contemporary life. There is, for instance, the portrait of
the good queen who devotes her time to looking after others, from the moment she arises and lights her own candle
to say her morning prayers, because she does not want to
disturb the slumbers of her serving maid. She later em-
broiders fine linen and talks informally with her ladies-in-
waiting; she receives her husband with a joyful face, speaking to him only of subjects she knows will give him pleasure.
As much as possible she keeps her daughters at her side, at
least when they have passed infancy, so that she can assure
herself that they will not be exposed to undesirable influences in their upbringing. She is able to rule the domain in
her husband's absence, making sure that she understands in
advance the problems which are to be brought before the
council so that she will be able to preside over it with dignity; she protects the rights of her son and heir coura-
geously if she is called upon to act as regent. The *chatellaine*
oversees the planting and harvesting at her manor, follows
with care the activities of her agents, especially the shearing
of the sheep, for one must protect oneself against unscru-
pulous shepherds. All this is described in a series of vignettes which recall the calendar scenes of such a manuscript as the Duke of Berry's *Très Riches Heures.* The
bourgeois wife helps her husband in his business, entertains
his friends (the exact opposite here of the wife in the Sixth
Joy of Marriage), sees to the supply of household linen,
keeps her serving-maids in hand (she is warned especially
about the dangers of letting them waste their days at public
lavoirs). One is left with an impression of great activity and
vitality. The women who are fulfilling their duties in such a
virtuous manner are seemingly well adjusted to their lives.
There is, of course, not even any thought of liberation from
this routine. It is only such deviations as idleness or envy, or
undue competition with their neighbors which makes them
unhappy. A modern woman might well take exception to

this state of affairs, but Christine and her contemporaries could scarcely have achieved anything by undertaking to overthrow a social system which was so entrenched in every aspect of life. At the same time, there is no doubt that the social ferment is already present which, as the record shows, eventually brought about the rise to power and influence of the middle classes and, ultimately, the French Revolution.

Christine herself was not unaware of the changing times. She reflects this attitude most clearly in her commentary on the pretenses of chivalry, and especially on the conventions of courtly love. Johann Huizinga had a good deal to say about this discrepancy between the real and the ideal, the illusion of a society based on chivalric ideas which clashed curiously with the reality of things. The chroniclers themselves, he points out, in describing the history of their times, tell far more of covetousness, cruelty, cold calculation, self-interest and diplomatic subtlety than of chivalry. Nonetheless, all of them as a rule, profess to write in honor of chivalry, which is the stay of the world.[36]

It is safe to say that Christine's eyes were open to the problem from the beginning of her literary career. Her contention was that, although chivalry might have made great lovers of men in the past, in the Paris of her day they were far more apt to be false to their fine vows and to boast in an ungallant fashion among themselves of their amorous exploits, thus endangering the reputation of any woman so foolish to believe their fine words. The persistence of this theme in Christine's writing leads one to believe that it was meant to be something more profound than the forerunner of *La Belle Dame sans Merci*.

Already in the *Cent Balades* there is the account of a love affair which went awry. It starts in Balade XXI. The lovers rejoice there in their newly-discovered emotion. Soon the knight is obliged to go to the wars in the Empire, though already they have begun to suffer from the wagging of malicious tongues, in Balade XXVI:

> Les mesdisans qui tout veulent savoir
> Car je suis gaye, cointe et jolie
> C'est tout pour vous que j'aim d'amour entiere . . .

The spiteful tongues are still active in Balade XXX, but in XXXII the lover finally departs. He remains away for a year and a half without sending any word to comfort the sorrowing lady who is left behind. Although in Balade L Christine denies that her little romance is to be taken seriously, one is not entirely convinced, for in LI she writes "Trop me deçut Amour par vostre chiere," and in LII she warns, for the first time, against false lovers:

> Sage seroit qui se saroit garder
> Des faulx amans qui ades ont usage
> De dire assez pour les femmes fraudes . . .

In her *Epître au Dieu d'Amour,* written in 1399, she seems less to be defending the honor of women than poking fun at Frenchmen who make vows to Cupid, but are nonetheless, false lovers, far inferior in all but a few notable cases, to the legendary lovers they pretend to emulate. This poem was of course followed by the celebrated Quarrel of the Rose, but in 1403 Christine wrote the *Dit de la Pastoure,* where a shepherdess is roundly deceived by a knight who passes her way and makes love to her in a traditionally idyllic setting. One can insist of course that Christine was merely developing a classic theme which enjoyed a renewed vogue at the beginning of the fifteenth century; that may be true in part, but taken together with her other tales of false lovers, it leads one to suspect that Christine had other intentions. Indeed, even Huizinga conceded that "A poem like *Le Dit de la Pastoure* of Christine de Pisan marks the transition of the pastoral to a new genre." [37]

Soon after, possibly in 1404, Christine undertook to write, at the request of one of her patrons—whom she does not name—the "Livre du duc des Vrais Amants." Here we have the fore-runner of the sort of psychological novel which would produce *La Princesse de Clèves* in the seventeenth century and all its descendants up to the present time. Christine's book, though still basically written in verse, is interspersed with letters in prose. This is an interesting device, in view of the fact that letters were a means by which medieval women could express themselves, as is well illustrated, for example, by the Paston Letters. It was still employed as a technique for novels in the eighteenth century. The plot concerns a young man who falls in love with his cousin, a lady married to a husband she does not love. The man suffers many pangs of love and very nearly persuades the lady to give in to his pleas. This turn of events is effectively prevented by the lady's childhood governess, the Dame de la Tour, who writes a long letter warning her mistress of the many practical perils created by an illicit love affair. The lady reconsiders, but as the couple truly loves one another, they continue a Platonic friendship which is a consolation to them both as the years pass. Was Christine trying to emulate the love of Dante for Beatrice? She certainly knew Dante's poetry, because she cites it as early as her letters in the Quarrel of the Rose. Did she by any chance know Petrarch's poetry for Laura? Certainly this concept of love seems more Italian than French at the beginning of the fifteenth century.

Although the situation suggests the *Princesse de Clèves* in several respects, Christine would have been very much against a confession to the husband; indeed she specifically warns against it in the *Trois Vertus*. The role of the governess is a novelty here, for the Dame de la Tour is the very antithesis of Trotaconventos, or Juliet's nurse, although they may be, in a sense, sisters under the skin, at least in that they belong to the Renaissance more than to the Middle Ages.

Christine was apparently so pleased with the letter written by the Dame de la Tour, that she used it again, almost *in toto*, at the end of the first part of the *Trois Vertus*. There is no denying that it is a good summary of ideas that Christine had expressed elsewhere to the same point. She speaks in particular of all the dangers which must be risked for a small amount of pleasure, and very uncertain pleasure at that. For the first time in French literature the victim of masculine trifling is having her say in public. It should be observed that it is not primarily any moral lapse which concerns Christine—although she duly warns of the inevitable damnation of the soul—but the fact that in the end the woman will have lost more than she can possibly gain, especially where men are so seldom to be trusted.

These are indeed bitter words, and Christine took occasion to repeat them in the *Cent Balades d'Amant et de Dame* which must have been written after the *Trois Vertus,* for the cycle appears only in the last of the major compilations of Christine's poetry, the British Museum Harley MS 4431, probably copied around 1410 or 1411. The tone of the "Lay de Dame" which closes the cycle has a note which sounds more than merely literary. The lady in question speaks of the price which must be paid in the servitude of love, but confesses the impossibility of mustering sufficient strength to resist temptation:

> O Amours dure et sauvage,
> Certes, qui te fait hommage
> Se met en divers servage,
> Et se peut bien attendre
> Que par ce dueil et dommage
> Lui vendra, c'est l'avantage
> Que tu fais au las courage
> Qui se laisse a toy surprendre
> Car ta puissance est trop forte,
>   Dure et diverse,
> Et si est de telle sorte
>   Et tant perverse
> Que tout cuer ou es aherse
>   Entre en la porte
> De dueil et en honneur morte
>   Il se reverse. . . .
>   (Roy ed., 3:308–9)

In writing the *Trois Vertus,* Christine apparently still considered it possible to resist the attraction of illicit love in courtly trappings. Although she addressed herself first of all to ladies of the court, she did not entirely overlook their humbler sisters, writing an interesting chapter in the third part of the "femmes de folle vie," admonishing them to give up their wayward lives (in which they were often subjected to physical abuse), to put on decent clothes and seek honest work for their ultimate salvation. In the summer of 1405 all aspects of human life must have seemed more hopeful than five or ten years later when France had been given occasion to witness nearly every sort of human depravity, the court dominated by a queen who stood for nearly all the vices Christine particularly condemned, the country torn asunder by rival factions which seemed to vie with each other in treachery.

At the very end of her life, Christine would again have her heart uplifted momentarily by the advent of Jeanne d'Arc. From her retreat in some convent, probably the Abbey of Poissy in the outskirts of Paris where her daughter had been a nun for many years, Christine hailed the savior of France who, to her delight, appeared in feminine form. So it was that she composed her *Dittie,* the first poem inspired by the exploits of the Maid of Orleans and, as far as we know, Christine's last public words.

Curiously enough the manuscript tradition suggests that the *Trois Vertus* was not an immediate success,[38] although the Duchess of Guyenne and her sisters led lives which frequently sound as if they came from its pages. Widowed at eighteen, Margaret was rescued with some difficulty from enemy territory and returned to live for a few years near her mother in Burgundy. In 1423 however, she was married by her brother, Philip the Good, for reasons of state, to Arthur of Richemont, younger brother of the Duke of Brittany, who had been a prisoner in England since the Battle of Agincourt. In a fashion worthy of Christine's precepts, she facilitated his liberation by refusing to marry him under any other conditions. It is possible that she may even have felt some personal attachment for him, as she had known him at the French court when both were young. She proved a devoted wife, protecting his interests when he fell from grace at Charles VII's court, supervising his estates in Parthenay while he was leading armies against the English and returning with him to Paris when the city reverted to French control in 1436. Her sister Anne, Duchess of Bedford, had resided in Paris as wife of the English regent, but had died several years before Margaret's return as the result of a contagion she had contracted visiting the poor in the Hôtel Dieu, again quite in accord with Christine's precepts. Medieval princesses must often have found themselves in such sad and ironic situations. There are only occasional glimpses of Margaret during her final years in Paris, where she died in 1442. A copy of her will, preserved in the Archives de la Loire Inférieure in Nantes,[39] reflects a touchingly generous spirit and a warm affection for those who surrounded her during her husband's almost continual absences. Here is the tribute of her husband's biographer:

> Richemont perdait la compagne de sa Jeunesse, de ses années d'épreuves, celle qui, veuve d'un dauphin de France, l'avait, par son choix, élevé au plus haut rang, celle qui avait encouragé son ambition, hâté sa fortune, partagé fidèlement sa disgrâce et secondé ses efforts. Le rôle de cette princesse dépasse la sphère du foyer domestique. En travaillant à réconcilier son beau-frère avec son frère, le duc de Bourgogne, en préférant à la cour le séjour de Paris, où elle représentait en quelque sorte la famille royale, elle avait rendu service au roi, à la France et mérite ainsi une place dans l'histoire de ce règne mémorable.[40]

Whether because of the *Trois Vertus* or not, she represented to a surprising degree the ideal princess whose portrait is drawn by Christine. And her earthly reward? Her husband re-married within the year and both he and her brother, Philip the Good, were too busy to carry out her final request, that her heart be buried at Notre-Dame-de-Liesse, a shrine in Picardy near her grandmother's favorite residence. She must have cherished happy memories of her early youth spent near the admirable Margaret of Flanders.

We know that there were copies of the *Trois Vertus* in the libraries of the Clèves and the Bourbons, families into which other sisters of Margaret married. It must also have been read towards the middle of the century by daughters of the middle class, to judge by the numbers of paper manuscripts which still exist, but its period of greatest popularity would seem to have been nearly a hundred years after it was written, when three printed editions were published between 1497 and 1536, all of them dedicated to

Anne of Brittany. At that time, when Italian manners were already coming into style, due importance was given to Christine's Italian origin. Not only the Duchess Anne knew Christine's book, but Anne of France, Margaret of Austria and Mary of Hungary owned copies and, whether through its influence or not, all exemplified qualities recommended by Christine. But since 1536 it has largely been forgotten. Styles changed and its immediate usefulness passed. Few books of its day however, give us a better insight into the lives of various sorts of women; and it tells us how at least one of them regarded those lives.

Let us return once more to the question of Christine's fundamental stand on the position of women in society. Certainly she would be astonished at the claims that are being made today. She never even mentioned equality between the sexes, and yet in the final analysis it is surprising to find her attacking many of the same attitudes in society which have more recently aroused the animus of Simone de Beauvoir or the members of the present generation devoted to Women's Liberation. She too objected to having women regarded as "sex symbols"; this is really the point of her disapproval of the *Romance of the Rose*. She believed that women were capable of acts of devotion and generosity, and that they were, above all, capable of playing a useful and unique role in the social order—as partners and often lieutenants of their husbands, as protectors and educators of the young, as examples to others of a life well lived. But she also thought that women should make a serious effort to merit the high regard of others; that indeed is why she wrote the *Livre des Trois Vertus*.

Notes

1. "Si nous jetons un coup d'oeil d'ensemble sur cette histoire nous voyons s'en dégager plusieurs conclusions. Et d'abord celle-ci—toute l'histoire des femmes a été faite par les hommes. . . . Quelques isolées—Sapho, Christine de Pisan, Mary Wollstonescraft, Olympe de Gouges—ont protesté de leur destin. . . ." (Paris: Editions Gallimard, 1949), 1:170.
2. *Le Livre des Trois Vertus et son milieu historique et littéraire* (Paris, 1912).
3. The most recent is Michel Mallat's *Genèse Médiévale de la France Moderne* (Paris,

1970) which has illustrations from the *Cité de Dames,* but does not mention *Le Livre des Trois Vertus.*

4. P. 148.

5. Lula McDowell Richardson, *The Forerunners of Feminism in French Literature of the Renaissance from Christine of Pisa to Marie de Gournay,* (Baltimore: The Johns Hopkins Press; Paris: Les Presses Universitaires de France, 1929). Kastemberg (diss., University of Heidelberg, 1909).

6. *L'Avision,* Bibliothèque Nationale fonds français 1176, fol. 60 and *La Cité des Dames* f. fr. 607, 2d Part, p. xxxvi: "Contre ceulx qui dient qu'il n'est pas bon que les femmes apprennent lettres".

7. *L'Avision,* fol. 53r.

8. *L'Avision,* fol. 62v.

9. *L'Avision,* fol. 37–38.

10. *The late Fourteenth century and the patronage of the Duke* (London: Phaidon 1967), 1:356–58 and passim. See especially *The Limbourgs and Their Contemporaries* (New York: George Braziller and the Pierpont Morgan Library, 1974).

11. *Bulletin de la Société de Paris et de l'Ile-de-France* (1967–68), 72–98.

12. See also S. Quicherat, *Procès de condemnation et de réhabilitation de Jeanne d'Arc,* S. H. F. (Paris, 1847), 4:513: "Ainsi, nous femmes innocentes, nous serons toujours maudi tes par les hommes qui se croient tout permis et au-dessus des lois, tandis que rien ne nous est dû. Ils sont entraînés par une dépravation vagabonde, et nous, si nous détournons tant soit peu le regard, on nous accuse d'adultère. Ainsi, ce sont des maîtres et non des maris. Nous ne sommes pas des épouses et des compagnes, mais des captives faites sur l'ennemi ou des esclaves achetées. . . ."

13. See Carla Bozzolo, "Il 'Decameron' come fonte del 'Livre de la Cité des Dames' di Christine de Pisan", in *Miscellanea e Richerche sul Quattrocento Francese,* Franco Simone, ed. (Torino: Giappichelli Editore, 1967), pp. 3ff.

14. "Moral Thought of Humanism," in *Renaissance Thought II* (New York: Harper & Row, 1965), pp. 44–45.

15. On the Boccaccio MSS see Patricia M. Gathercole, "Illustrations on the French Boccaccio Manuscripts" in *Studi sul Boccaccio* (Firenze: Sansoni, 1963), pp. 405–7.

16. ". . . depuis l'an MCCCIII[xx] XIX que je commençay, jusques à cestui CCCC et cinq, ouquel encore je ne cesse, compillés en ce taudis quinze volumes principaux . . .", *L'Avision,* fol. 52r.

17.   Helas! ou donc trouveront reconfort
         Pouvres vesves, de leurs biens despoillees,
         Puis qu'en France qui sieult estre le port
         De leur salut, et ou les exillees
         Seulent fouir et les desconseillees,
              Mais or n'i ont plus amistié?
         Les nobles gens n'en ont nulle pitié,
         Aussi n'ont clers le gregeigneur ne li mendre,
         Ne les princes ne les daignent entendre.

Maurice Roy, ed., *Oeuvres poetiques de Christine de Pisan* (Paris, 1886), 1:213.

18. *Le Livre des faicts du bon messire Jean le Maingre, dit mareschal de Boucicaut,* publ. par J. F. Michaud et J. J. P. Poujoulat, in *Nouvelle Collection des mémoires,* (Paris, 1836), 1st series, vol. 2.

19.   Helas! Mais quel fortune amere
                          Cuert sus a femme, et quel misere,
                          Quant pert mari bon et paisible,
                          Qui preudons l'avoit et sensible
                          Selon soy, et qui l'avoit chiere! . . .
                          Et ainsi la dolente veuve
                          Sera semonce et adjournee
                          En plusiers cours et malmenee
                          Par abusemens et plais querre
                          Contre elle, d'eritage et terre
                          Desheritee et desnuee . . .
                                        (vv. 6983–7005),

(*Le Livre de la Mutacion de Fortune* par Christine de Pisan, publié d'après les manuscrits par Suzanne Solente, II [Paris: A. & J. Picard, 1959], p. 93.)
20. John Bartier, *Légistes et gens de finances au XVe siècle:* les conseilliers des Ducs
de Bourgogne Philippe le Bon et Charles le Téméraire, Académie royale de
Belgique, classe des lettres et des sciences morales et politiques. Mémoires. 2d
series, vol. 50, fas. (Bruxelles, 1955), pp. 341 ff.
21. In both the *Mutacion de Fortune* and the *Trois Vertus,* Christine speaks of
former friends who are no longer kind when one is a widow:

                     Et tel l'a mainte foiz chuee
                     Et flatee et honneur lui fait,
                     Et moult si offert en tout fait
                     En temps que le mari vivoit,
                     Qui grant estat et bel avoit,
                     Qui a present le doz lui tourne.
                              Mutacion de Fortune (vv. 7006–7011)

"Vous trouvez communement durté, pou de pris et de pitie en toute personne,
et tieulx vous souloient honnourer au temps de vos maris, qui officiers, ou de
grant estat estoient, qui, ores en font peu de compte, ou pou les trouvez amis."
Le Livre des Trois Vertus, Boston Public Library, Boston MS. 1528 fol. 82r°.
22. *Les Honneurs de la Cour* in La Curne de Sainte-Palaye, *Mémoires sur l'Ancienne
Chevalerie* (Paris, 1826), 2:135–219.
23. *The Waning of the Middle Ages* (New York: Doubleday, Anchor Books, 1956), p.
52.
24. "Pour Madame de Berry . . . et pour toutes semblablement, car entre les
roynes, princesses, baronnesses, dames, damoiselles du noble sang de France, et
generalement le plus des femmes d'honneur frappes de ceste pestilence, en cestui
francois royaume, a cause de tant de diverses morts ou prises de leurs prouchains,
si comme maris, enfans, freres, oncles, affins et amis, les uns deffaults par bataille,
les autres trespasses naturellement en leurs lis, comme de maintes pertes et autres
diverses infortunes et aventures obliquement, puis en un temps, survenues, aviser
comment se aucune chose proposer et remener a memoire pourroit savoir et estre
valable a aucun reconfort." *L'Epistre de la prison de vie humaine* (Bibliothèque Nationale fonds français 24786, fol. 37). See S. Solente, "Un traité inédit de Christine

de Pisan, *l'Epistre de la prison de vie humaine"*, in *Bibliothèque de l'Ecole des Chartres* 75 (1924): 263–301.

25. For the background of this incident, see L. Mirot, "L'Enlèvement du Dauphin et le premier conflit entre Jean sans Peur et Louis d'Orléans," *Revue des questions historiques* 96 (1914): 415–19; also C. C. Willard, "An autograph manuscript of Christine de Pizan?", *Studi Francesi* 27 (1965): 452–57.

26. See Richard Vaughan, *John the Fearless: The Growth of Burgundian Power* (London: Longmans 1966), pp. 247–48.

27. A good description of this prince is to be found in Maurice Rey, *Les Finances Royales sous Charles VI: Les Causes du Déficit, 1388–1413,* Bibliothèque générale de l'Ecole pratique des hautes Études. Sciences, économiques et sociales (Paris: S.E.V.P.E.N., 1965): "Ce Valois qui reçut les enseignements d'un prêtre réputé, d'un Fenèlon avant le temps (dont les principes d'éducation nous sont connus), qui toute sa vie cotoya d'illustres guerriers, ne témoigna jamais de vertus morales. Sa conduite politique a fait l'objet de critiques unanimes. Ses pêchés de jeunese n'ont pas su mériter l'indulgence. Il fut aux yeux de tous un médiocre doublé d'un 'faux homme et traître,' un faible, presque un dégénéré qui acheva de se déconsiderer en prêtant l'oreille à des personnages tarés" (p. 278).

28. Hedwige de Polignac Chabannes et Isabelle de Linares, *Anne de Beaujeu* (Paris: Crépin-le Blond, 1955), p. 153, cited from text published by A.-M. Chazaud (Paris, 1878).

29. "Car il n'est plus grant coquerie que veoir a personne, qui qu'elle soit, grant et oultrageux estat, et en scet bien qu'il ne lui apertient ou qu'il n'y a de quoy le maintenir, et le temps est ores venu qu'on ne voit autre chose. Et se telz gens ont de la povrete par decouste, et que mal leur en preigne, on ne les doit plaindre, car plusieurs se desertent et mettent a povrete par telz oultrages qui fussent bien aisez se amodereement voulsissent vivre. Et plus grant honte y a plusieurs, c'est des debtes que souvent font aux cousturiers, drapiers, et orfevres, desquelles sont a la fois executez, et fault qu'ilz baillent une robe en gages pour l'autre avoir. . . ." (Boston Public Library MS 1528 fol. 68v.)

30. See Huizinga, p. 161, referring to Froissart's *Chroniques* for the year 1395; also *Les Quinze Joyes de Mariage,* ed. Joan Crow (Oxford: Oxford University Press, Clarendon Press, 1969), pp. 54–55.

31. ". . . Et ains que elle voise nulle part, se elle est sage, soit bien aviser ou, avec qui, comment et qui y doit estre ou elle va, ne de trouver ces pelerinages hors ville pour aller quelque part jouer ou mener la gale en quelque compaignie joyeuse n'est fors pechie et mal a qui le fait, car c'est faire ombre de Dieu et chape a pluie, et tieulx pelerinages ne sont point bons, ne aussi tant aller trotant par ville a joene femme, au lundi a Sainte Avoye, au jeudi, je ne scay ou, au vendredi a Saincte Katherine, et ainsi aux autres jours. Se aucunes le font n'en est ja grant besoing." (Boston Public Library MS 1528 fol. 79r.) See also fol. 90r: "Si ne lui sont bien seans tant de compagnies faire par ville, ne trotter à ces pellerinages trouvés sans besoing, qui ne sont fors toutes despenses sans besoing et neccessité."

32. *Les Honneurs de la Cour,* pp. 172–80.

33. "Cy aprez s'ensuivent les parties des draps d'or, de soye, de laine, tapisserie, broderie, vaisselle et autres choses necessaires pour le fait de la gesine de mademoiselle de Rethel et de Jehan de Rethel Monsieur, son fils, dont ma dite dame accoucha a Arras, au mois de janvier, l'an mil IIIIe et deux, prises et acheptées a

Paris par Jehan Chousat, receveur des finances de monseigneur le duc de Bourgogne, des marchands et autres personnes, cy aprez en ce rolle desclarées . . ." in E. Petit, *Itineraires de Philippe le Hardi et de Jean sans Peur,* (Paris, Imprimerie Nationale, 1888), pp. 568–73.

34. *Les Quinze Joyes de Mariage,* ed. Joan Crow, pp. 14–21.

35. "Car sans faille les orgueilz et estas ne furent oncques en toutes manieres de gens depuis les grans jusques aux mendres si oultrageux que ores sont, et ce puet on veoir par les croniques et anciennes hystoires . . ." (Boston Public Library MS fol. 80r).

36. *The Waning of the Middle Ages,* p. 67.

37. Ibid., p. 135.

38. C. C. Willard, "The Manuscript Tradition of the *Livre des trois vertus* and Christine de Pizan's Audience," *Journal of the History of Ideas* 27 (1966): 433–44.

39. Published in Eugène Cosneau, *Le Connétable de Richemont, Artur de Bretagne (1394–1458)* (Paris: Hachette, 1886), pp. 586–96.

40. Cosneau, pp. 329–30.

Woman in the Marginalia of Gothic Manuscripts and Related Works

PHILIPPE VERDIER

Université de Montréal

The documents in this paper are essentially borrowed from the remarkable inventory and illustrations of *Images in the Margins of Gothic Manuscripts* by Lilian M. C. Randall.[1] One can find there the first extensive catalogue raisonné of realistic, satirical, or fantastic scenes and figures used as line endings, illustrations between lines and as bas-de-page culled from 226 manuscripts, mainly English, Flemish and French (Picardy and Paris), and ranging from devotional books, Psalters and Hours (or a combination of both), theological and canonical texts, historic works, didactic, legal and scientific tracts, romances, songs, and poems. The sources of such fanciful marginal and in-text illustrations seem more often than not elusive and irrelevant to the text they frame. They may derive also (in the guise of visual comments or rather free digressions) from the *Dialogues* of St. Gregory; the *Fables of Aesop,* which had been translated into Latin elegiacs by Alexander Neckam and into the vernacular by Marie de France; a number of lives and passions of the saints; the *Physiologus* and *Bestiaries;* fables and fabliaus; the epic *Renard the Fox; Roman de Renard;* and, above all, from proverbs and exempla or moral comments used in sermons by predicant monks, usually placed preferably toward the end in order to quicken their already half-lethargic audiences.[2] The *Sermones Vulgares* of Jacques de Vitry (d. 1240) are worth a particular mention in this connection because in 1208 their author became associated with the priory of Oignies, founded in the Sambre valley by four brothers from Walcourt, one of them the goldsmith monk Hugo.[3] Hugo and his workshop at Oignies established a new style and technique in silverwork that spread through northern France and were characterized by peopled scrolls enlivened by hunting scenes and by nielloed plaques featuring grotesques and "grylles." [4] Exemplum 60 of Jacques de Vitry—a gallant meeting of a young man and a nun—is reflected, *mutatis mutandis,* in the oaristys of a Franciscan caressing a woman spread across his frock, in a Picard Psalter (ca. 1290).[5] It was chosen to top, as a crest, the illustration (two Dominican monks) painted inside the capital *B* of the word opening Psalm 127 (which, according to the Vulgate, promises "domestica felicitas" to pious men: "Beati omnes qui timent Dominum, qui ambulant in viis ejus").

The marginalia of Gothic manuscripts is almost always an eccentric world, at times like an underworld, parasitic on texts and commenting on them obliquely with a devious humor, extending from a surrealistic imagination to a surreptitious criticism of the "establishment" in contemporary society and a more or less brazen anticlericalism. Parallels between narration and illustration are more incidental than regular, even in manuscripts of *Lancelot, The Grail* and *The Romance of Alexander.* The most tantalizing problem raised by the marginalia is that of focusing them, as visual footnotes to the text, and the text itself, to a common ground. From the sociological point of view they cannot be quoted without reservation as prima facie evidence because the documents they "adorn" have to be deciphered as symbolical comments made in a tongue-in-cheek, bantering way. They are secretly interlaced with the main illustration of the

text—a vignette or decorated initial—and they co-exist with
the text, but on a distinct psychic and interpretative level.
Semi-abstract and semi-monstrous patterns, they anticipate
the creations of Hieronymus Bosch and like them they teem
with outcrops of the unconscious. They offer a considerable
variety of tests of medieval sexual behavior, but their eroticism is couched in a light or redeemingly comic vein and
they certainly do not play the wanton with women as sex objects.[6] They would rather appear as the naive exponents of
a woman's freedom movement fighting against the definition of her condition by the Church or against the rules
edicted by man. Healthy counterparts to the conventions of
courtly love, the marginalia cunningly avoid the pitfalls of
the then prevailing misogyny.[7] In getting the upper hand,
the woman may wear her consort's pants and fight for her
right to appropriate them, whereas the husband, like a fool,
will sit on eggs.[8] The occasionally inverted image of the
relationships between woman and man is just one facet of
the topsy-turvy world mirrored in the marginalia. They add
up to one in which all the opinions generally received are
permuted and reversed: it has become a world of "choses a
anvers," as Chrétien de Troyes had already observed in
Cligés (c. 1170). A daring instance is that of a bull milking a
naked woman.[9] This trend toward a seemingly irrational attitude betraying the subversive spirit was given free rein in
the marginalia, which began to run wild during the last
third of the thirteenth century in the English, Flemish and
northern French manuscripts. It assumed its literal expression in the *Fatrasies d'Arras,* the *Sottes Chansons de Valencien-
nes;* in Germany the "verkehrte Welt" gave birth to the
Lügendichtungen. Alanus ab Insulis was aware of the consequences of such a reversal of values and warned against it in
his *Anticlaudianus* (c. 1185), although he was not loath to use
"exempla" in sermons.[10] In such an environment of coun-
terfeits, the ape, that most insolent plagiarist and distorter
of a creation made by a good and rational God, plays a key
part.[11] The monkeys and their hybrid brothers that had
proliferated over the capitals of Cluniac cloisters were
anathematized by St. Bernard, not only from the point of
view of religious decorum but in the name of aesthetic de-

cency, in his *Apologia ad Guillelmum Sancti Theoderici abbatem* (c. 1127): "in claustris coram legentibus fratribus quid facit illa ridicula monstrositas, mira quaedam deformis, formositas ac formosa deformitas? Quid ibi immundae simiae . . . quid monstruosi centauri? Quid semihomines?" [12] For their lack of realism St. Bernard condemned in the name of realism such fantastic hybrid figures: "Sub uno capite multa corpora, et rursus in uno corpore capita multa . . . hinc in quadrupede cauda serpentis, hinc in pisce caput quadrupedis. Ibi bestia praefert equum, capram trahens retro dimidiam, hic cornutum animal equum gestat posterius" with a vehemence in defending true representation distorted by morbid imagination, recalling the vituperation of Vitruvius, the classicist, against the proto-mannerist intrusion of grotesques into Roman art: "sed haec, quae ex veris rebus exempla sumebantur, nunc iniquis moribus improbantur, nam pinguntur tectoriis monstra potius quam ex rebus finitis imagines certae." Pointing to the "coliculi dimidiata habentes sigilla [the medieval "grylles"] alia humanis, alia bestiarum capitibus" painted on the walls, Vitruvius passed sentence on them without appeal: "haec autem nec sunt, fieri possunt nec fuerunt." [13] The medieval grotesques shared with the lecherous monkeys the stigma of uncleanliness, which did not prevent the babewinnes (babewyns), as they were called, from invading not only the manuscripts, but the royal plate, ecclesiastical garments, religious architecture, and the borders of stained glass windows in churches.[14]

In Gothic art the marginalia represent to a large extent the continuation of the Hellenistic revival of the peopled scrolls of antiquity [15] found in romanesque sculpture and illumination. Their fauna derives in direct line of descent from the one transmitted in the coils of the twelfth-century capitals and in the mazes of foliage painted within the initials of manuscripts from the eleventh through the thirteenth centuries. With the coming of age of the Gothic spirit, the spirals burst open and spilled their contents all over the folios or, procession-like, along the carved cornices [16]; the hybrids or "grylles," the grotesques and "drôleries" [17] of manuscript decoration were born. There was, however, a precedent for the marginalia, insofar as they depict scenes related to the text as an interplay of associative imagery. They are found in the Byzantine monastic Psalters with marginal illustrations.[18] The first Byzantine marginal Psalters, decorated in the second half of the ninth century, and those of the eleventh and later centuries,[19] even if they were luxury books produced in scriptoria close to the court, are imbued with a sense of the picturesque which appealed to the monastic mind, and a rampant realism verging at times on caricature, as with the shadow puppets. Most striking is the abundance of their tiny illustrations: 260 subjects are depicted in the *Chludov Psalter* (Historical Museum, Moscow), 106 in *Pantocrator 61* (Mount Athos), 90 in the *"Bristol" Psalter,* and 400 (in 207 folios) in the *Theodore Psalter* (both in the British Museum, the latter from the monastery of St. John Studion, dated 1066), and 375 in the *Vatican Psalter* (ca. 1092). By comparison, the tiniest Hours of the fourteenth century, those of Jeanne d'Evreux (1325–28?) at the Cloisters, New York (209 folios measuring 3-1/2" high and 2-7/16" wide) display about 900 marginal motifs. The Byzantine marginal Psalters seldom depict comments or images "ad litteram" of the psalm verses,[20] as do the *Utrecht Psalter* and its copies. Their iconography is typological, hagiographical or, for the oldest Psalters, filled with references to the iconoclastic controversy.[21] The marginal visual glosses exhibit a very free treatment and sometimes a sense of humor, as when St. Zozymus averts his face while giving a dress to a swarthy and gaunt naked Mary of Egypt, in illustrating the eighth verse of Psalm 54 (AV Ps. 55:7: "Yea, I would wander afar, I would lodge in the wilderness"),[22] or when the heron nests, like St. Simeon Stylites, on the top of a column strutting over her eggs, surrounded by the fluttering birds of the Lord's fir trees (Ps. 103 [104]: 16, 17).[23] Images, instead of being rooted in the text, can be grafted onto it through a secondary association, as in folio 104 of *Pantocrator 61,* a marginal comment to the sixty-ninth verse of Psalm 77(78): "Et aedificavit sicut unicorninium sanctificium suum" (according to the Vulgate translation), a unicorn, symbol of Christ made flesh, nestling its muzzle against the breast of a woman whom a Greek inscription identifies as the nursing Theotocos.[24]

The complex relationships between text, main illustrations, margins, and bas-de-page, are exemplified by the description of the office of the Virgin in the *Hours of Jeanne d'Evreux*, a manuscript given to Jean Pucelle and traditionally dated between 1325 (when Jeanne d'Evreux married Charles IV) and 1328 (the date of the King's death).[25] Its decoration is unusual in that in a dual presentation the Infancy of Christ and the Passion face each other.[26] The pair, the Annunciation and the Arrest of Christ, is most puzzling.[27] The standing Virgo Annuntiata and the kneeling angel are two features derived from Sienese iconography. The Holy Ghost overshadows Mary through a trap door in the ceiling, and the doll's house (where the Annunciation is taking place) is uplifted by two angels as if it were the miraculous "casa di Loreto."[28] In the margins angels play musical instruments. In the initial D of "Domine labia mea aperies" a queen kneels in her oratory, her pet dog near her.[29] Furthermore, this oratory-letter is guarded by a seneschal and blossoms into leaves sheltering animals evoking the idea of fertility: a rabbit, a monkey and a squirrel. The bas-de-page displays a scene combining two buffeting games played between young men and women: "frog in the middle" and "qui fery."[30] On the facing folio one sees the Betrayal of Christ with the rubric: "Incipiunt hore sancte marie . . ." between two grotesque herms, and in the bas-de-page two warriors who, mounted on a goat and a ram, are tilting at the "quintaine", a keg or water butt, a contraption swivelled on a post used for the training of jousters in Italy. The tilting and buffeting game, combining violence and deception,[31] may substitute in the manuscript for the mocking of Christ, which in the fourteenth century could be acted out or represented as a "chappefol," a sort of tag and blind man's buff. Pucelle also commented most irreverently on the Annunciation as a matter of "touch and go" in which the girl kneeling before the squatting youth repeats the revolutionary iconographical feature of the angel kneeling before the standing Mary. The other girl, pressing both hands on the young man's head, recalls the threat announced to the serpent in Genesis: "Inimicitias ponam inter te et mulierem . . . ipsa conteret caput tuum." (3:15).[32]

An inverted religious mood ("à anvers") is rampant on practically every folio of the *Hours of Jeanne d'Evreux*. On folio 45, verses 10–13 of Psalm 148 for the Hours of the Virgin: "volucres pennate . . . principes terre . . . juvenes et virgines . . . laudent nomen Domini," have suggested three overhanging line endings: a gargoyle-like woman whose coat hangs down like a wing, washing her head, from where the rinse drips into a basin proffered by a contortionist, while a Saracen with falchion and shield protects his head with a bucket.[33] No less irreverent is the decoration of the litany in an English book of abbreviated hours for Augustinian use, ca. 1300, in the Walters Art Gallery. The "omnes sancti pontifices et confessores" are represented by two chess players, one of them a half-naked sharper who has lost his shirt to his smarter opponent; the "omnes sancti monachi et heremite" by the she-wolf suckling and licking Romulus and Remus, and the "omnes sancte virgines et vidue" by a stymied monkey, astride a bear tethered to a post.[34] On f. 103 of the part reserved for the Hours of St. Louis in the *Hours of Jeanne d'Evreux,* under a vignette of the French king disciplined by his confessor, a musician-Phyllis rides a hooded centaur-Aristotle, pious masochist walking on all fours to the beat of the viol on the bas-de-page.[35] There may also be a humorous allusion to the voluntarily restricted sexual relations between Louis IX and his wife, Marguerite de Provence. In exemplum 15 of Jacques de Vitry's *Sermones feriales et communes* Aristotle has an affair, not with Phyllis, but with Alexander's wife, who managed to take revenge on the philosopher for having reproached her husband for being immoderately in love with her to the point of neglecting public affairs: from the Church's point of view Alexander was committing adultery with his own wife.

Together with the "frog in the middle" and "qui fery," "hot cockles" ("hautes coquilles") were frequently represented in marginalia and were carved on fourteenth-century ivory writing tablets made in Paris.[36] In this game a young man would bury his head in a lady's lap and thus blindfolded had to surmise who had struck at his back from behind. The pattern of its representation in works of art corresponds to the killing of the unicorn in the bas-de-page of manuscripts and on the small ends of ivory composite caskets of Paris origin, the other side of which is decorated with scenes borrowed from romance and allegory.[37] The unicorn is the symbol of the virginal incarnation of Christ. It had sought refuge in a maiden's bosom where it was pierced by the huntsman's spear. Its death announces Christ's crucifixion. On the ivory plaques the maiden is wont to hold a mirror—the "spotless" mirror of the Song of Songs and the litany of the Virgin, which may be also interpreted as a crown or as the "chapelet" of courtly love. In the French translation of the *Physiologus* which is attributed to Pierre le Picard, verse 11 of Psalm 91 "et exaltabitur sicut unicornis cornu meum", is rendered "ma corone est ensi essauchié comme l'unicorne." [38] In the ivory caskets the killing of the unicorn is sometimes carved on the same panel as the subject of King Mark spying from a tree on Tristan and Iseult, who watch his reflection in the pool. Eros lurking in the foliage looks from above at the killing of the unicorn in a carved bracket of the western facade of the cathedral at Lyons.[39] The assimilation of the unicorn hunt into a myth of courtly love is evinced in the *Bestiaire d'Amour* of Richard de Fournival: "Love, skilled hunter, has placed in my path the young girl, in whose sweet fragrance I fall asleep and I die of the death that is my destiny." [40] On an enamelled roundel, a Paris work ca. 1320, in the Bayerisches Nationalmuseum, Munich, the hunter who transfixes the unicorn is perched on a tree, while the maiden holds a mirror in which her own face is reflected.[41] The mirror, as an emblem, may be invested with opposite meanings: prudence or self-knowledge; truth, *vita contemplativa;* or, on the contrary, vanity, Venus, Luxuria.[42] On fol. 97v. of the second volume of a Flemish psalter in the Bodleian Library, Oxford, a repentant woman proffers a mirror as a comment on verse 39 of Psalm 118: "amputa oprobrium meum quod suspicatus sum," and under verse 41 ("Et veniat super me miseria cordia tua domine"), a youth, in the bas-de-page, jumps on the "frog" between two admiring women.[43]

On folio 117 of a Picard psalter in the Bibliothèque Nationale, Paris, the opening of Psalm 97, "Cantate Domino canticum novum quia mirabilia fecit," is illustrated in the two-storied capital C of Cantate by the creation of Eve out of Adam's rib (conforming to Genesis 2:21–22) and with priests singing choral song: [44] "Li prestre qui cantent en sainte esglise," says the rubric below the bas-de-page, where one sees girls wearing surcoats embroidered with red hearts dancing to a viol or crowning a lover kneeling in adoration with a "chapelet." The implication is that not man but woman is highest among the "mirabilia" which God made. On the other hand, the parallel drawn between the Church born on Mount Calvary out of the blood and water that issued forth from the pierced chest of Christ, and the birth of Eve out of the sleeping Adam, was a time-honored symbol.[45] In the illumination, Eve at her birth wears a hairdo which makes her a sister of the girls painted in the bas-de-page, merry-makers of the regained garden of delights, and a forebear of the Venuses of Lucas Cranach, the more naked looking because they wear nothing but a hat. The parody (or is it an *eulogium* of all women in Eve?) is underlined by a brace of "grylles," a siren (half bird and half woman), and a male feathered hybrid perching on the upper framework.

A more traditional rendition of Eve is given in the margin of f. 169 on the third part of the *Livre de Lancelot del Lac* (ca. 1280) in the library of Yale University. Poised on one of those flexible stems, which in manuscript decoration are the ancestors of the modern mobiles, Eve spins and rolls up the wool of her distaff around a spindle while Adam is busy delving.[46] In the English *Psalter of Queen Isabella* (1305–8) in Munich, Naamah, a name which in Hebrew means the pleasant woman, is represented weaving.[47] "And Zillah, she also bare Tubal-Cain, instructor of every artificer in brass and iron: and the sister of Tubal-Cain was Naamah," according to Genesis 4:22 in the King James version of the Bible. Zillah was the second wife of Lamech, who, through Adah, his first wife, had engendered Jubal, the inventor of music.[48] Tubal-Cain, the unkempt smith, embodied in gothic art the proletariat which rose as the result of the progress achieved in metallurgy during the twelfth century.[49] At a time when women had not yet entered the textile industry and when the love code of southern France still had not conventionalized the lyrical expression of passion, the "chansons de toile" (weaving songs), which exalted the unrestricted physical dedication of women to the men with whom they had fallen in love, began with descriptions of women sewing and embroidering.[50] Curiously enough, the themes constantly recurring through the chansons de toile (e.g., the maiden who weaves, who is accused of unfaithfulness, who humbles herself before her supercilious lover, comes back pregnant from the fountain) follow a pattern analogous to that of the Annunciation to the Virgin in the apocryphal gospels and to the suspicion cast on her when in the custody of Joseph she was weaving the veil of the Temple in his house.[51] Western medieval iconography did not miss the point made in the *Protoevangelium* of James (10:1) and in *Pseudo-Matthew's Gospel* (8:5), that the purple and scarlet that fell to the lot of Mary among the other "undefiled virgins of the House of David" who were commissioned to "make a curtain for the temple of the Lord," signified that she was "the Queen of Virgins" and betokened her blemishless chastity,[52] but the scene was shifted from Joseph's house to the uncontroversial temple where Mary lived as a child.[53]

Women holding a distaff and a spindle are painted in the margins of manuscripts engaged in every kind of activity. Distaff and spindle are the "arma mulieris" used by women while spinning, combing, carding, and winding the wool or the linen thread—or while beating their husbands. Whether they were busy at home, in the country, and in town, or in workshops, women employed in the textile industry were numerous in Flanders, in northern France, Champagne and Normandy. In Paris their condition as workers was protected by regulations in the *Livre des Métiers* of Etienne Boileau (1261–69). These regulations, forbidding them to be employed as fullers, were confirmed by letters of patent by Philippe VI in 1349.[54] According to an ordinance of October 1281, the "tisserandes de toiles" were in competition with men. The Paris register of tax-payers (*rôles de la taille*) lists an entry in 1292 of two "fileuses de laine", three "pigneresses" and, in 1300, of one "fileuse de laine," two "ouvrieres en laine," one "pigneresse de laine," and two "pigneresses" of other textiles. Combing linen and hemp was tantamount to a woman's trust: three "cerencesses" (from the verb "serancer," in German "schrenzen") are mentioned in 1292. The silk industry was completely dominated by women: eight "fillaresses de soie" are registered in 1292 and thirty-six in 1300. The making of silk belts and alms purses—the "bourses" or "aumônières sarrazinoises" copied from oriental costumes via Sicily and the Kingdom of Jerusalem—was the exclusive responsibility of a women's guild.[55] A royal ordinance of Philippe le Bel lists 124 names of "faiseuses d'aumônières sarrazinoises." In the making of men's leather purses a woman was authorized to help her husband, when he was the head of an "ouvrouer" (workshop), and to succeed him in his business if he died. On the same bas-de-page of f. 59 of the *Romance of Alexander,* painted by Jehan de Grise, Bruges, 1338–44, in the Bodleian Library, a young lady offers her heart to a grateful young man and an older man presents a purse to the lady, who turns her head in a gesture of rejection.[56] Does she refuse a partnership in business or rather a dishonest proposition? [57] In the motets and refrains, as well as in the Minnekästchen and in the French ivories deriving from them, the initiative is taken by the young man who makes "l'offrande du coeur." [58] Thus the two scenes contrasted in the bas-de-page of the *Romance of Alexander* would stress the spontaneous love of the young woman, bypassing the conventional give-and-take of courtly love, and censuring the sensuous or interested response on man's side. How many of such implied critical remarks were added to manuscripts by women? [59] Of the two most beautiful surviving French silk "aumônières sarrazinoises," one is kept in the Museum at Hamburg and the other in the treasure of the cathedral at Troyes. The later is embroidered with an extraordinary subject: a dream. In the upper part of the purse a woman is dreaming, that is, a winged figure is approaching her in her sleep. Below, the same woman and her friend, or a rival, are seated on either side of a kind of execution block on which a heart is exposed. The two women are wielding a woodsman's saw as if they were halving the heart. An arm holding an axe emerges from a cloud above them.[60]

Certain women's professions were easily open to joke or libel; foremost are those of bath attendant (estuveresse) and midwife (this one was more influential in society when she was a prostitute), or the combination of midwife and doctoress (miresse) in one person.[61] In an early fourteenth-century Flemish Psalter and Book of Hours in the Walters Art Gallery a woman is closing the door of an "étuve" (bathing hut) on a nude man. Another naked man is lurking behind a tree and a female attendant stoops under the weight of two pails of hot water. On f. 75 of the *Romance of Alexander* in the Bodleian Library, a naked woman invites her friend, who has already disrobed, to enter the bathing hut into which a character wrapped in a bath towel is vanishing. On the right part of this scene of hydro-therapeutic mimicry, the man and woman are embracing in the tub before which the curtains have been drawn.[62] Bath establishments had the reputation of being houses of ill repute, and great artists of the fifteenth and sixteenth centuries envisioned them as subjects for voyeurism.[63]

On f. 135 of the first volume of the Psalter and Book of Hours of Joffroy d'Aspremont and Isabelle of Kievraing of the diocese of Metz (before 1302), one of the midwives of the aprocyphal gospels is bathing Christ in a tub that assumes the value of a baptismal vat, as we infer from Psalm 118:29 written above ("viam iniquitatis amove a me"). On f. 10 of the second volume (kept in the National Gallery of Victoria, Melbourne) a woman is bathing a girl already grown with budding breasts and the angel of the previous illumination is holding a lighted candle. Should we read an allusion to the bath given to the bride, symbolizing the Church, before her union with Christ, into Psalm 44:14–15, written above the scene? It reads "omnis gloria ejus filiae regis ab intus, in fimbris aureis, circumdata varietate. Adducentur regi virgines post eam" (these were clearly related to the Coronation of the Virgin from its early formulation in Gothic art).[64]

On f. 28 of an early Franco-Flemish Book of Hours in the Walters Art Gallery the Annunciation is glossed in the margin by two hybrid angels playing the organ and a viol, two men playing a shawm and a trumpet, and two other men respectively balancing a basin and training an ape. A "mire" (physician) looks at a urinal presented by an ape. There is no doubt that we are confronted here not with the pregnancy test of today but, as the custom is described in Brantôme's *Femmes Galantes*,[65] with a virginity test. On f. 13 of the Picard manuscript (lat. 10435, already quoted, in the Bibliothèque Nationale, Paris), "ma demiselle di Biencourt" has an appointment with an ape holding a urinal, mocking as it were the golden chalice proffered by "Saint eglise," painted inside the initial opening of the Psalm on the same folio. The marginalia around the Visitation on f. 28 of the Franco-Flemish Book of Hours in the Walters Art Gallery are supplemented by young monkeys attending a medical course and a nude prudishly turning away from two apes decoying a bird. That is explained by f. 75v of another Franco-Flemish Psalter and a Book of Hours in the Walters Art Gallery, where Psalm 79 ("oratio pro vinea Domini va-stata") and the subsequent Psalm 80, announcing Israel's domination, are glossed upon by a mire holding a urinal, an ape with a bird cage and an ape who has just snared three birds into a clapnet [66]—and by f. 66 of the East Anglian *Peterborough Psalter,* ca. 1300, where the advent of the Lord's justice promised in verse 8 of Psalm 97 is visualized by a girl holding a bird cage.[67] Although the symbolism of the bird in a cage is polyvalent, pointing, according to the context, to the condition of the soul jailed in the body, or to its self-redemption in its cell and subsequent readiness for the "vita contemplativa," it allegorizes mainly the Word made flesh.[68]

The great majority of women were deprived of education "for their own sake." The lawyer Philippe de Navarre expressed the common view of the thirteenth century in terms completely in keeping with Arnolphe's philosophy in Molière's *L'Ecole des Femmes,* "Toutes fames doivent savoir filer et coudre, car la pauvre en aura mestier et la riche conoistra mieux l'ovre des autres. A fame ne doit on apprendre letres ne escrire, si ce n'est especiaument pour estre nonain: car par lire et escrire de fame sont maint mal avenu." [69] The marginalia are replete with women's chores: in a two-volume Flemish Psalter in the Bodleian Library she is represented stirring the pot, a naked brat lying across her lap, while her elder child fans the fire with bellows, a sad footnote to life's miseries "a generatione in generationem" of Psalm 89 (". . . but woman's work is never done"); or she is helplessly looking at an ape helping itself to pablum.[70] She also warms her baby at the hearth and rocks him in his cradle following the intercourse that twice preceded both scenes.[71] The sad looking and aging woman who, in the Bodleian Library Flemish Psalter, appears as a bust portrait at the beginning of King Ezechias's complaint (Isaiah 38), is suspiciously sniffed by a rabbit as she wistfully reminisces on carnal pleasure, depicted in the bas-de-page.[72] Women also stir the churn, knead the dough, cook waffles with a waffle iron, beat the laundry, or pound the pestle in the mortar, while the husband roasts the meat on a spit.[73]

Scenes of poultry farming in the back yard are frequent. In the Psalter painted for Geoffrey Luttrell, ca. 1341, the wife of the farmer feeds chicken [74] while squeezing her inseparable emblem, the distaff, under her left arm. On another page she is sagging under the weight of a flour sack she went on foot to pick up at the mill (whereas the husband rides a horse to bring the corn); and three women reap the wheat with sickles,[75] a telling comment to verse 12 of Psalm 95, written above this famous bas-de-page: "gaudebunt campi et omnia quae in eis sunt." In a Franco-Flemish Book of Hours of the early fourteenth century in the Walters Art Gallery, the month of July is illustrated with a woman wielding a rake, while her husband, armed with a pitchfork, manages to make hay, laying his right hand on her breast; and the month of September is characterized by a farmer sowing and his wife leading the horse that pulls the harrow.[76] The climax of the topsy-turvy world is reached through folios 137–48 of the *Smithfield Decretals* of Gregory IX, in the British Museum, where the husband fetches water, washes dishes and does the laundry, grinds corn, bakes bread, spins, and is beaten by his wife after the performance of each chore, which it would have been incumbent upon a wife to do.[77]

Woman's sceptre, the distaff, may be used by her in the

marginalia for striking at a cat eating out of a bowl, inter-
vening between two dogs or two cocks fighting, or for chas-
ing the fox who has grabbed Chanticleer. In the second
branch of *Roman de Renart,* it is the farmer, Constant des
Noes, who runs after Renart, brandishing a stick, and who
will blame his wife for not having taken the same weapon.[78]
Malkyn, who in Chaucer's *Nun's Priest's Tale* chases the fox
"with a dystaf in hir hand" (line 564), descends from a
marginal drôlerie, or from the popular tale behind it. In the
illustration of the *Smithfield Decretals,* a manuscript of the
glossed decretals of Gregory IX, written in Italy but illuminated in England (perhaps at St. Bartholomew's, Smithfield,
in London, in the second quarter of the fourteenth century), the fox flees twice with a goose and the farmer's wife
strikes him with her distaff and spindle; [79] the goose says
"quec" in the same scene from f. 149v of the *Gorleston Psalter,* as in a much later popular lyric, dating ca. 1492: "He
toke a gose fast by the nek and the gose thoo began to
quek." [80] The goose stands for the pious simpleton, one of
the gullible fowl to which Renart, mitred and holding a
bishop's crozier, has just delivered a sermon, as we see not
only in the *Smithfield Decretals,* but also in *Queen Mary's
Psalter* and the *Gorleston Psalter.*[81] In the person of Renart
are stigmatized the abuses of the Church in raising money,
and in the farmer's wife fighting with a distaff the most
vocal protest of the country people.

In a Book of Hours of Maestricht, ca. 1300, the authori-
tarian air of an abbess is lampooned by a marginal painting
showing her erect on her throne, her distaff stuck on her
right as a pennant and the cat hastening to bring her
spindle, whereas an abbot, also enthroned, holds a distaff.[82]
A squirrel disapprovingly turns his back, tail down, on this
despicable representation of the *clerici conjugati, uxorati.*[83]
Jean Pucelle designed a scathing comment on verse 76 of
the canticle of Zacharias in the first chapter of Luke, "in
sanctitate et justicia coram ipso omnibus diebus nostris," in
the shape of a cleric astraddle a line ending in a gargoyle,
who holds a distaff and unwinds the thread to a cat, which
paws at the spindle.[84] In a northern French Psalter and
Hours a knight squats, like Hercules, at the foot of a medi-

eval Omphale who, fingering the thread of her distaff, is gracefully, if precariously, poised with one foot on a curlicue shooting forth across the bas-de-page. Or the positions are permuted and a hooded villain stands and spins while a seated woman sets the reel into motion.[85] In a Flemish Psalter and Hours in the Walters Art Gallery a hybrid woman, the symbol of those "who sit in darkness and in the shadow of death," lifts her distaff and her outstretched crane's neck toward a man who lunges at the page, "oriens ex alto," holding a distaff and letting the reel, which looks like a lantern, be pecked at by the crane's bill.[86]

On f. 226 of Robert de Boron's *Histoire de Merlin*, in the Bibliothèque Nationale, Paris, and on f. 329 of the Yale *Lancelot del Lac*, the woman turns her traditional attributes, the distaff and spindle, into a jousting weapon and charges at a defenseless knight clad in chain mail.[87] On f. 100v of the Yale *Lancelot*, the lance of a tilting Dominican breaks against her shield, and on f. 224 of the *Breviary for Marguerite de Bar* (part 1, Yates Thompson MS 8 in the British Museum), a peasant woman, armed only with a lance and riding a goat, dismounts a fully armed knight astride a ram.[88] Such tilting females, coming from the aristocracy or from lower classes, represent argumentative women and, more particularly, married ladies (*baillistres*), dowager duchesses or countesses who, replacing their absent or incapacitated husbands, fought more fiercely against their vassals than did the liege lords.[89] On ladies highest on the social ladder, rougher men may take revenge: on f. 86 of the *Rutland Psalter*, for instance, a lady wearing her "touret" like a crown and her distaff as a scepter, lets fall her hand of justice, the spindle, from her perch at the see-saw-like top of a ducking stool, while a yokel is hacking away at the immobilizing wedge at the lower end of this version of the wheel of fortune, with the set purpose of having her take a plunge.[90] In the marginalia knights are very often represented as being afraid of snails. This slander which harks back to the free-for-all debacle of the Lombards before Charles the Great's host in 772, picked up momentum with the diffusion in northern France and in England towards the end of the twelfth century of the poem *De Lombardo et*

Lumaca, the barbs of which were levelled against the hated Lombard usurers and pawnbrokers.[91] On f. 15v of a Book of Hours for the use of Therouanne, in which each of the Passion hours is preceded by a poem in Picard dialect, a woman entreats a knight not to use his lance or bow against a snail; in the left margin, a woman dances to the call of a pipe and of a cowbell rung by a messenger of the devil.[92] On f. 40v of the Metz Pontifical for Reynard de Bar, Bishop of Metz (1302–16), a woman pleads with a knight confronting the snail with spear and buckler.[93] But "scribit Herodotus quod mulier cum veste deponit et verecundiam," [94] and on the bas-de-page of f. 86v–87 of an English Book of Hours of the first quarter of the fourteenth century in the British Museum (Harley MSS 6563) a stark naked female warrior marches with spear and buckler against a snail slowly moving to meet her. The image is "prima facie" an allusion to its context in Psalm 131:17–19, "illuc producam cornu David . . . inimicos ejus induam confusione" (Then I shall make a horn to sprout for David . . . his enemies I will clothe with shame). But there is more to it, as the snail enjoyed the reputation of being an androgynous fornicator.[95] True to medieval tradition, a curé reminds his parishioners of its unique privilege in the sermon quoted by Jean-Jacques Brousson in his *Anatole France en pantoufles.* The sexological triad: knight, woman and snail partaking of male and female nature, is made clear when, on two confronting folios of a Flemish Psalter, a knight drops his sword at the sight of a snail protruding its horns, and a woman willingly absorbs with a basket the shock of the horns of a charging ram. On the borderline between the two folios, a grotesque referee of the two uneven contests holds, instead of the herald at arms' trumpet, an erotic bagpipe with an enormous drone.[96] Armed with the same basket, the woman can bait a ram or arouse the animal paradigm of chastity, the unicorn.[97]

On f. 10 of the *Saint Graal,* written and illuminated by Pierest dou Tielt at Tournai (1351), two women are jousting against each other with their distaffs. They are naked and, like the grotesque riders tilting at a "quintaine" under the Betrayal of Christ in the *Hours of Jeanne d'Evreux,* they ride a goat and a ram.[98] In the Breviary for Marguerite de Bar, quoted above, the knight riding the ram is dismounted by the woman riding a goat. The naked woman riding a goat carved on a bracket in the southern arm of the transept of the cathedral at Auxerre undoubtedly embodies Luxuria, as she wears a chapelet or roses and strokes the horn and tail of her hairy steed.[99] In the bas-de-page of the Graal manuscript the erotic element is emphasized by two monkeys enlisted as heralds at arms. One blows a trumpet and the other plays a bagpipe. The sexual connotation was added to a theme in which it was originally lacking; it is patterned after a Hellenistic one of two riding erotes confronting each other symmetrically on both sides of an axis made of the tree of life.[100] There is a curious reminiscence of it on f. 7 of a Ghent Missal (1366) in The Hague, where two naked men, one armed with a spoon and a basket and mounted on a goat, and the other armed with a pointed shield and stick, face off, about to charge each other.[101] But some eroticism is implied here and, conversely, when the riders are naked women astraddle animals of manifold sinful reputation who joust with distaffs and spindles, the sexual innuendo is also turned against chivalry as a sport.[102] The images take over the debunking of chivalry initiated in the *fabliaus*. Impatience of tournaments must have been increasing among the country people and a few radicals among women of the aristocracy.[103] On f. 16 opening the Psalms in the *Psalter and Hour of Yolande*, Vicomtesse de Soissons, a manuscript from the Amiens region, ca. 1290, of the two heralds at arms painted on the bas-de-page, one wears a fool's cap and the other rides a lion led by Cain, who has just killed Abel. Here the allusion to the outdated trials by wager of battle is substantiated by the direct relation of the marginal image to the duel between David and Goliath, which is represented within the B of *Beatus Vir* of the first verse of Psalm 1.[104] Of course, satirical comment is absent from the main illustration of manuscripts and from the sumptuous objects reflecting the rules and ways of life of aristocratic patrons. Sir Geoffrey Luttrell had himself painted on f. 202 of his Psalter (ca. 1340), being armed for the lists by his wife and daughter. On f. 8v of *Le Roman de la*

Poire (Paris, Bibliothèque Nationale, fr. 2186, Paris or Picardy ca. 1260) the departing knight wears on his helmet the colors of his lady's scarf. The lady puts the helmet on the kneeling knight, a scene recalling an actual knighting performed by a lady, on the engraved silver "print" from a mid-fourteenth century mazer, reset towards 1500 in a silver dish belonging to Bermondsey Abbey.[105] On the enamelled foot of the "Coppa del Torneo," a rock crystal hanap richly mounted in the second quarter of the fourteenth century (in the Poldi-Pozzoli Museum, Milan), a woman presents the two champions their lances.[106·]The bellicose character of the woman arming, or stripping herself for the lists, is echoed in the pugnaciousness assumed by Frau Minne. On f. 61v of a *Picard Psalter* (in the Bibliothèque Nationale, Paris, lat. 10435), "me dame de Renti" (Renty is near Saint-Omer) shells her lover with roses, a feature frequently found on the ivory caskets and mirrors; on the top of f. 38v a hybrid woman bombards a hybrid man with roses. On f. 30 of an early fourteenth-century Flemish Book of Hours in the library of Trinity College, Cambridge, a man and woman are kneeling right and left of Eros, but the winged god points his arrow towards the man only.[107] The lover may kneel before Frau Minne as she is about to pierce him with an arrow, or stand his ground passively under the protection of a shield.[108] On f. 256v of a north French Psalter in the Walters Art Gallery, a hybrid woman, armed with sword and shield, fights back a grotesque apocalyptic dragon with seven heads on its tail—an amazing drôlerie, imbued with a rather awkward religious symbolism, since in Gothic art the Virgin either as Theotocos or crowned by Christ may trample the dragon underfoot, but the fight against the dragon threatening the woman, who in chapter 12 of *Revelation* designates the Virgin, is carried out exclusively by Michael and his angels.[109]

The equal footing, and more often than not, the more than equal footing with men, enjoyed by women on the highest rungs of the social scale is emphasized in scenes of falconry and chess-playing. On f. 12 of the second part of Marguerite de Bar's *Breviary* (in the Bibliothèque Municipale, Verdun) a woman and a falconer wreathed with ivy

are training a cast of short-winged unhooded hawks, provided with jesses and bell, to come to the lure. The woman
has received the hawk, correctly, on her gloved left hand.
The falconer holds his hawk, as an eastern falconer would
do, on his bare right hand. Woman as a falconer is included
as a part of a *Jeu des Dames* cycle in the *Taymouth Hours* in
the British Museum.[110] The theme runs parallel to the
motif of an amorous conversation on riding, and is
frequently carved on the backs of ivory mirrors.[111] In a bas-
de-page of a psalter from the region of Amiens of the end
of the thirteenth century (in the Pierpont Morgan Library
in New York) both lovers are riding, but the lady holds the
falcon on her gloved left hand and, in relation with the two-
column text, she has been given heraldically the pride of
place, dexter.[112] On the back of an ivory mirror in the
Louvre, exceptionally carved with four figures, the lovers
are playing chess. Behind the young man stands a friend
holding a falcon, and behind the young woman a lady-in-
waiting is holding the chapelet of roses. The favorite topics
of elegant life: falconry, and of courtly love: crowning, are
blended into that of chess-playing.[113] Even then, the game
of chess remained under constant attack on the part of the
Church and the moralists,[114] an attitude reflected in the
marginalia; on f. 112 of the *Romance of Alexander* in the
Bodleian Library, above the chess players a monkey is
strumming on a jaw bone, that is, the weapon of Cain "that
did the first murder." [115] On f. 40 of Jacques de Longuyon's
Voeux du Paon in the Pierpont Morgan Library, a mermaid,
one of those alluring females who destroy man's enterprises
and soul with their fair enticing song, plays a jawbone with
a pair of tongs.[116] On some ivory mirror backs representing
the game of chess played between a young man and
woman, the lady, still holding in her left hand the pieces
taken from her opponent, raises in surprise her right hand
as her adversary is making the decisive move leading to her
being checkmated.[117] This turning point of the game has
been interpreted as having been inspired by an episode in
the thirteenth-century Chanson de Geste, *Huon de Bordeaux*,[118] in which Huon plays chess against the daughter of
the Saracen admiral, Yvorin. High are the stakes: should

Huon lose the game, he shall be beheaded. If he is the winner, he will gain the lady's favor and money. He loses, but his opponent is moved by his beauty. In the representations of the game the man usually wins, or the two opponents are men and one of them, having pawned everything in the game but his trunk hose, engages the other in a brawl.[119] In a northern French breviary (1288) a similar pattern had already been used to depict a licentious fight during a dice game, in which a nun resists the importunate gesture of a cleric.[120]

In the marginalia the animals assume a human appearance and the image of man becomes distorted into the monstrous. A strange osmosis has taken place, attractive and repulsive at the same time. As of the middle of the twelfth century the interest begins to shift from the allegorizing and theological view of the animal world, inherited from the *Physiologus,*[121] towards a more sympathetic approach, borne out of a feeling of secret congeniality between beast and man. In his *Speculum,* the Cistercian Ailred, who became abbot of Rivaulx in 1147, complained, not so many years after the celebrated *Apologia* of St. Bernard, that monks were partial to "cranes and hares, does and bucks, magpies and crows, not indeed for any Antonine or Macharian purpose, but for more womanly delights." [122] The *De Natura Rerum* of Thomas de Chantimpré, written in the middle of the thirteenth century, had many editions, and a French moralizing version of his treatise, *Liber de monstruosis hominibus. La manière et les faitures des monstres,* was published between 1290 and 1315.[123] The magnificent English bestiaries of the twelfth century open with paintings of scenes of the creation which would befit a scientific textbook of natural history,[124] but in the Bible painted by William of Devon (an artist possibly attached to Henry III), the hexameron contained within the initial I of *In principio* opening the Book of Genesis, is completed in the margin by a wonderful zoo where animals real or grotesque, hunting or pacing, are confronted with a bishop, a monk, a hunter and hybrid creatures bridging over the species.[125] In the *Bestiaire d'Amour* of Richard de Fournival the threefold nature of woman is compared with the threefold nature of the wolf.[126] In a bible of the fourteenth century in Brussels, the introductory letter of St. Jerome, "de omnibus libris divine ystorie," sums up the themes parading in the margins of Gothic manuscripts: a hunt; an ape holding a urinal and an angel playing a bagpipe near the Virgin and Child; two hares tilting above King Arthur and, in the bas-de-page, the falconer and his lady; the coronation of the youth by his girl; two lovers embracing, and musicians; and, below, a fantastic animal orchestra whooping it up, and a wild *stantipes* of hares and monkeys.[127] The dances are no less wild in the *Romance of Alexander* painted by Jehan de Grise; however, among men wearing masks of horned or long eared animals like sorcerers, the women joining hands with their partners seem to have kept, with their daily attire, all their wits about them.[128]

Dominated by the woman, the world of lovers exists in an innocence which is shared with their favorite animals. On a bracket of the facade of the cathedral at Lyons, carved ca. 1300, near the lady with a unicorn, a young man and woman caress each other's chins. As their coat of arms per pale, he holds a falcon and she a pet dog.[129] In an English bestiary of the thirteenth century the *sirena* and the *onocentaurus* are conniving to cause navigators mischief.[130] But on the tailloir above a capital in the church of Saint-Denis-Hors at Amboise, the merman and mermaid, reconciled with the world and forgetting it, are about to exchange a kiss.[131] On f. 110 of a *Roman de la Rose* of the mid-fourteenth century in the Bibliothèque Nationale, Paris, they embrace, as do the centaur and centauress on a beautiful carved boss of the nave vault in Lincoln Cathedral (1240–53).[132] Deeply human, although half animal, a wild man and a hairy wild woman, walking on all fours, happily meet nose to nose on f. 64v of a treatise on nobility written for Walter de Milemete in 1326–27 for presentation to Edward III (Christ Church Library, Oxford).[133] Three line endings of the invocation "Sanctus, sanctus, sanctus" in the *Hours of Jeanne d'Evreux* are decorated with wyvern-like creatures. Two twist into a caduceus and kiss.

Such line endings were imitated by enamellers. The buckle plate of a lady's belt kept in the Baden Baden Museum is provided with a siren (a bird-woman) cast in silver, and a plaque enamelled on basse taille silver with a hybrid woman, her hair caught back in a net and her armless body ending in a lioness's hindquarters. The hanging part of the belt, the mordant, is enamelled with a hybrid man, the male counterpart of the fantastic female creature. When the belt was hanging, the centaur-like creature enamelled on the mordant would seem to be crawling upwards to his mate, the centauress of the buckle. The enamelled letter A studding the belt's silk material repeats the initial of the lady's first name, or, more exactly, her patronage emblem.[134] The belt, a marriage gift, is possibly the work of Jean Pucelle in Paris.[135] In the Archaeological Museum at Spalato are kept fragments of a French lady's belt with enamelled plaques showing women, young men and women, two loving couples, grotesque birds, a siren and a centauress similar to the one crawling on the Baden Baden belt.[136] Another enamelled belt, kept in the Cleveland Museum, which is decorated with scenes of love and music and with grotesques, betrays the French fashion dominating in Milan at the court of Gian Galeazzo Visconti.[137] Such belts are worn by the Virgin holding the Child in fourteenth-century statues, either showing only the buckle plate or revealing the mordant when the mantle falls open instead of being wrapped up. In vestimentary terms they recall the prophecy of God in Ezechiel: "This gate shall remain shut; it shall not be opened and no one shall enter by it; for the Lord, the God of Israel, has entered by it; therefore it shall remain shut" (44:2).[138] In the statue of the Virgin and Child at Bouxières-aux-Dames in Lorraine, one of the most remarkable exponents of the mysterious matrimonial bond between the Virgin and Christ, the child has pulled up his mother's belt and looks at it with the deepest concentration as if it were a phylactery with a message written on it.[139] Such a blend of mundane and religious symbolism was not exceptional. A lady's girdle, set with enamelled apes and a grotesque hunt, forms part of the mitre of William of Wykeham, who was elected to the see of Winchester in 1366.[140]

In Germany a tradition observed until modern times

holds that upon the announcement of her engagement the
future bride should wear a belt kept in the church and return it after the wedding night, when her husband has un-
tied it.[141] King Lear was archaeologically sound when he
said of women, referring to a similar custom and costume:

> Down from the waist they are centaurs
> Though women all above,
> But to the girdle do the gods inherit,

but he was mad at them and out of touch with the true medieval spirit when he added:

> Beneath is all the fiend's.[142]

NOTES

1. Berkeley and Los Angeles: University of California Press, 1966, pp. viii, 235;
739 fig. Index to subjects, pp. 45–235. A second edition is forthcoming.

2. See the bibliography in Jurgis Baltrušaitis, *Réveils et Prodiges: Le Gothique Fan-
tastique* (Paris: Armand Colin, 1960), p. 355, n. 13, and Lilian M. C. Randall, "Exempla as source of gothic marginal illumination," *The Art Bulletin* 39 (1957):
97–108.

3. Th. T. F. Crane, *The Exempla or Illustrative Stories from the* Sermones Vulgares *of
Jacques de Vitry,* Folklore Society Publications, vol. 26 (London, 1890); François
Courtoy, "Le trésor du prieuré d'Oignies aux soeurs de Notre-Dame à Namur et
l'oeuvre du frère Hugo," in *Bulletin de la Commission Royale des Monuments et des Sites*
(Brussels, 1952), pp. 125–28.

4. Courtoy, pp. 119–258, figs. 2, 4, 16, 25, 43–44. Compare the reliquary arms of
St. Landelin at Crespin (Nord) in Jean Taralon, *Les Trésors des églises de France*
(Paris: Caisse Nationale des Monuments Historiques, 1965), p. 4, those at The
Cloisters, New York, in *The Metropolitan Museum of Art Bulletin* 6 (1948), fig., p.
243, and those at Binche (Belgium) in *Les Monuments Historiques de la France* (Paris,
1966), 1–2, fig. 76, p. 99; also the book cover of the Carolingian so-called St. Aure
Evangeliary in the Arsenal Library, Paris (MS 1171): J. J. Marquet de Vasselot,
"L'Orfèvrerie et l'Emaillerie aux XIIIè et XIVè siècles," in André Michel, *Histoire
de l'Art, depuis les premiers temps chrétiens jusqu'à nos jours,* vol. 2, pt. 2 (Paris: A. Colin,
1906), p. 926.

5. Abbé Victor Leroquais, *Les Psautiers manuscrits Latins des bibliothèques publiques de
France,* vol. 2 (Paris: Macon, 1941), p. 95. *Bibliothèque Nationale Les manuscrits à peintures du XIIIè au XIVè siècle,* no. 68 (1955):35–36. Together with the illustrations
are given the names and birth places of various attractive "demiseles" and "dames"
involved in amusing and sometimes embarrassing situations. On folio 187 of the

Smithfield Decretals in the British Museum, the monk treasurer is put in stocks with the lady who was his accomplice in the robbing of the treasure: Randall, "Exempla . . . ," fig. 2 and p. 103.

6. Obscaena and scatologica are specially reserved for making fun of nuns; see the index of Lilian Randall and numerous marginalia in a XIVth-century MS of *Le Roman de la Rose* (fr. 2556), in the Bibliothèque Nationale, Paris.

7. On women as embodiments of the "sexus lubricus" see the books of Carlo Pascal, *Poesia latina medievale* (Catania: F. Battiato, 1907), p. 151, and *Letteratura latina medievale* (Catacia: F. Battiato, 1909), p. 107. In a passage of Bernard of Cluny's *De Contemptu Mundi,* the woman is "res male carnea vel caro tota." See also Edgar De Bruyne, *Études d'Esthétique Médiévale* (Bruges: De Tempel, 1946), 2:196–98.

8. F. 30v of a mid-fourteenth century MS (William S. Glazier 24, Pierpont Morgan Library, New York) of Jacques de Longuyon's *Voeux du Paon,* precisely that book which established the cult of the "nine worthies" before Eustache Deschamps added the "nine heroines" as co-stars. As a drôlerie in the *Hours of Jeanne d'Evreux* (1325–38) in The Cloisters, New York, a wife runs away with her man's pants. See also Richard H. Randall, "Frog in the Middle," *The Metropolitan Museum of Art Bulletin* 16 (1958), fig., p. 275, where a translation appears from the Flemish for the proverb illustrated by Peter Brueghel the Elder: "Where the woman wears the pants and holds up the upper hand, there John [also a slang name for the male genitalia] must always dance to the tune of their command." In her article "A Mediaeval Slander," Lilian M. C. Randall examines the overtones of cowardice and homosexuality in the libel "Anglais cové," or "Angli caudati" (meaning both 'tail' and 'hatching' Englishmen): *The Art Bulletin* 42 (1960):25–38. The illustrations of the slander are all found in manuscripts of northern France and Flanders. Shall we surmise that the ones in the Psalter of Gui de Dampierre and in a Psalter and Hours from Ghent (*Art Bulletin* 42 [1960], fig. 2 and p. 27) were inserted by a pro-French illuminator? Gui de Dampierre, count of Flanders (1280–97) took sides with Edward I against Philip the Fair. The egg-hatching motif took many forms in proverbs and art. The carved misericord in Saint-Seurin at Bordeaux is interpreted as illustrating the popular saying "Sit on the eggs and let the hen escape": Victor Henry Debidour, *Le bestiaire sculpté du Moyen Âge en France* (Paris: Arthaud, 1961), fig. 381. Pity for a debilitated hatching man pervades the short story of Guy de Maupassant, "Père Toine."

9. See Flemish Hours of the early XIVth century in Trinity College Library, Cambridge, MS B. 11–22f. 118 v; published in Lilian M. C. Randall, *Images in the Margins of Gothic Manuscripts,* fig. 93. One may suspect a play on the words between *emulgentia* (milking) and *indulgentia* (indulgence) as suggested by a book listed by Rabelais in Saint-Victor Library, the *Boudarini Episcopi. De emulgentiarum profitibus enneades novem cum privilegio papali* (See Pantagruel, Bk. VII). It is only at the time of *Piers Plowman* (1363) that an inflation of indulgences resulted into a depreciation of their purchase cost down to a penny by the pound (for pons poundmele, A. II. 198).

10. "In fine vero debet uti exemplis ad probandun quod intendit, quia familiaris est doctrina exemplaris," *Summa de Arte Praedicatoria, Patrologia Latina,* J. P. Migne, ed., vol. 210 (Paris, 1855), col. 114 (Henceforward *PL*).

11. Horst Woldemar Janson, *Apes and Ape Lore in the Middle Ages and the Renaissance* (London: Warburg Institute, University of London, 1952). Apes play an ac-

tive part in exempla and proverbs, the origin of which sometimes remains obscure, as the popular saying that after their death spinsters, like apes, lead the souls of bachelors to hell. See the ejaculation of Katherine to Baptista in *The Taming of the Shrew*, 2. 1. 34, and that of Beatrice to Leonato in *Much Ado about Nothing:* "I will even take sixpence in earnest of the berrord and lead his apes into hell . . . and there will the devil meet me, like an old cuckold, with horns on his head, and say 'Get you to heaven, Beatrice, get you to heaven. Here's no place for you, maids': so deliver I up my apes, and away to Saint Peter" (2. 1. 45–50). The maid delivering up her apes is carved in a wooden misericord in Bristol cathedral. See Mary D. Anderson, *Misericords: Medieval Life in English Woodcarving*, (Hammondsworth, Middlesex: Penguin Books, 1954), fig. 36 and p. 21. The scene is connected with another saying recorded by Congreve: "Heav'n has no rage, like love to hatred turned/ Nor Hell a fury, like a woman scorned" (*The Mourning Bride*, [1697] 3. 8).

12. Migne, *PL* 182. 915–16. After his reconciliation with Saint Bernard, Abbot Suger did not hesitate to flank the typological and anagogical stained glass windows in the ambulatory of the abbey church at Saint Denis with grisaille windows showing a diapered pattern of gryphons. He had a good advocate for doing so, Denys the Pseudo-Areopagite, who in his *De Caelesti Hierarchia* had contended that negative symbols, because they are the farthest removed from God, are most apt to evoke Him in absentia. In the footpath of Denys, Hugh of Saint Victor distinguishes between a "modus figurativus decens et conveniens" and "alter discrepans, inconveniens et indecorus. Alter per similia, alter per dissimilia signa." De Bruyne, *Études*, 2:215. Concerning the grisaille windows at Saint Denis, see Louis Grodecki in: *De Artibus Opuscula XL: Essays in Honor of Erwin Panofsky* (New York: New York University Press, 1961), p. 174 and n. 40.

13. *De Architectura* 7.5. On this passage and a related one in Horace's *Ars Poetica* (1. 5) in the controversy about grotesques in the Renaissance, see Nicole Dacos, *La Découverte de la Domus Aurea et la Formation des Grotesques à la Renaissance*, Studies of the Warburg Institute, vol. 31 (London: The Warburg Institute, The University of London; Leiden: E. J. Brill, 1969), pp. 121–35.

14. Joan Evans, *English Art 1307–1461* (Oxford: Oxford University Press, 1949), pp. 38–44. Phillipe Verdier, "Les bordures à décor simiesque d'un vitrail normand" [Monkey Business in a Norman Stained Glass Window], *Montreal Museum of Fine Arts* 4, no. 1 (June 1972). In April 1344 the provençal architect and sculptor, Jean de Loubières, received payment for having carved four "babuini" above the main entrance of the Pope's Palace, at Avignon; see Enrico Castelnuovo, *Un pittore italiano alla corte di Avignone, Matteo Giovannetti e la Pittura in Provenza nel secolo XIV* (Turin: Einaudi, 1962), p. 104 and n. 1. Rabelais must have been familiar with marginalia made of what Chaucer calls "subtil compassinges" (a play on the words compass-geometrical design, and singe-monkey) and "babewinnes," because in his catalogue of the Saint-Victor library he gives the treatise *De baboinis et singis* to Marmotretus (a nickname made of Marmotret, a commentator of the Bible, and a marmot, meaning an ape), with glosses by the Franciscan Des Orbeaux, a Poitiers professor. See *Oeuvres complètes de Rabelais*, Bibliothèque de la Pléiade (Paris: Nouvelle Revue Française, 1965), p. 196, n. 1.

15. J. M. C. Toynbee, "Peopled scrolls: a Hellenistic motif in imperial art," *Papers of the British School of Athens*, vol. 18, n. s. 5 (1950), reprint pp. 1–43. J. Baltrušaitis, *Réveils et Prodiges*, pp. 150–52 and 201–2, and fig. 37 (p. 152) illustrating marginal

images in the *Hours of William de Brailes,* 1220–24, still tied by a sort of umbilical to the initials that generated them.

16. See Francis Wormald, "The Tickhill Psalter," *The Burlington Magazine for Connoisseurs* 79 (1941):134. See in Baltrušaitis, *Réveils et Prodigés,* pp. 178–80, figs. 26–28, friezes of grotesques substituted for capitals and creeping along cornices. Some time after the grotesque decoration was on the wane, they had a Hellenistic revival in the *Hours of Charles the Noble* (Charles III, 1361–1425, king of Navarre) in the Cleveland Museum of Art, thanks to the marginal decoration attributed to Zebo da Firenze. The nude figures and the putti cavorting among the scrolls come directly from the jambs of the Porta della Mandorla of Santa Maria dei Fiori (the cathedral of Florence), the northern backlash being responsible for the transformation of a putto into a Mannken Pis (folio 175). See William D. Wixom and Emanuel Winternitz, "The Hours of Charles the Noble," *The Bulletin of the Cleveland Museum of Art* 52 (1965):84–91; Charles Seymour, *Sculpture in Italy, 1400 to 1500,* The Pelican History of Art, (Hammondsworth, Middlesex: Penguin Books, 1966), pp. 31–35, pl. 4; Millard Meiss, *French Painting in the Time of Jean de Berry* (London and New York: Phaidon, 1967), p. 229.

17. The *Songes drôlatiques de Pantagruel où sont contenues plusieurs figures de l'invention de maistre Francois Rabelais,* published in 1565, contributed to the fortune of the term "drôleries," which is of medieval vintage. The grotesques of the *Songes drôlatiques,* not invented by Rabelais (who died twelve years before), picked up the tradition of the Gothic marginalia through the motifs of Peter Brueghel the Elder, which had been engraved by Hieronymus Cock and Peter van der Heycher. See André Blum, *L'Estampe satirique en France* (Paris: M. Giard & E. Brière, 1918), p. 238; Bertrand Guégan, "Rabelais et les Songes drôlatiques de Pantagruel . . . ," *Arts et Métiers Graphiques,* no. 34 (1933):15–22.

18. Suzy Dufrenne, *L'illustration des psautiers grecs du moyen-âge, vol. 1, Pantocrator 61, Paris Grec 20, British Museum 40731,* Bibliothèque des Cahiers Archéologique No. 1 (Paris, 1966); Dufrenne, "Psautiers byzantins," *L'Oeil* 167 (November 1968): 2–9, 86.

19. N. Malickj, "Le psautier à illustrations marginales du type Chludov est-il de provenance monastique?", *Mélanges Th. Uspensky,* vol. 2, no. 2 (Paris, 1932), pp. 235–43; André Grabar, *L'Iconoclasme Byzantin Dossier archéologique* (Paris: Collège de France, 1957), pp. 196–203, 214–33. Late "monastic" Psalters with marginal illustrations include Hamilton MS 78 A 9 in the Kupferstichkabinett, Berlin, and W. 733 in the Walters Art Gallery, Baltimore, which is a link between an eleventh-century prototype and the Russian Psalter of 1397 in the Leningrad Public Library (codex 1252 F vi). See Dorothy Miner, "The monastic Psalter of the Walters Art Gallery," *Late Classical and Mediaeval Studies in Honor of Albert Matthias Friend Jr.* (Princeton, New Jersey: Princeton University Press, 1955), pp. 232–53.

20. The *"Bristol" Psalter* (British Museum 40731) is an exception to the rule.

21. In an analogous manner, the marginalia of Gothic manuscripts censure viciously and pornographically the mores of the Knights Templars. See Lilian Randall, *Images,* p. 219, and references to figures.

22. British Museum, Additional MSS, 19352 f. 58. Dufrenne, "Psautiers byzantins," fig. 6.

23. Paris, Bibliothèque Nationale, Grec 20, f. 12; Dufrenne, *L'illustration des psautiers,* pp. 44, pl. 37.

24. Dufrenne, ibid., p. 30, pl. 16.

25. On the Jean Pucelle problem see the recent articles by Florens Deuchler, "A Magnificent Manuscript—A Historical Mystery," and E. H. Flinn, "Jean Pucelle— Facts and Fictions," in *The Metropolian Museum of Art Bulletin* 29 (1971):253–56 and 257–60.

26. The same unusual procedure is followed in a Book of Hours for Metz of the second half of the fourteenth century, Paris, Bibliothèque Nationale, lat. 1403; Victor Leroquais, *Les Livres d'Heures Manuscrits de la Bibliothèque Nationale* (Paris, Mâcon: Protat Frères, 1927), 1:239–41, pl. XLIX–LXV.

27. F. 15v–16, reproduced as figs. 2 and 3 in *The Hours of Jeanne d'Evreux Queen of France at The Cloisters,* Intro. James Rorimer, a facsimile digest (New York: The Metropolitan Museum of Art, 1957).

28. Such an interpretation was advanced by Erwin Panofsky in *Early Netherlandish Painting* (Cambridge, Massachusetts: Harvard University Press, 1964), p. 30 and n. 1., Kathleen Morand has objected that caryatid figures are frequent in the *Hours of Jeanne d'Evreux* and that Pucelle could as well have taken inspiration from caryatid angels in the Genesis page of Philip the Fair's Bible (Paris, Bibliothèque Nationale, lat. 248), which is one of the iconographic sources of the Bible written in 1327 by Robert de Billyng and illuminated by Jean Pucelle, Anciau de Sens and Jaquet Maci. See *Jean Pucelle* (Oxford: Oxford University Press, 1962), pp. 41–42, 45.

29. A pet dog sits on the mantle of Yolande de Soissons, kneeling before a statue of the Virgin and Child, and seems to join in her prayer, on f. 232v. of her *Psalter and Hours* (M. 729 in the Pierpont Morgan Library, a manuscript from Amiens?), c. 1290. The squirrel is a favorite pet of royal and aristocratic ladies; see Lilian Randall, *Images,* p. 215. In the late series of the tiles inlaid at the royal abbey of Chertsey, Surrey, a crowned lady holding a squirrel, tentatively identified as Queen Eleanor of Castile, d. 1290, stands between St. Edmund and St. Thomas a Becket. See J. S. Gardner and Elizabeth Eames, "A Tile Kiln at Chertsey Abbey," *Journal of the British Archaeological Association,* 3d Series, vol. 17 (1954):24–42, pl. XII a. The squirrel has been adopted by the Virgin and the Child in a Norman statue of the early fourteenth century recently acquired by the Museum of Fine Arts, Houston, Texas. See *Art and the Courts: France and England 1259 to 1328,* The National Gallery of Canada, no. 62, pl. 84 (Ottawa, 1972).

30. Lilian M. C. Randall, "Games and the Passion in Pucelle's Hours of Jeanne d'Evreux" *Speculum* 42 (1972):246–57. Randall, *Images,* p. 103. In the *Romance of Alexander,* illustrated by Jehan de Grise (MS 264 in the Bodleian Library), the frog game is represented four times; once, on f. 97v, it is played by four girls alone; cf. R. H. Randall, "Frog in the Middle," *The Metropolitan Museum of Art Bulletin,* volume 16 (1958):272, fig. 272.

31. On folio 95 of an Anglo-French Book of Hours (from Canterbury? Egerton MS 1151, British Museum), the hunter who in the bas-de-page treacherously shoots from behind at a heron corresponds to Judas, who slips behind Christ in the Betrayal scene painted in the initial above. *Art and the Courts* 2, no. 25, pl. 38. Pucelle did not represent the Mocking of Christ in the *Hours of Jeanne d'Evreux,* but only the Flagellation, facing the Nativity (f. 53v and 54). The framework of the Flagellation is supported by two caryatid figures, one being a bald tormentor with a whip. Under the Nativity, merrymaking constitutes only a part of the marginalia. Other figures are of a sinister character. A tumbler balances a pole which is the

mirrored image of the thin column of the Flagellation, and a monstrous high priest trains a dog to the tune of a jaw bone, a weapon of murder. Under the previous illustration showing Christ before Pilate, f. 34v, a bald centaur-like creature uses the tail of a dog as the blowpipe of a bagpipe and one of its legs as the chanter. The dogs of the Nativity and Christ before Pilate's pages are, under the guise of drôleries, cryptic references to verse 17 of Psalm 21 which applies to the Passion: "Quoniam circumdederunt me canes multi; concilium malignantium obsedit me." (The *Hours of Jeanne d'Evreux,* facsimile edition, New York: The Metropolitan Museum of Art, 1957), fig. 8, 9, and 6. Emanuel Winternitz, "Bagpipes for the Lord," *The Metropolitan Museum of Art Bulletin* 16 (1958):276–86.

32. The motif of the young lady pressing her hands on the youth's head in the frog game was copied, although in a much less spirited manner, in the bas-de-page under the Annunciation f. 39 of the *Hours of Jeanne II Queen of Navarre,* a manuscript illuminated by a follower of Pucelle some time after the artist's death, in 1334. K. Morand, *Jean Pucelle,* pp. 48–49, pl. XVIIc. The location of this manuscript is unknown.

33. Frog in the middle, blind-man's buff, spinning the top, field hockey, stilts and a game in which a girl holds one of her legs with her hands and is about to kick a youth with the other, are enamelled on a French ewer in the National Museum, Copenhagen, which shows also three rows of grotesques, one on the lid, two on the foot and above it hybrids, half-centurs and half-dragons, male and female, one of them making an obscene gesture, and all happily playing bells, the horn and the trumpet. The ewer was made in the same workshop as the enamelled French chalice and paten also in the National Museum, Copenhagen: see Mouritz Mackeprang, *Vases sacrés émaillés d'origine française du XIVème siècle conservés dans le Musée National du Danemark* (Copenhagen: Markus, 1921). Concerning the ewer, see Marie Madeleine Gauthier, *Emaux du Moyen Age occidental* (Fribourg: Office du Livre, 1972), Cat. 204, color plate p. 255. It could be the work of Jehan de Toull (on this goldsmith see Gerda Panofsky Soergel, "Ein signierter Pariser Silberemail-Kelch um 1330," *Munuscula Discipulorum: Kunsthistorische Studien Hans Kauffmann zum 70. Geburtstag 1966,* ed. Tilmann Buddensieg and Matthias Winner [Berlin, 1966], pp. 225–33) or, of Pucelle himself. Around the reliquary crown from the abbey of the Paraclet (in the treasure of Amiens cathedral), the receptacles of relics from the True Cross, the Holy Crown, of SS. Margaret and Agnes are interspersed with translucent enamels in concave hexagonal collets, displaying a woman astride a piebald horse, male and female hybrids and animals; see Taralon, *Les trésors des églises de France,* no. 62.

34. Florence McCulloch "The funeral of Renart the Fox in a Walters Book of Hours," *The Journal of the Walters Art Gallery* 25–26 (1962–63):14, figs. 2–3. The bridled bear is the companion of the jugglers, i.e., the apes, and the implication seems to be that the ape will spirit out to hell, with the virgins, the non-remarried *viduae;* cf. n. 11 above.

35. In *L'Histoire du Graal* of Robert de Borron, a Picard manuscript in the Bibliothèque Nationale (Paris, fr. 95), Aristotle and Phyllis appear twice: on f. 61v Phyllis, an elegante, with her hair bulging out in two "boursettes," rides Aristotle and whips him; on f. 254 Aristotle, wearing his scholar's cap and seated at his desk, turns back his head towards the young woman who wears a "chapelet" and is about

to crown the philosopher with another one—a caricature of the Evangelist inspired by his symbol which comes back to the source of the theme: the poet inspired by the muse. The piggy-back ride of Phyllis on Aristotle will be treated in later medieval art as a scene of matrimonial fun performed by a bourgeois couple. In a din-anderie plate owned by Judge Irwin Untermeyer, New York, the wife has laid bare the buttocks of her husband, who holds the spindle and the reel, and gives him a sound thrashing. See *Medieval Art from Private Collections: A Special Exhibition at the Cloisters,* The Metropolitan Museum (New York 1968), no. 122. Compare a miseri-cord in King Henry VII's chapel at Westminster Abbey in Anderson, *Misericords,* fig. 43. On the bourgeois attire of Phyllis, see Wolfgang Stammler, *Reallexikon zur deutschen Kunstgeschichte,* 1:1036 f. The source of Phyllis's piggy-back ride is not ex-emplum 15 of Jacques de Vitry, but *Le Lai d'Aristote,* composed by the Norman poet Henry d'Andely, in the first half of the thirteenth century, followed by the Middle High German poem *Aristoteles und Fillis* and Ulrich von Eschenbach's *Alex-andreis* (see Jane Campbelle Hutchinson, "Housebook master and the folly of the wise man," *The Art Bulletin* 48 [1966]:75–76).

36. L. Randall, *Images,* p. 111. Raymond Koechlin, *Les ivoires gothiques français* (Paris: A. Picard, 1924), vol. 2, nos. 1171, 1173, 1176. The "kokilles" games is de-scribed by Froissart in *L'Epinette amoureuse,* verses 217–18.

37. Randall, *Images,* fig. 664–67. *Art and the Courts,* no. 83 (with the bibliography).

38. Jean Avalon, "L'Annonciation à la Licorne," *Pro Arte* 5 (1946): 341–48.

39. Debidour, *Le bestiaire,* fig. 317.

40. Verdier, "Les ivoires de Walters Art Gallery," II, *Art International,* vol. 7, no. 4 (1963):29, fig. 1. In the *Bestiaire d'Amour* the symbol of the pelican in piety, mean-ing Christ dying on the Cross, is transferred to the woman who opens her breast and her heart to her well-beloved. More prosaically, on f. 213 of a Flemish Book of Hours in Trinity College Library, Cambridge (B. 11. 22), above the pelican rend-ing its heart to feed its youngsters, a woman opens her treasure chest (Randall, *Images,* fig. 553). As the text reminds us: "omnia operatur unus atque idem spiritus dividens singulis pro sic vult" (*I Cor.* 12:11).

41. M. M. Gauthier, *Emaux,* Cat. 208, fig. p. 260. A hunt involving a fox, two stags, a hind and a unicorn, is enamelled on the silver gilt mount of the Bruce horn of Savernake: See Sir Charles James Jackson, *An Illustrated History of En-glish Plate Ecclesiastical and Secular,* vol. 2 (London, 1911), pp. 589–613. The Bruce horn is held to have been the tenure horn of the Savernake forest. One of the methods of transferring inheritance "sine scriptis" since Anglo-Saxon days was to convey the title in frank almoin, or in fee, or in serjeantry through the trans-mission of a horn. The *cornu potatorium* which John Goldcorne presented to the guild of Corpus Christi, Cambridge, ca. 1347, was hereafter used at Corpus Christi College on feast days as a *poculum caritatis;* see Jackson, *Illustrated History of English Plate,* p. 109. The curious inscription enamelled on the French horn containing the relics of St. Ursula's eleven thousand virgins, in the treasure of St. Servatius in Maestricht:

> Bien dot il estre gentil de drot
> Ke le serf se met a la mort
> Nul ne doit che corne porteer
> Il n'est dine pour prendre le singler

indicates that wearing the horn was disapproved in hunting animals which, like the boar, were devoid of the christological association applying to the stag.

42. Oiseuse of the *Roman de la Rose,* with her hair well combed and holding a mirror, is equated with Luxuria: J. V. Fleming, *The Roman de la Rose: A Study in Allegory and Iconography* (Princeton, New Jersey: Princeton University Press, 1969), reviewed by William Calin: *Speculum* 47 (1972):311–13. The slut of Babylon in the Angers tapestry of the Apocalypse is represented like the hybrid woman of f. 29 of the *Ormesby Psalter* (Bodleian Library, Douce 366; L. Randall, *Images,* fig. 249) holding a mirror and a comb which denote lecherous coquetry. In Superbia, one of the seven deadly sins mirrored in God's eye, painted by Bosch (Prado, Madrid), the devil holds the mirror to the woman as she complacently fixes her coif.

43. L. Randall, *Images,* fig. 210.

44. Lat. 10435 f. 117 *Manuscrits à Peintures,* Bibliothèque Nationale (1955), no. 68. Jacqueline Rambaut-Buhot, *Les trésors de la Bibliothèque Nationale,* Editions filmées d'art et d'histoire (1958).

45. On the iconographical transmission from Byzantine prototypes of the motif of Eve's birth, see Pierre du Colombier, "Sur la transmission des schémas de composition au moyen âge," *Gazette des Beaux Arts* 6th ser., vol. 72 (November 1968): 255–58.

46. L. Randall, *Images,* figs. 5–6. The Yale manuscript contains also *La Queste del Saint Graal* and *La Mort au Roy Artus.* See *The Yale University Library Gazette* 29, no. 3 (January 1955):103–5.

47. Bayerische Staatsbibliothek, Cod. Gall. 16, f. 20v; L. Randall, *Images,* fig. 724.

48. Tubalcain was often confused with Jubal, as in Vincent de Beauvais's *Speculum Doctrinale* 16:25. In fourteenth century iconography, hammering at his anvil, he became the inventor of the musical scale.

49. See the passage in Bartholomaeus Anglicus's *De Proprietatibus Rerum* quoted in Jacques Le Goff, *La civilisation de l'occident médiéval* (Paris: Arthaud, 1964), p. 259.

50. Alfred Jeanroy, *Les origines de la poésie lyrique en France au moyen âge* (Paris: Librairie Hachette, 1925), pp. 125ff.

51. Benjamin Harris Cowper, *The Apocryphal Gospels* (London: David Nutt, 1897), pp. 12, 43–44.

52. Jacqueline Lafontaine-Dosogne, *Iconographie de l'enfance de la Vierge dans l'Empire byzantin et en Occident,* Académie royale de Belgique. Classe des beaux arts. Memoires. 2d ser., fasc. 3–3b (Brussels: Palais des Académies, 1965), 1:182, 2:132.

53. Cope of St. Louis of Anjou, embroidered with gold thread and multicolored silks, of the end of the thirteenth century in the basilica at Saint-Maximin (Var): *Trésors,* no. 642; *Grandes Heures of Jean de Berry* (1409), Paris, Bibliothèque Nationale, lat. 919, f. 34; Book of Hours from the workshop of the Master of the Boucicaut Hours, Oxford, Bodleian Library, MS Douce 144, f. 19 (1407). In both manuscripts an angel brings food to Mary at the loom in the Temple. See Millard Meiss, *French Painting in the Time of Jean de Berry,* fig. 234; II, *The Boucicaut Master* (New York, and London: Phaidon, 1968), fig. 51. In MS 453 of the Pierpont Morgan Library in New York, which was illuminated by the Master of the Bedford Hours, Mary combs the wool while in the margins the angels ministering to her within wreathed roudels locate the main scene in the Temple precincts. On the bas-de-page of Hours illuminated by artists of the "Bedford" atelier, in the Walters Art Gallery (W 281), Mary combs the wool in a "hortus conclusus." See Dorothy

Miner, *Illuminated Books of the Middle Ages and the Renaissance* (Baltimore: The Walter's Art Gallery, 1949), no. 99, pl. XL.

54. Andrée Lehmann, *Le rôle de la femme dans l'histoire de France au moyen âge* (Paris, 1952), under the chapter: "Industrie texile," pp. 438–45.

55. The *opus anglicanum,* an embroidery made of multicolored silks and gold or silver gilt threads, with pearls and precious stones, was the occasional pastime of ladies and nuns, but as of 1260 the most sumptuous work was executed for the church and export by men and women in London, following a seven-year apprenticeship. See Grace Christie, *English Medieval Embroidery* (Oxford: Oxford University Press, Clarendon Press, 1928).

56. Bodley 264: Randall, *Images,* fig. 407–8.

57. Cf. f. 132v of the mid-fourteenth century *Roman de la Rose* in the Bibliothèque Nationale, Paris, fr. 25526, where an aroused man, probably a cleric, offers a purse to a seduced nun (Randall, *Images,* p. 191).

58. See for example on the Arras tapestry, "L'ofrande du coeur," in the Musée de Cluny, Paris (first quarter of the fifteenth century), which is close to three tapestries in the same museum from a set of "Cinq pièces à sujets courtois" once in the castle of Canche in Britanny.

59. Françoise Baron has re-examined from the point of view of the arts the rôles de la taille, "Enlumineurs, peintres et sculpteurs parisiens des XIIIe et XIVe siècles d'apres les rôles de la taille," *Bulletin Archéologique du Comité des Travaux Historiques et Scientifiques,* n.s. 4 (1968 [Paris, 1969]):37–121. Around 1300 one finds four enlumineresses, one peintresse, eight ymagières. In a later period of the fourteenth and fifteenth centuries studied by the same author after the archives of the Saint Jacques-des-Pèlerins hospital, one more peintresse and one more ymagière are registered. See *Bulletin Archéologique,* n.s. 6 (1970 [Paris, 1971]), 77–115. Christine de Pizan wrote in chap. 41 of the first book of her *Livre de la Cité des Dames* (ca. 1405): "a propos de paintrerie, je cognois aujourd'hui une femme que on appelle Anastaise, qui tant est experte et aprise à faire vignetures d'enluminure en livres et champaignes d'histoires [bas-de-pages with stories in a landscape] qu'il n'est mencion d'ouvrier en la ville de Paris . . . qui point l'en passe." Bibliothèque Nationale, Paris fr. 607. *Manuscrits à Peintures* (1955), no. 162. Henri Martin, *La miniature française du XIIIème au XVème siècle* (Paris and Brussels: Van Oest, 1923), p. 75. One of the greatest painters of manuscripts of the fourteenth century, Jean Le Noir—"Pucelle reincarnate," as Millard Meiss called him (exhibition review, *The Art Bulletin* 38 [1956]:191)—worked with his daughter Bourgot.

60. *Art and the Courts,* no. 96, pl. 125.

61. A. Lehmann, *Rôle de la Femme,* under chapter: "Mèdecine et soins," pp. 471–76.

62. Randall, *Images,* fig. 393. The scene jovially comments on verse 2 of Psalm 109 written above the bas-de-page: "virgam virtutis tuae emittet Dominus ex Syon." The alliteration virga/virgo has been rendered familiar with the diffusion of the iconography of the tree of Jesse in gothic art. (Arthur Watson, *The Early Iconography of the Tree of Jesse* [London: Oxford University Press, 1934]). In the second illustration (Randall, *Images,* fig. 392) a maid also brings two pails of hot water to the lovers, anticipating the taylorized service pleasantly intimated in parallel episodes of Aubrey Menen's *Abode of Love.* Scantily clad girls take tender care of King Wenceslas as his bath attendants in the margins of the Wenceslas Bible in the Na-

tional Library, Vienna (Cod. 2759–64): See Julius von Schlosser, "Die Bilderhandschriften König Wenzel I," *Jahrbuch der Kunsthistorischen Sammlungen des Allerhöchsten Kaiserhauses* (1893), pp. 214 ff.

63. "Que nus ne nulle du dit mestier ne soustiegne en leurs mesons ou estuves bordiaus de jour ne le nuit, mesiaus ne mesèles, reveurs, ne autres gens diffamez de nuit," Etiénne Boileau, *Livre des Métiers*, René de Lespinasse et François Bonnardot, eds. (Paris, 1879), part 1, art. LXXIII. Jan van Eyck in his painting of a public bath, which Bartholomeo Fazio saw before 1455 in Cardinal Ottaviano's house, added a convex mirror to allow the onlookers to share with the patrons the view of a woman's back: "eximia forma feminae e balneo exeuntes occultiores corporis partes tenui linteo velatae notabili rubore, e quis unius os tantummodo pectusque demonstrans, posteriores corporis partes per speculum pictum lateri oppositum expressit, ut et terga quemadmodum pectus videas," *De Viris Illustribus* (Florence, 1745), p. 46. The medieval theme of the bath with its erotic undertones was taken over in the "appartement des bains" in Francis I's Fontainebleau palace. See *L'Ecole de Fontainebleau*, Editions des Palais Nationaux (Paris, 1972), Cat. nos. 323, 411, 415, and p. 479.

64. Beatus Amadeus Lausannensis Episcopus (1140–1159), Homilia VII: De Beatae Virginis obitu, assumptione in caelum, exaltatione ad Filii dexteram, in *PL* 188. 1340–41. Dom Odon Cassel, "Die Taufe als Brautbad der Kirche," in: *Jahrbuch für Liturgiewissenschaft* 5 (1925):144–47.

65. V.g. the test imposed by Ferdinando I de'Medici on his wife Christine de Lorraine on the first night of their marriage, Brantôme, *Les Dames galantes,* ed. Maurice Rat (Paris: Garnier Frères, 1955), p. 112.

66. W. 82. See Randall, *Images,* fig. 10.

67. Brussels, Bibliothèque Royale, MS 9961-2. Randall, *Images,* fig. 118; cf. fig. 729.

68. V.g. ´on the mosaic of the Glorification of the Virgin at Santa Maria del Trastevere, Rome, ca. 1140. Øystein Hjort, "L'oiseau dans la cage: Exemples médiévaux à Rome," *Cahiers Archéologiques* 18 (1968):21–31. Hélène Toubert, "Le renouveau paléochrétien à Rome au début du XIIème siècle," ibid., 20 (1970): 145–48. On f. 201v of MS 44–18 of the Art Museum, Princeton University, the ape decoying birds with a bird paradoxically demonstrates the lesson of verse 9 of Psalm 31: "Nolite fieri sicut equus et mulus quibus non est intellectus" (Randall, *Images,* fig. 7).

69. *Les quatre temps de l'homme.* See Charles Jourdain, "Mémoire sur l'éducation des femmes au moyen âge," *Excursions historiques et philosophiques à travers le moyen âge* (Paris, 1888), p. 463 and n. 2.

70. Oxford, Douce, 6.f.22 (in the right margin a woman carries a heavy load of firewood in a basket); Douce 5, f. 29. See Randall, *Images,* fig. 702, 700.

71. Aristotle, *De Historiis Animalium,* French, late thirteenth century, Merton College, Oxford, MS O.1.3 f. 65v (Randall, *Images,* fig. 405).

72. "In dimidio dierum meorum vadam ad portas inferi . . . non aspiciam hominem ultra," a good Latin diagnosis of menopause as pause o'men, vv. 10–11. Douce 6 f. 160v (Randall, *Images,* fig. 404).

73. F. 4v of the second part of the Psalter and Hours of Joffroy d'Aspremont and Isabelle Kievraing, Victoria National Gallery, Melbourne, 1254/3 (see Randall, *Images,* fig. 432). The husband wears in the guise of a hairdo a pair of seraph's

wings, because, so near to the hearth, he has acquired the seraph's fiery nature. In the same bantering vein, an ape stirs the churn with a bishop's crozier in a Franco-Flemish manuscript in the British Museum (Add. 30029, f. 19, 89; Randall, *Images,* fig. 54).

74. A similar scene is painted next to the one of the cock chaperoning his hens on the top of the frame of an illuminated page in the *First Bible of Charles the Bald,* ca. 846 (Paris, Bibliothèque Nationale, lat. 1. Baltrušaitis, *Réveils,* p. 49 on Carolingian *drôleries,* fig. 31A.B.). Exchanges between Ireland and northern France would account for the grotesques multiplying within the lines of the Sacramentary of Gellone and the Books of Kells, the latter being conspicuous for its generous borrowings from the poultry farm; see Francoise Henry, *Irish Art in the Early Christian Period* (London: Methuen, 1943), pp. 143–44 and p. 144, n. 1.

75. British Museum Add. 42130 ff. 166v, 158, 172v: Randall, *Images,* figs. 697 and 701 (cf. fig. 698: F. 10v of the *Smithfield Decretals* in the British Museum).

76. W. 88, ff. 10, 12. In this manuscript the pictures of peasant life, like the famous ones in the *Luttrell Psalter* in the British Museum (ploughing f. 170, sowing, f. 170v, harrowing f. 171, stacking sheaves, f. 173, harvest cart, f. 173v, of which the monkey waggoner of f. 126 affords a malicious foretaste), inject into the traditional iconography of the months, as it had been defined in church art, an idyllic vision of country life not contrary to its comic facets, in which indulged an aristocracy becoming dissatisfied with the deeds of prowess of chivalry and courtly love. See Johan Huizinga, *The Waning of the Middle Ages* (London: E. Arnold, 1937), chap. 10. Much before Louis XVI and Marie Antoinette, Edward II enjoyed farming, smiths' work, digging and thatching: Thomas Frederick Tout, *The Place of the Reign of Edward II in English History* (Manchester: Manchester University Press, 1914), p. 9.

77. Lilian M. C. Randall suggests that the sequence is based on that taken over in Wright's *Chaste Wife,* ca. 1462 (ed. F. J. Furnivall, Early English Text Society, vol. 12 [1965]).

78. Robert Bossuat, *Le roman de Renard* (Paris: Hatier-Boivin, 1957). In f. 21 of the French manuscript Douce 360 in the Bodleian Library, Constant des Noes runs after the fox with a big stick, but his wife is the first to arrive at the rescue: Kenneth Varty, "Reynard the Fox and the Smithfield Decretals," *Journal of the Warburg and Courtauld Institutes* 26 (1963): 352, pl. 40 c.

79. British Museum, Royal 10 E. IV, f. 49v and f. 175, Varty, "Reynard," pls. 37 d and 39. The subject is also represented in a stained glass panel at York Minster, ca. 1315, and in a carved misericord in the cathedral at Ely, in 1338: Varty, p. 353, and pl. 40 d.

80. Randall, *Images,* p. 101, s. v. "Fox and goose." The text of Cambridge University Library MS Ee, 1.12 is reproduced in *Lyrics of the XIVth and XVth Centuries,* ed. Russel Hope Robbins (Oxford: Oxford University Press, Clarendon Press, 1952), pp. 44–45.

81. *Smithfield Decretals* f. 49v; *Gorleston Psalter* ff. 47, 49v, 128, 143v; *Queen's Mary Psalter* (British Museum, Royal 2 B. VII) ff. 157v–158.

82. British Museum, Stowe MS 17, f. 34, ff. 34, 113. Randall, *Images,* fig. 524, 121. The church may be under attack through the figure of the abbess, because distaff and spindle, the attributes of Eve, were given to the new Eve, Maria, who impersonates the church. Maria or Ecclesia holds the cross staff, the spindle and the dis-

taff on an ivory plaque in the Metropolitan Museum, New York, which is classified with the school of Charles the Great: *Karl der Grosse, Werk und Wirkung, Zehnte Ausstellung unter den Auspizien des Europarates* (Aachen, Düsseldorf : Schwann, 1965), no. 524, fig. 102; cf. f. 40v of the *Sacramentary of Petershausen,* a Reichenau manuscript (ibid., no. 474).

83. On the contempt in which married clerics were held, see Etienne Gilson, *Héloise et Abélard* (Paris: Vrin, 1938), p. 46 ff.: Robert Génestal, *Le privilegium fori en France du décret de Gratien á la fin du XIVe siècle* (Paris: E. Leroux 1921); Philippe Delhaye, "Le dossier anti-matrimonial de l'*Adversus Jovianum* et son influence sur quelques écrits du XIIème siècle," *Medieval Studies* 13 (1951):74.

84. *Hours of Jeanne d'Evreux,* f. 51. See Randall, *Images,* fig. 120.

85. Arras, Diocesan Museum, MS 47, ff. 32, 208v. Randall, *Images,* figs. 734–35.

86. W. 82. f. 192v. Randall, fig. 90. The couple forms a fantastic bracket connecting verses 78–79 of Zacharias' canticle in the first chapter of Luke with the short Psalm 53: "Dominus susceptor es anime mee," v. 6. It resembles the grotesques designed to replace lines omitted by the scribe. See Florence McCulloch, "The Funeral of Renart," pp. 19, 21, fig. 5, 6. Compare also the beginning of "la passion nostre seigneur . . . mise du latin en francois," f. 246v. of the *Hours of Bonne de Luxembourg* (The Cloisters Collection, New York, 69. 86.), where St. Peter's cutting off of Malchus's ear in the Arrest of Christ painted in the vignette, is related to the cock of his triple denial above, with the help of a "turncoat" figure who lets his sword hang in the left margin and confronts the cock with a lantern. At the opposite end of the framework roosts an ominous owl, the night bird of ill repute: Florens Deuchler, "Looking at Bonne of Luxembourg's Prayer Book," *Metropolitan Museum of Art Bulletin* 29 (February 1971), fig. p. 274. An ape holds an owl as a falconer would hold a hawk on f. 175 of the *Smithfield Decretals,* showing on the other side Renart the deceiver fleeing with the goose.

87. Randall, figs. 708–9. Fr. 95, Robert de Borron, contains *L'Histoire du Graal* (f. 1), *L'Histoire de Merlin* (f. 113), *Les Sept Sages de Rome* (f. 380) and a *Chronique Fabulante,* extending from Adam to Emperor Tiberius, translated from the Latin by André le Moine: *Bibliothèque Nationale Manuscrits à peintures* (1955), no. 57.

88. Randall, *Images,* figs. 706, 710.

89. See the deeds of Mahaut, countess of Artois, and of others in A. Lehmann, *Rôle de la femme,* pp. 213–18.

90. The Psalter in the Duke of Rutland Collection at Belvin Castle, English, midthirteenth century, is a pioneering book in the development of drôleries. The man hacking at the ducking stool—Randall, *Images,* fig. 731—looks as if he were mumbling verse 11 of Psalm 83 written above him: "elegi abjectum esse in domo Dei mei magis quam habitare in tabernaculis peccatorum."

91. Lilian M. C. Randall, "The Snail in Gothic Marginal Warfare," *Speculum* 27 (1962):358–67. Twenty-nine manuscripts illustrating the libel are listed in the appendix. Towards the end of the fifteenth century the epic fight of the "lymasson" was retold in the *Compost and Kalendrier des Bergers.* A woodcut stages a woman with a distaff and two soldiers attacking the snail entrenched on the top of a column in an edition of 18 April 1493: Arthur Mayger Hind, *An Introduction to a History of Woodcut: With a detailed survey of work done in the Fifteenth Century* (London: Constable, 1935), 2: 650, no. 2.

92. Randall, *Images,* fig. 311. Victor Leroquais, *Les livres d'heures manuscrits de la Bibliothèque Nationale* (Paris, Mâcon: Protat Frères, 1927) 2: 158. Bibliothèque Nationale *Les Manuscrits à Peintures* (1955), no. 79. There is a sacrilegious association between the anguish shared by the woman and the knight who braces himself for an attack on the snail, and the sweat of Christ on His way to Calvary: "li sueurs de son front iusq (ues) a tierre coroit" as one reads in the text immediately above the bas-de-page. The cowbell is the emblem of the woman who, enfeoffed to the devil, leads the carol (*corea*): Cf. exemplum CCCXIV in Jacques de Vitry (cf. ed., Th. T. F. Crane, note 3).

93. Fitzwilliam Museum, Cambridge, MS 298; Randall, *Images,* p. 138.

94. Saint Jerôme, *Adversus Jovinianum, PL* 23.279.

95. The nostalgia of the androgynous human being, made perfect in the image of God before Eve was separated from one of Adam's ribs, lingers in the depiction of the Insulinde's androgynes in the diary of Jean de Mandeville's fabulous travels (1322–56). Naked human beings are painted in their primeval state of innocence, the male organ hanging over that of the female on f. 195v of the luxurious copy, *Le Livre des Merveilles,* illustrated mainly by the Master of Marshal Boucicaut's Hours, and presented by the Marshal to Jean de Berry as a new year's gift in 1413 (Paris, Bibliothèque Nationale, fr. 2810; cf. Philippe Verdier, "Jean le Magnifique duc de Berry," *Médecine de France* 15 (1950), fig. p. 21. In the *De Natura et Dignitate Amoris* of William of Saint-Thierry, the unity of the self is recaptured in the reconciliation of *animus et anima* and through the interacting consciousness of *sponsus* and *sponsa.* The treatise was written against the separate and selfish "amor carnalis et degener" for which Ovid, then widely read, gives the recipes in *Ars Amatoria;* see Etienne Gilson, *Théologie mystique de Saint Bernard,* Études de philosophie médiévale, vol. 20 (Paris: Liège, 1934), p. 88, n. 1; E. de Bruyne, *Études* 2:162. The myth of the androgynous primitive nature of man and of the striving of the self to reconquer its lost unity is told by Aristophanes in Plato's *Symposium* (189c–193d).

96. Copenhagen, Royal Library, GKS 3384 8° f. 160v–61. Randall, *Images,* fig. 307. On the erotic meaning of the bagpipe, to which Aretino is a witness, see Jacques Combe, *Jheronimus Bosch,* trans. Ethel Duncan (London: B. T. Batsford, 1946), p. 19, n. 50. Professor Terence Scully of Waterloo Lutheran University kindly sent me the copy of a fourteenth century rondeau, in the tradition of the pastourelle, in which "muser" is used "à double entente" (to play the bagpipe and to have fun). Here is the first stanza:

> Robin, muse, muse, muse,
> car tu y pues bien muser.
> Or sofle en ta cornamuse,
> Robin, muse, muse, muse.
> Je te donray une muse
> Se tu le sauras sofler:
> Robin, muse, muse, muse,
> car tu y pues bien muser.

At a line ending the *Hours of Jeanne d'Evreux,* a cross-legged bagpipe player is blowing an instrument equipped with a very long chanter shaped like a fool's "marotte," recalling that "marotte de fou fait bonheur de femme" [*Metropolitan Museum of Art Bulletin,* 16 (June 1958), fig., p. 276]. On fig. 24 of the *Picard Psalter* (in the Bibliothèque Nationale Paris, lat. 10435), "dame marote la bele," naked, exhibits her back to a sphinx-like character, while "me dame de Morvel" (Morvel is a township near Arras) dances to the tune of a bagpipe played by a hybrid man.

97. Randall, *Images,* figs. 712–13.

98. Paris, Arsenal, 5218, f. 10. Randall, *Images,* fig. 719. In the vignette one sees Galahad welcomed at the gate of the "blanche abeie" and behind the church altar "un escu a une croix vermeille," which no knight shall be permitted to bear "s'il n'est li mieldres chevaliers qui soit au monde." See *La Queste del Saint Graal,* ed. Albert Pauphilet (Paris: Melun, Librairie D'Argences, 1949), pp. 26–30. The two tilting women in the bas-de-page jokingly anticipate the fight between King Baudemagus and "li bons chevaliers a armes blanches" for the right to wear the miraculous shield, whose pedigree harks back to Joseph of Arimathia.

99. Debidour, *Le bestiaire,* fig. 447.

100. Successive revivals of the theme or its pattern are: a south Italian ivory plaque of the eleventh century in the Metropolitan Museum of Art, New York (The Cloisters 66–171) and romanesque capitals at Mozac and Bourbon l'Archambault (Debidour, p. 323, fig. 446).

101. The Hague, Meermanno-Westreenianum Museum, MS 10 14. Randall, *Images,* fig. 461.

102. In the second stanza of the rondeau quoted in n. 96, the shepherdess answers Robin: "Je ne say fere fuszée/mais je say fere si four," the play on the words being between *fere fuszée* ("I cannot do my yarn on the reel") and *fere fourt* ("but I have tow on my distaff").

103. Sensitive to public opinion, the church abolished tournaments for a very short time with Clement V's bull "Passiones miserabiles" (1313). Philippe le Bel answered by having one of his publicists write the treatise *De torneamentis et justis* in defense of the sport (unique manuscript in the Vatican Library, Regina lat. 1642). After John XXII's advent the ban on tournaments was lifted.

104. William D. Wixom, *Treasures of Medieval France* (Cleveland: The Cleveland Museum of Art, 1967), pp. 170–71 ff.

105. C. J. Jackson, *Illustrated History of English Plate,* 2: 460–61, figs. 525–26.

106. The coppa is stamped with the Avignon hall mark and may have been made by a goldsmith from Paris called to the court of Clement V. Marie Madelaine Gauthier, *Emaux,* Cat. 196, fig. 197, p. 250.

107. MS B 11.22 f. 30, in Randall, *Images,* fig. 398. Among the sexual symbols are notably two bagpipes and, in the line endings, two foxes. In Gauguin's paintings and sculptures the fox, according to a tradition of the South Seas, stands also for Luxuria.

108. Randall, *Images,* fig. 400–401. On f. 118 of the already mentioned Psalter and Hours of Joffroy d'Aspremont and Isabelle de Kievraing, the uneven fight appears as the reverse of the image sustained by the allegorical figure of Penance in the *De Quincey Apocalypse* (Lambeth Palace MS 209): Penance, covering herself with a shield on which the emblems of the Trinity are emblazoned, resists "les suggestions del diable."

109. W. 45 f. 256v. On the iconography of the passage in the Apocalypse, "et signum magnum apparuit" (12, 1), see Ernst Guldan, *Eva und Maria, Eine Antithese als Bildmotiv* (Graz, Cologne: Böhlau, 1966), pp. 102–5. In the painted altar-piece of the Apocalypse in the Victoria and Albert Museum, the "woman clothed with the

sun, with the moon under her feet, and on her head a crown of stars" does not represent the Immaculate Conception, but the Church, whose son, emperor Heraclius, will kill Chosroes II, King of Persia. This interpretation comes from the illustrated *Commentary on the Apocalypse* of Friar Alexander, Franciscan in Bremen, which covers historical events up to 1232 and up to 1249 in the *ne varietur* edition. See Claus M. Kauffmann, *An Altarpiece from Master Bertram's Workshop in Hamburg*, Victoria and Albert Museum Monograph no. 25 (London: H.M.S.O., 1968), p. 39 (subject 29). Alexander's *Commentary* was responsible for the new tenor, militant and optimistic, of the English painted Apocalypses; see Peter Brieger, *English Art: 1216–1307* (Oxford: Oxford University Press, Clarendon Press, 1957), pp. 159–61.

110. Yates Thompson MS 13 ff. 72v–75v, in Randall, *Images*, fig. 229.

111. The two lovers of Villard de Honnecourt's drawing are seated on a synthronos, of the kind shared by Christ and the Virgin in the Coronation. Indeed, the lady makes the same deferent gesture towards her lover as Mary towards Christ in the Coronation iconography. J. B. A. Lassus, *Album de Villard de Honnecourt,* ed. Léonce Laget (Paris, 1968), pl. xxvi.

112. M. 796 f. 106, in John Plummer, *Liturgical Manuscripts for the Mass and the Divine Office* (New York, 1964), no. 47, pl. 17.

113. Raymond Koechlin, *Les ivoires gothiques francais*, vol. 2, no. 1053, pl. CLXXX.

114. Jean de Joinville relates in his *Histoire de Saint Louis* that, as the fleet of the seventh crusade was crossing the Mediterranean, the king threw overboard the chessboard and ivory pieces of his brother, the comte d'Anjou, and Gautier de Nemours. The moralizing tendency underlines the allegorical poem *Le Eches Amoureux*, written between 1370 and 1380. The background of a vignette in Gautier de Coincy's *Miracles Notre Dame*, purposely shows a checky pattern behind the scene of "la nonnain qui lessa l'abbeie et s'en ala au siècle": Paris, Bibliothèque Nationale, nouv. acq. fr. 24541 f. 93, in Henry Focillon, *Le peintre des miracles Notre Dame* (Paris: P. Hartmann, 1950), pl. XXIII.

115. Randall, *Images*, fig. 104. Cf. Shakespeare, *Hamlet* 5.1.86–87. The earliest appearances of the jaw bone as Cain's weapon are on the Irish crosses. See Arthur Kingsley Porter, *The Crosses and Culture of Ireland* (New Haven: Yale University Press, 1931), p. 121: "Cain took in his hand the jawbone of a camel, so that he slew Abel" (*Book of Lecan*). Meyer Schapiro interpreted *cinbán* ('jawbone') as a kind of alliteration of Cain bana: Cain the slayer. "Cain's jaw bone that did the first murder," *The Art Bulletin,* 24 (1942):210–11. This etymology indicates how collective unconsciousness builds images out of associated sounds, as in sleep dreams are born out of words phonetically contiguous that release the "double entente" mechanisms (described by A. A. Brill, *Basic Principles of Psycho-Analysis* [New York: Washington Square Press, 1968], pp. 138–44). Tongue twisters, contrepèteries, and Jean des Entomeures's "matière de bréviaire" tie in with their texts many incongruous marginalia.

116. William S. Glazier Collection MS 24 on deposit at the Pierpont Morgan Library, in Randall, *Images*, fig. 520. In the bas-de-page f. 13 of the *Tenison Psalter* in the British Museum (Add. 24686, begun before 1284 for Alfonso, the son of Edward I), an ape is doing a handstand on the tail of a mermaid suckling her offspring. Romanesque mermaids are carved on the northern sides of churches, which is associated with the fall of man. Cf. examples at Saint-Germain-des-Prés,

Paris, and the abbey church of La Sauve Majeure (Gironde), in May Vieillard-Troiekouroff, "Les zodiaques parisiens sculptés d'après Le Gentil de la Galaisière astronome du XVIIIè siècle," *Mémoires de la Societé Nationale des Antiquaires de France*, n.s., vol. 4 (1968), pp. 173–74, fig. 2; P. Bonnet-Laborderie, "Fenêtre ouverte sur la Gironde romane," *Archéologia* 100 (1966):84–85.

117. Margaret H. Longhurst, *Catalogue of Carvings in Ivory, Victoria and Albert Museum* (London, 1929), pp. 46–47, pls. XLII, XLV. See W. D. Wixom, *Treasures of Medieval France*, p. 206.

118. Raymond Koechlin qualified this interpretation in "La partie d'échecs de Huon de Bordeaux et les ivoires français du XIVème siècle," a contribution to the *Mélanges Emile Berteaux* (1924), which he quoted in anticipation in his *Ivoires gothiques français*, vol. 2, no. 1044. It is not out of the question that the episode in Huon de Bordeaux, like other chess games described in the *Roman en prose de Tristan, La Vengeance de Radiguel,* and the *Fabel du Dieu d'Amour,* were in the minds of chess players and influenced the representations of the chess game in the marginalia and ivory carvings. On f. 76v of the *Luttrell Psalter,* a king plays backgammon with a woman. In the tapestry "Le jardin d'amour," 1460–70 (a Basel work in the Historical Museum, Basel), the lady who plays chess wears a queen's crown and makes the gesture of surprise usual in ivory carvings. Two lovers also play cards; see Jean Lanz, "Tapisseries gothiques," *Orbis Pictus* no. 20 (Lausanne, n.d.), p. 15. V, VI.

119. Florence McCulloch, *Funeral of Renart*, p. 1, fig. 2. Randall, *Images*, figs. 66, 103, 105, 151.

120. The Library of Heidelberg University, Cod. Sal. 9, 51, f. 272v, in Randall, *Images*, fig. 51.

121. The metrical *Physiologus* of Theobaldus (Abbot of Monte Cassino, 1022–35?) was translated into old English: Eduard Adolf Ferdinand Maetzner, *Altenglische Sprachproben* (Berlin: Weidmann, 1867), vol. 1, pt. I, p. 55 ff.

122. *PL* 195.572. The earliest English Bestiary, Bodleian Laud. Misc. 247, written in a Canterbury script in the first half of the twelfth century, omits already the pictorial comparisons with the life of Christ. See Talbot Rice, *English Art 1100–1216* (Oxford: Oxford University Press, 1953), p. 88.

123. On the editions of Thomas de Chantimpré and on the manuscript fr. 15106 in the Bibliothèque Nationale, Paris, see *La manière et les faitures des monstres* in J. Baltrušaitis, *Réveils . . .* , pp. 258–60, and notes 57, 58, pp. 360–61.

124. Bodleian Library, Ashmole 1511, and Aberdeen 24; British Museum MS Harley 4751, and Bodleian 764. Thomas Sherrer Boase, *English Art 1100–1216,* (Oxford: Oxford University Press, Clarendon Press, 1953), pp. 295–96.

125. Baltrušaitis, p. 149, fig. 35 B. On the *Bible of William de Devon*, see G. F. Warner, *Illustrated Manuscripts in the British Museum*, 1st series (1899), and P. Brieger, *English Art: 1216–1307*, pp. 157–58.

126. In fr. 15213 of the first half of the fourteenth century in the Bibliothèque Nationale, Paris, the *Bestiaire d'Amour* comes after *Ysopet*, the French translation of the fables after Aesop adapted in Latin by Alexander Neckam (1157–1217).

127. Brussels, Bibliothèque Royale, 9157. Baltrušaitis, fig. p. 51. The stantipes—*estampie*—was a gliding dance, of courtly character, danced longways—*stehenden Fusses*—in contrast to the *ductia*, where the players led in a round dance. On its rhythm see Catherine Keyes Meyer in her introduction to *Medieval English Carols*

and Italian Dances, New York Pro Musica, Decca Records, D L 9418 (Library of Congress cat. R 62-1204).

128. Baltrušaitis, fig. B pp. 212–13.

129. Debidour, *Le bestiaire,* fig. 360.

130. British Museum, Sloan 278; Baltrušaitis, p. 133, fig. 20 B. The *sirena* is designed as a mermaid and the *onocentaurus,* instead of being half a man and half an ass, is a merman with a bow. The Latin text still refers to Isaiah 14:22 and 34:14, as in earlier versions of the *Physiologus.* In Isaiah, the cursed cities of God's enemies, Babylon and Edom, have been razed into a wasteland, in which the satyrs (goat demons) and the sirens (hybrid birds and women) will dance and howl.

131. Debidour, *Le bestiaire,* fig. 331.

132. C. J. R. Cave, "The Roof-bosses in Canterbury Cathedral," *Archaeologia* 84 (1935), pl X, fig. 7.

133. *De Nobilitatibus Sapientiis et Prudentiis Regum* MS E. II (92) f. 64v. In Randall, *Images,* fig. 694.

134. Erich Steingräber, "Ein Frauengürtel aus dem frühen 14. Jahrhundert," *Kunstchronik* 12 (1959):89–91. *Art and the Courts,* no. 60, pl. 82, pp. 144–45.

135. On the supposed activity of Pucelle as a goldsmith and the connection between his drôleries and the decoration of Parisian enamels made between ca. 1320 and 1334, the date of his death, see Marie Malelaine Gauthier, *Emaux,* p. 258.

136. *Starohrvatska Prosvjeta,* Ser. III, 2 (Zagreb, 1952):227–29.

137. Gauthier, *Emaux,* no. 240, p. 247 and fig., p. 296.

138. Von J. Adolf Schmoll gen. Eisenwerth, "Lothringische Madonnen Statuetten des 14. Jahrhunderts" in *Festschrift Friedrich Gerke,* ed. J. A. Schmoll (Baden-Baden: Holle, 1962), pp. 134–35 and n. 28.

139. Ibid., fig. 20. William H. Forsyth, "Medieval Statues of the Virgin in Lorraine related in type to the Saint-Dié Virgin," *Metropolitan Museum Studies* 5, pt. 2 (1936):235–38, fig. 9. Thirteenth and fourteenth century statues of Virgins were frequently provided with belts, clasps or orphreys enriched with translucent enamel. See Louise Lefrançois-Pillion, "Deux statues gothiques au musée de Salins-de-Jura," *Gazette des Beaux Arts,* ser. 6, vol. 20 (1938) pp. 201–7; Jean Taralon, "Le trésor d'Evron," *Les monuments historiques de la France* (1962), 1: 32–34, figs. 4–8. On Assumption Day the cathedral of Pisa was entirely girdled with the "sacra cintola." Made in the second half of the thirteenth century, the cintola was adorned with precious stones, silver plaques on enamelled ground and "de plique" enamels. It cost 8000 florins and was so heavy that it had to be carried by two men. A few fragments survive: M. M. Gauthier, *Emaux,* Cat. 155. *L'Europe Gothique XIIè–XIVè siècles: Douzième Exposition du Conseil de l'Europe* (Paris, 1968), Cat. 461. The girdling of Pisa cathedral was the most extravagant of those prophylactic rites studied by P. Saintyves in "Le tour et la ceinture de l'église," *Revue Archéologique* 5th ser., vol. 15 (1922), pp. 79–113.

140. J. Evans, *English Art,* p. 38.

141. Karl Weinhold, *Die deutschen Frauen in dem Mittelalter,* 2d ed. (Vienna: Gerold's Sohn, 1882) 1: 388.

142. 4.6.126–29.

Illustrations

As it has not been possible to treat each illustration included in this text individually, and, moreover, since not every illustration here included can be assigned to marginalia, it appears appropriate to introduce these illustrations in a short preface and to begin by summarizing some parts of the foregoing essay which are essential to such a preface.

Verdier begins his essay by addressing himself to formalistic, methodological, and historical matters touching on the relationship between text and marginal illustration, the realistic yet semi-abstract nature of these representations, possible methods of interpreting the marginalia by attempting to find a common ground between miniature and marginalia or text and marginalia, the development of motif and style, the transmission of compositional devices, and related aesthetic matters. From these considerations he turns to the world represented in the marginalia—most often a topsy-turvy world—and, more specifically, to woman's place in it. In the course of the essay it becomes clear that whatever her given position may be, it cannot be called passive: from the lowest to the highest rungs of the social scale she participates actively in the world around her. Through motifs, iconographical similarities, compositional devices, and other means, links are established between women on all rungs of this ladder, even when those on a lower rung parody those occupying a more elevated place. Despite this secret sympathy which connects all women and renders the attempt to arrive at distinct categories so frustrating, it is possible to distinguish among the depictions of medieval women belonging to various social strata.

There are, first of all, miniatures depicting the sacred precinct, showing the *Virgo Annuntiata* or *Theotocos* or other sacred persons (evident in figs. 1 and 10). While *ars profana* does not enter the miniature itself, the marginalia of hours, psalters, and breviaries abound with depictions lampooning representatives of the church or the sacred domain (e.g., fig. 3, where a cleric and a nun engage in profane love, while the secular lover genuflects before his lady; fig. 9, where a midwife washes a young girl in the manner Christ is washed in fig. 8; fig. 10, where a naked Dominican is visible; fig. 15, where a woman tilts with a Dominican, gaining victory over him; and fig. 23, where a hybrid woman, confronting the apocalyptic dragon, usurps the place traditionally belonging to the angel Michael).

Moving to the second realm, the secular domain, involving the life of woman of the upper social class, we find representations without visible parody of the hunt, falconry, *amour courtois*, chivalry, games, religious devotion, and other activities of the courtly life. In fig. 1 woman is seen in prayer, in fig. 25 playing chess, in fig. 6 engaged in courtly love, in fig. 24 in falconry, and in figs. 20, 21, and 22 she is seen participating in the chivalric life. Absent from the portrayal of women of the highest stratum engaged in these activities is the subversive spirit pulsating in marginalia depicting the life of women of the rising bourgeoisie and the peasantry. The portrayal of these women constitutes a major concern of the essay.

Women held a recognized and regulated position in various industries, chiefly in the textile industry. Working as professionals, they dominated the silk industry, making silk belts and alms purses (fig. 6) which influenced the design of enamelled belts (figs. 2, 27). Other professions enjoyed lesser repute, such as that of bath attendant (fig. 7) and midwife-doctoress (figs. 8, 9). An example of woman's physical labors corresponding to popular representations of labors of the months is illustrated in fig. 12.

Woman's physical pleasures may be expressed in activities like the dance (fig. 17), while her carnal pleasures are conveyed more obliquely through rabbits and snails (figs. 16,

17) and horns (woman baiting unicorn, fig. 18), as well as goats and rams (fig. 19).

The motif of the joust (figs. 13–16) is one of the major vehicles by which Verdier is able to crystallize popular contemporary discontent with authority and unpopular practices, such as trial by wager. Aided by her ever-present distaff (figs. 11, 14, 19), woman in many depictions represents the mettlesome rising proletariat critical of both clergy and court.

Finally, there are the fantastic and real creatures (figs. 10, 16, 18, 23, 26, 27) deployed most frequently in the parody of human—often woman's—foibles (figs. 3, 10, 11). While the ape plays the leading role (figs. 4, 10, 11, 19), other animals are well represented (figs. 3, 11, 16, 18, 26, 27). Generally more entertaining than didactic, hybrid, grotesque creatures combining frequently feminine and animalistic features populate this *mundus inversus* (figs. 3, 11, 23).

Verdier concludes his presentation aptly with enamelled belts (figs. 2, 27) which unite the full range of contraries: sacred and profane symbolism, real and fantastic feminine representations, the peasant girl wearing the belt before her marriage and the Virgin wearing it to signify the gate closed by God. By inseverably joining these contraries, the vehicle fittingly encapsulates the polyvalent symbolism relating to woman's role in the Middle Ages.

RTM

Fig. 1. Psalter and Book of Hours of Yolande de Soissons: Yolande de Soissons kneeling before a statue of the Virgin and Child.

The Pierpont Morgan Library, MS. 729, fol. 232v.

164

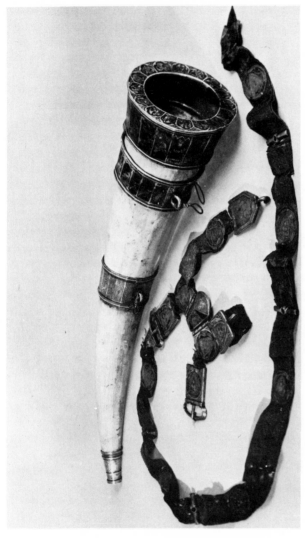

Fig. 2. Savernake Forest Tenure Horn, Hunt, and Unicorn.
Courtesy, Marquess of Aylesbury.

165

Figs. 3a and 3b. Comments on Psalm 127:1 and Ps. 129:1.
Bibliothèque Nationale, Paris; MS. Latin 10435, f. 158–158v.

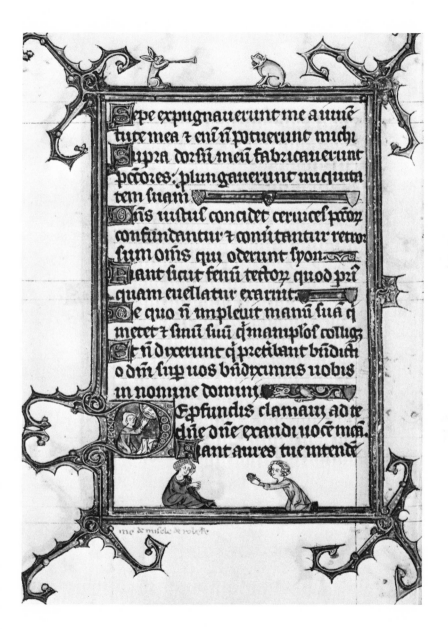

Fig. 4. Misericords: Ape and grylle.

Haarlem, Grote Kerk, 1512.

Figs. 5a and 5b. Line fillers in a Litany: Book of Hours and Psalter.

The Walters Art Gallery; 10.102, f. 29–29v.

pro nobis

Omnes sancti innocentes orate p nobis.

Sancte stephane.
or.

ance laurenti.
oro.

Sancte vincenti.
or.

ance fabiane.
or.

ance sebastiane.
or.

Sancti iohannes z paule. orate pro nobis.

Sancti cosma z damiane orate pro nobis.

Sancti geruasi z prothasy. orate p nob.

Omnes sancti martyres orate pro nob.

Sancte siluester.
or.

Sancte Gregori.
or.

Sancte martine.
or.

Sancte augustin.
or.

Sancte ambrosi.
or.

Sancte jeronim.
or.

Sancte sicholae.
or.

Omnes sancti pontifices z confessores

Fig. 6. "Aumônière Sarrazinoise," The Dream.

Troyes, Treasure of the Cathedral.

Fig. 7. Bathing Hut and estuveresses, Psalter and Hours.

The Walters Art Gallery; 10.82, f. 100

Fig. 8. Midwife washing Christ.

The Bodleian Library, Oxford; MS. Douce 118, f. 135.

Fig. 9. Woman washing young girl.
National Gallery of Victoria, Melbourne; MS. 1253/4, f. 10. The Aspremont Hours.

Fig. 10. Visitation and marginal drolleries, Book of Hours.
The Walters Art Gallery, W. 104, f. 28.

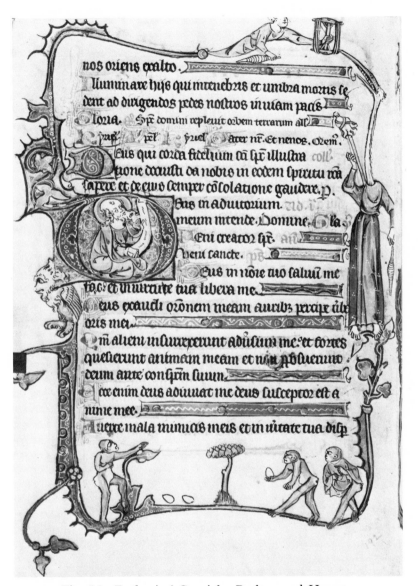

Fig. 11. Zacharias' Canticle, Psalter and Hours.
The Walters Art Gallery; W. 82, f. 192v.

Fig. 12. Reaping, *The Luttrell Psalter.*

British Museum, London; Additional MS. 42130, f. 172b
Courtesy, British Library Board.

Fig. 13. Woman dismounting knight, Breviary for Marguerite de Bar.

London, British Museum, Yates Thompson MS. 8, f. 224.
Courtesy, British Library Board.

Fig. 14. Woman charging knight, *Lancelot del Lac.*
Yale University Library, Yale MS., f. 328, fig. 709

Fig. 15. Woman and Dominican tilting, *Lancelot del Lac.*
Courtesy, the Beinecke Rare Book and Manuscript Library, Yale University, Yale MS.,
f. 100v, fig. 706

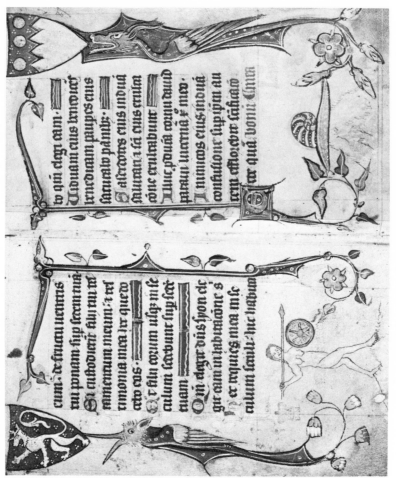

Fig. 16. Woman fighting snail.
British Museum, Harley MS. 656 ff., 86v–87.
Courtesy, the British Library Board.

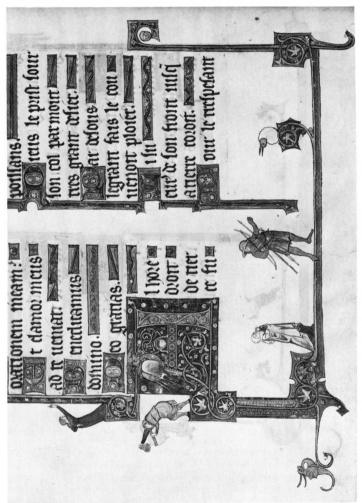

Fig. 17. Woman, knight, and snail.
Bibliothèque Nationale, Paris, MS. Latin 142 4 f., 15v.

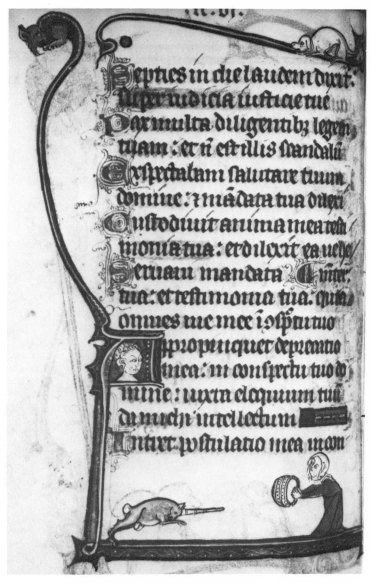

Fig. 18. Woman baiting unicorn.
Bibliothèque Municipale, Nancy; MS. 294, f. 20

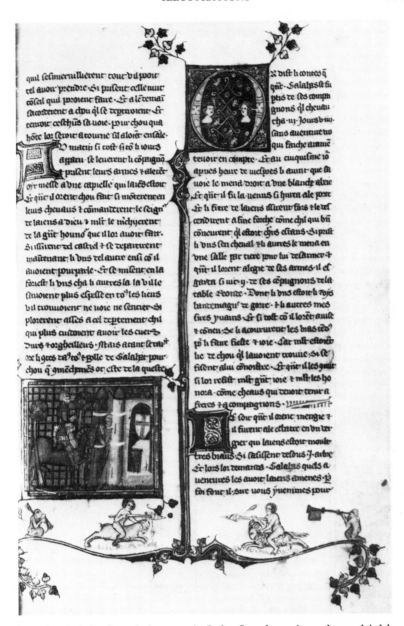

Fig. 19. Galahad and the mock fight for the miraculous shield.
Arsenal, Paris; MS. 5218, f. 10.

Fig. 20. Departure of Geoffrey Luttrell for the lists, *Luttrell Psalter*.

British Museum, London; Additional MS. 42130, f. 202v.

Fig. 21. Departure for tournament, *Roman de la Poire.*
Bibliothèque Nationale, Paris; MS. fr. 2186, f. 8v.

Fig. 22. Central Part of Silver Bermondsey Dish.
Bermondsey Parish Church, London.

184

Fig. 23. Hybrid Apocalyptical Woman, Psalter.
The Walters Art Gallery, W 45, f. 256v

Fig. 24. Falconers.
Bibliothèque Municipale, Verdun; MS 107, f. 12.

Fig. 25. Mirror Back: Lady and gentleman playing chess.
*The Cleveland Museum of Art; 40.1200, "Purchase from the
J. H. Wade Fund."*

Fig. 26. Line endings to Sanctus, Sanctus, Sanctus, *Petites Heures* by Jean Pucelle, made for Jeanne d'Evreux

The Metropolitan Museum of Art, The Cloisters Collection; Purchase, 1954; fol. 31, p. H.

Fig. 27. Belt for a lady's dress.

Courtesy, Markgräfliche Badische Verwaltung, Zähringer Museum, Baden-Baden, Germany.

Index

Aesop, *Fables of,* 121
Alamanni, laws of, 7, 8, 9, 16
Alanus ab Insulis, *Anticlaudianus,* 123
Albertus Magnus, 11, 16
Ailred, *Speculum,* 141
Alexander, 127. *See also Romance of Alexander*
Aliénor de Poitiers, *Les Honneurs de la cour,* 104, 108
Allegory, in Petrarch, 75; in *Nibelungenlied,* 24 f.
Amour courtois. See courtly love
Anastaise, 95
Andreas Capellanus, *De amore libri tres,* viii
Anne de France, 106, 116; *Enseignements d'Anne de France,* 106
Anne, Duchess of Bedford, 114
Anne of Brittany, 116
Anticlericalism
in marginalia, 122, 135, 141
Antifeminism, 41, 50, 95, 116, 141, 142. *See also* misogyny
Ape. *See also* monkey. In marginalia, 123, 124, 133, 134, 142, 143, fig. 4, 169, fig. 10, 174, fig. 11, 175, fig. 19, 181
Aristotle. And Phyllis, 127; "On Length and Shortness of Life," 2, 10, 11
Arma mulieris (distaff and spindle), 129, 130, 134, 135, 136, 137, fig. 11, 175, fig. 14, 177, fig. 13, 176
Augustine, Saint (and Augustinian thought), 36, 57, 69, 70, 79; and Petrarch, 70, 73, 79, 80, 88

Aumonières sarrazinoises, 131
Averroes, 10 f.

Babewinnes (*babewyns*), 124
Beauvoir, Simone de, 90, 116
Bédier, Joseph, 44
Beguines, 11, 16
Belt, 142 f.; ennamelled belts, fig. 2, 167, fig. 27, 187
Béroul, *Tristan,* 57
Bestiaries, 122; *bestiairies d'amour,* 141
Binni, Walter, 76
Blancheflor, 45
Boccaccio, 66, 94, 99, 100; *De Claris Mulieribus,* translation of, 97; *Decameron,* 97
Boileau, Etienne, *Livre des Métiers,* 130
Boron, Robert de, *Histoire de Merlin,* 136
Bosch, Hieronymous, x, 123
Bosco, Umberto, 74, 75, 77
Boucicaut, Maréchal, 103
Breviary for Marguerite de Bar, 136, 138, 139
Brousson, Jean-Jacques, *Anatole France en pantoufles,* 137
Brunhild, 26, 33, 35, 36
Burn, A. R., 3

Calcaterra, Carlo, 67, 69, 70, 71, 72, 73, 74, 76, 77, 79, 80
Caricature, in marginalia, 125
Carnal pleasures, woman's. *See also* sexual behavior. In marginalia, fig. 16, 178, fig. 17, 179, fig. 18, 180, fig. 19, 181

189